PUBLISH AND PROMOTE YOUR EBOOK IN A DAY

PUBLISH AND PROMOTE YOUR EBOOK IN A DAY

DARIN JEWELL AND CONRAD JONES

THAMES RIVER PRESS

Publish and Promote Your Ebook IN A DAY

THAMES RIVER PRESS
An imprint of Wimbledon Publishing Company Limited (WPC)
Another imprint of WPC is Anthem Press (www.anthempress.com)
First published in the United Kingdom in 2013 by
THAMES RIVER PRESS
75–76 Blackfriars Road
London SE1 8HA

www.thamesriverpress.com

A CIP record for this book is available from the British Library.

ISBN 978-0-85728-166-1

This title is also available as an eBook

This book is dedicated to
Aidan Joshua Souleiman Jewell
and
Aimee Elizabeth Emine Jewell

CONTENTS

1

HOW TO PUBLISH AND SELL YOUR EBOOK

How to polish your work and build marketing hooks into it, add depth to your characters, format and convert your book into ebook format.

There has never been a better time to publish and sell your own book. Despite being excited about uploading your book and getting it out there on sale, stop for a few hours and read the pointers in this guide. They will make you think about your book as a commercial product, which is essential before you publish. Hindsight is a great thing and we are offering you the opportunity to benefit from our experiences so that you can get it right the first time around. Using our years of experience in the digital book world, you can make your manuscript as good as it can be and avoid some of the pitfalls which are easy to stumble into.

Before formatting your book, you should consider certain ways in which you can amend your work in a few simple ways, which will greatly improve its marketing potential. Whether you are writing for pleasure or for commercial gain, polishing your product before you upload will pay dividends very quickly. There are some crucial mistakes and omissions that are often made by self-publishing authors and this guide will help you to identify and avoid them. It will also give you some essential marketing tips, which you should incorporate into your manuscript before you publish it as a digital download. It has already taken hundreds of hours to create your book, and by spending just a few more hours you can make it as marketable as possible. You will increase its chances of reaching its intended market, attract more readers and ensure its commercial success by:

- writing hooks into your book
- hitting the ground running
- choosing your words wisely
- showing rather than telling
- adding depth, colour and sense
- turning factoids into facts

Write Hooks Into Your Book

When writing your book, if you want your book to sell you need to look at it from the perspective of the people who you want to read your book. Hundreds of books are published every day and it is difficult to make your book stand out from the rest. Writing hooks into your book gives readers a reason to pick yours up first. You have to give your target market an incentive to read your work. Think about why they would want to buy it besides the fact that you think it's a good book. What will make them identify with the characters or recognise the sites mentioned in the book? With this in mind (and with your marketing approach in general), start by focusing on your local readers first, whether that is your family and friends or a potential fan base from a large group or organisation connected to you. If you can build a loyal readership in a place of employment, big city or even a small town to start, then you are on to a winner.

A good example of this is vicar-turned-author G.P. Taylor and his book *Shadowmancer*. When he completed the manuscript, Reverend Taylor was told no publisher would be interested in a parable about Christianity and black magic set in the eighteenth century. He decided to ignore templated rejection letters from publishers and the naysayers and publish the book himself. He sold his Harley-Davidson to cover the cost of self-publishing the book. The novel's popularity spread gradually by word-of-mouth as parishioners, friends and neighbours recommended it to fellow readers. This local groundswell of support and subsequent positive reviews and media coverage eventually lead Faber & Faber to offer to publish the book, after which it spent 15 weeks at the top of the British book charts, making Reverend Taylor a millionaire and much sought-after literary talent. He sold the US rights to his book for £314,000, which is said to be more than three times J.K. Rowling's US advance for the first Harry Potter story. He then signed a four-year deal for £3.5 million with Faber in the UK and Putnam in the US. The film rights to *Shadowmancer* were sold for £2.25 million, and his book has now been translated into more than twenty different languages.

The lesson of this story is start local, then go regional, national and finally international. You may not have eighty parishioners and God on your side to strengthen your resolve in the marketing of your manuscript, but you will find that your nearest and dearest are often glad to help endorse, review and recommend your book, especially if you add local flavour in a subtle or seemingly disguised way. Remember that word-of-mouth will sell more books than any other media. If a fan of your novels tells their family and friends that a local landmark or street name, river, cathedral or train station is in the story, then they can visualise the book as it progresses. It also gives you a hook into the local media, which is really important.

Local landmarks, street names or areas will give you a hook into the local media vehicles. You will have to try to build personal relationships with local journalists, editors, radio personalities and their associates, which are priceless when you are releasing a new book or have a book-signing coming up. So if you have a local interest in your book, then the press are more willing to listen to you when you call. An important point to remember is, unless you're a celebrity, your book is not news, however interesting and informative it is, until you've built up a grassroots following. Don't be disappointed if your local television station does not call you back or your local newspaper leaves you on hold until you finally hang up.

Any successful author has had more doors slammed in their face than they can remember but as your local fan base and social network grows, then so does the news value. When any author launches their first book, nobody wants to know; you have to start on the bottom rung and take one step up the ladder at a time, working hard at building interest in you as a brand. Writing hooks into your books helps to achieve this.

If you have any links to large organisations, then mention them in the book. For example, at the end of Conrad Jones's *Soft Target*, the local football derby is targeted by terrorists. Liverpool is a city full of football fans, blue and red. We are talking about millions of fans. Using the clubs in the book gave it a hook into the corporate side of the clubs and they invited Conrad to do book signings at their pre-match corporate dinners. Likewise, incorporating a scuba diving centre in the Lake District, which has thousands of members, also helped to generate sales of the book in the early days. They distributed bookmarks and sent emails to their members telling them that the dive centre was mentioned in his book. These hooks are case specific but the key point is to think about the content of your book and look for the hooks that can get your foot in the door. Conrad didn't put these places and organisations into the story by accident; he did it intentionally to make marketing his book easier. Use the places in your book to help you reach pockets of interest.

Similarly, you should place the names of friends, family and your main readers in your ebook. You can use given names or second names only if they have asked you to put them into the storyline. If you want someone to tell everyone that they meet about your book, put them in it. It's often said that when someone looks at a photo, the first person they look for is themself. Similarly, if you subtly mention one of your friends or fans in your book (not just in the acknowledgements, but in the narrative itself), you'll be surprised at how favourably they'll review your book and how many times they'll mention it to others, and there's nothing better than a good recommendation, which is known today as "viral marketing."

Be careful not to associate their character with their actual names. If done correctly, this generates word of mouth and builds sales. For instance, if your brother is named Stanley Timothy Parker and you write thrillers, you might want to add in Major Stanley Timms to the terrorist taskforce. Another example is Sylvia Blythe, a detective in *The Child Taker*. The name is the maiden name of a big fan who also writes reviews for every novel that Conrad writes. If you can build that kind of loyalty from readers then you will sell ebooks to the people they talk to and good recommendations and reviews are priceless. Hooks help sell books.

Hit the Ground Running

You need to grab the attention of your reader in the first paragraph so they'll want to read more. If you spend too much time in setting the scene and developing the characters, you'll lose your readers after a few pages. Rather, you need to grab their attention and hold it throughout your book. Let your characters, through their dialogue and actions, convey to the reader what's around them, what situation they're in and who they are. If you look at your story objectively and don't believe that the first chapter excites or intrigues the reader (with novels) or informs the reader (with non-fiction), change it or create a prologue that does.

Your opening sentence, opening paragraph, opening page will set the tone for the rest of your book. If your book starts at a gradual pace and builds up momentum and leads to an unforgettable twist at the end, the problem is that some readers and reviewers will read the beginning and not bother to read on. Start with an action scene in novels rather than setting the scene and introducing the characters; start straight in with practical tips or advice with business books/guides rather than spending the first few chapters explaining the theory behind the practice. Hook your readers on the first page, make sure you add hooks every few pages and keep the action moving so that they stay captivated throughout the book.

> *Exercise 1. Take half an hour to think about the names and places in your book. Could you place marketing hooks into it?*

For example:
Could a female character in the book have their name tweaked to become your sister, auntie, friend, work colleague?

Could a character visit a local landmark or could you mention a famous street name in the novel?

Are there any football teams, organisations, companies or recognisable brands mentioned in the text?

Choose Your Words Carefully

You can write a masterpiece that is worthy of literary accolades and awards the world over but if it does not speak to your target audience then you are wasting your time creating it in the first place. Be careful to keep your story flowing and the language understandable. If readers have to look up more than one word in a chapter then the writer has already lost their interest. Using longwinded, flowery sentences can irritate readers, as can the use of obscure words, which have to be explained.

A classic example of this is Stephen Hawkings's *A Brief History of Time*. Hawking approached an editor with his ideas for a popular book on cosmology. The editor was doubtful about all the equations in the draft manuscript, which he felt would put off laypersons and buyers in airport bookshops that Hawking hoped to reach. The editor warned him that for every equation in the book the readership would be halved, eventually persuading Hawking to drop all but one equation: $E = mc^2$. In addition to Hawking's notable abstention from presenting equations, the book also simplifies matters by means of illustrations throughout the text, depicting complex models as diagrams. No doubt Stephen was frustrated by the editor's demands but the commercial aspect of the book has to be the priority.

You can find similar problems in Robert Ludlum's Bourne thrillers. The films are full of non-stop action and are ultra-exciting but the books are difficult to read and the vocabulary is over-complicated. Keep it simple; the storyline is more important to the reader than your superior knowledge of vocabulary or insider jargon.

Don't get too wordy. With ebooks you can provide a good amount of information in a succinct way. Resist the urge to weave in too many plots or offer too much conventional wisdom unless it is specifically pertinent to the main storyline or product or service that you are selling, and then only if it is relevant/applicable to the target audience. Descriptions of characters and places are important but keep the narrative flowing as you can lose the reader by being overly descriptive and too clever with overly complicated plotlines or delivering an overdose of unexpected twists.

Authors often write novels with characters speaking in their local dialect, which can make it difficult to read (especially if you don't speak the local dialect) and slow the pace of the book. It's like having subtitles in movies – people generally go to see action movies to relax and be entertained, not to have to read off the screen and therefore miss some of the action. Likewise, if a reader is struggling to follow the discourse or dialogue in a novel, they're much more likely to put down the book than take the time to learn the lingo. A great example of how to include authentic character-spoken accents without causing readers to struggle to understand the local dialect is *Moby-Dick* by Herman Melville.

Similarly, it's generally a good idea to temper too much crude language in action novels, which might put off or offend potential readers. In *The Bourne Identity*, there are thirty uses of the word "s—t," two uses of the word "f—k," a few uses of "damn," "hell," and over a dozen exclamatory uses of God's name in vain. Do they really add to the atmosphere or action? In hard-hitting or gritty books like Irvine Welsh's *Trainspotting* or *Porno* there needs to be the right measure of expletives to accurately reflect the language used by the characters. But if the book is replete with harsh language or expletives on most every page, it'll put off readers, retailers and magazine reviewers (with ebooks, e-tailers and e-zines reviewers).

Exercise 2. Are there words in your book that can limit your readership? Will a layperson reading your book have to either pass over the words without knowing what they mean (and thus the meaning is lost) or take the time to look up the words in the dictionary (and thus the flow is lost)?

Can you change them to everyday speak to broaden your readership? If the language is only understandable to some, can you change it so it is understandable to many? Are you using terminology to try to distinguish yourself or terms that might be offensive to your readers? If so, your book will have limited appeal.

Show Not Tell

Allow your readers to experience the story through actions, thoughts, senses and feelings rather than through author exposition, summarisation and description. Don't drown the reader in adjectives, but allow readers to experience your ideas by interpreting events in the story. Nobel Prize-winning novelist Ernest Hemingway was a notable proponent of the "show, don't tell" style. In his own words, "the dignity of movement of an iceberg is due to only one-eighth of it being above water." The "dignity" Hemingway speaks of suggests a form of respect for the reader, who should be trusted to develop a feeling for the meaning behind the action without having the point painfully laid out for them.

As alluded to previously, rather than setting each scene and portraying the landscape through detailed descriptions, let your characters set the atmosphere and scene through their own words, and define themselves through their actions. Let your characters tell the story, rather than you telling it for them from a third-party perspective. If you use the narrative to paint the scene, your book will read like a film script. Your readers need to get into the minds of the characters and identify with them, but if you're describing it then they'll feel removed from the action.

Think about writing in an active voice rather than using passive descriptions. Adding just a few key phrases here and there could make all the difference to your novel. For instance:

Asda was busy that day, packed with shoppers. (Passive)

'I could barely move in Asda that day; the other shoppers streamed up and down the aisles like rats in a maze,' Stephanie said in an irritated tone. (Active)

Both sentences say the same thing but the second is spoken by a character in the book; this both gives her and the narrative more depth and allows the reader to visualise her speaking. Remember that readers like "show, don't tell" so be careful not to overuse the narrative to describe the setting when you could use a key character to do it better, while giving depth to the character at the same time. For instance:

The woods looked dark and spooky as the light faded. (Tell)

Sarah turned and looked towards the woods. The dark shadows made her shiver with fear as the sun sank behind the mountain. (Show)

Once again, both sentences say the same thing but the second allows us to visualise the scene and get a sense of what the character was feeling at the time. On a similar theme, when establishing the year in which the chapter is set, you can use a brief description in the narrative or, preferably, you could use the action to show the reader what year it is. For instance:

Paul left school in 1983 and could still vividly remember the journey home after his last day. (Tell)

Paul remembered the day he left school like it was yesterday. He had said goodbye to his best friend when his uncle turned up at the bus stop in his brand new 1983 plate Ford Capri. 'Nice car, Uncle Dave, have you been robbing banks again?' Paul had teased.

'Just picked it up this morning. Get in and less of your cheek or you can walk home,' his uncle grumbled. (Show)

Exercise 3. Consider the following: Place, time and setting.

There are two essential dimensions to the setting of any book: place and time. If you have written a novel set in the present, the time in which your story is set is relatively straightforward and the tenses used are easy to check. However, if you are writing fiction that spans the lifetime of a character or goes back to events of a character's past then you will need to pay special attention to tenses to ensure readers always know what time each chapter or paragraph is set in or it could easily become confusing.

Do not take it for granted that the reader knows where the story is up to and avoid having more than one person speaking in any single paragraph as it can leave readers wondering who is speaking at any given point in the narrative. You will know who is speaking as the author, but the reader may not.

Add Depth and Colour to Your Characters

Every character in your book will have many dimensions but have you described them fully, irrespective of their role in the plot? You know the characters, what they look like, what they wear and what their traits are, but have you conveyed this to the readers? Are they relaxed and laid back or dark and dangerous? Could a few more adjectives give them more depth and make your book a better read?

Another dimension often left under described are the places and things that have a presence, despite not being "living" things. For instance:

New York, vibrant, exciting, noisy but dark and dangerous at times.

London, historic, multicultural, old, tired and scruffy around the seams.

The harvest moon, glowing, mysterious, with a dark side.

Honda Fire Blade, powerful, unforgiving, eye-catching lines.

Use descriptive "humanising" words for some inanimate objects as well as your human characters. Some writers do not pay due attention to the setting because they are keen to get stuck into the storyline. You know where the story takes place and the setting is a clear in your mind, but is that clarity of vision conveyed through the writing? You can be sure that a drab setting is dull and one-dimensional at best and unclear or confusing at worst. You have to make sure the reader knows where he or she is at every juncture, and your descriptions should help them navigate their way through the scenes alongside your characters. You can be subtle or you can be direct as long as you use good descriptions along the way. For example:

John crossed the street, wearing a black suit and carrying a holdall. Beneath his arm was a copy of the local newspaper.

The setting, time and place could be enhanced considerably with the use of some "show" techniques and some well-placed adjectives.

> *John had to wait for a line of black-cabs to roar by before he could cross the street. As he reached the halfway point, a double-decker splashed rainwater over his highly polished shoes and the trousers of his black suit were soaked to the knees. The Adidas holdall, which he was carrying, felt heavy. Beneath his arm was a copy of the local paper, the* Manchester Evening News.

> *Exercise 4. Spend a half hour taking one paragraph from each chapter in your book and enhance the setting or add depth to the characters.*

Make use of your characters' five senses to enhance the setting. This applies throughout the manuscript but especially when your characters are in places like the dark, the woods, undercover and so on. Describing the sights, sounds and smells will enrich the scene for your readers. If the characters are on the beach or in a fish-and-chip shop, a fun fair or a morgue, what stench or aroma can they smell? Smells are evocative when setting the scene, so do not underestimate how powerful writing them into the setting can be.

Pick a paragraph in your book and imagine what sounds you would hear while the action was taking place. You do not have to be overly descriptive but the odd line here and there will add more depth to your narrative. If your characters are in the woods, can they hear the breeze in the trees? If they are near the sea, are the waves lashing against the rocks? If they are on a bridge near a railway station, could they feel the rush of air from a passing train? During a fight scene, can they feel the crowd closing in on them?

Novels *should* have colourful characters with vibrant scenes, and rich characters and colourful scenes, that are smelly, fragrant, noisy, silent, silky, slimy, bitter, sweet – and always highly visual. Write from your characters' perspectives and don't assume the reader knows what's in your mind, that he or she can imagine what the characters are feeling. Show the readers your imaginative world through the characters' eyes.

> *Exercise 5. Check if your characters are using their senses fully in your book. What can they see, feel, smell and taste?*

Check Your Facts

Research is vital and a lack of proper research is a mistake made by many authors. Readers are intelligent and if you insult their intelligence with a blatant error then it will spoil their enjoyment of your book. If your character is holding a Glock 17, then make sure you know it fires 9 mm ammunition and how many bullets can be slotted into a magazine. That may sound obvious to some but if you mention that your character "flicked off the safety catch and opened fire" then some clever-clogs will inevitably review your book and point out that a Glock 17 doesn't have a safety. If you are not sure, Google it. All the information any writer could ever need is available on the Internet. If you are writing about a meeting at the White House, chances are that you have never been in there and neither have your readers. However, a quick look on Google images will show you the colour of the wallpaper and which pictures are actually on the walls. To add authenticity, you can add a single well-researched detail. For instance:

John gazed up from the desk at Lincoln's portrait and his fingers felt the scorch mark left on the veneer by Clinton's cigar.

Both facts are made up but your readers need to believe that you know what you are writing about to be convinced by the storyline. Suggesting that President Clinton burnt the veneer is difficult to verify and hints that you have an intimate knowledge of the Oval Office. So don't be afraid to take some liberties. Invent just what you need to set the scene but keep it real. Make sure you give clear facts, and keep them pithy and precise. If you use real events in your book to make it seem authentic, then make sure you know the details.

Also, be careful with the overuse of clichés. The English language is full of clichés and we are all guilty of using them unwittingly. Clichés are nothing other than laziness and readers don't usually respond well if a book is riddled with them. Instead of saying "The worst case scenario," just say "at worst." Rather than saying "At the end of the day," better to say "ultimately." And don't overuse the thesaurus. There's a temptation to always search for a synonym. But generally, the simple, more direct word is better. Show that you know, but don't show off what you know.

Exercise 6. Revisit some of the "factoids" or descriptions stated in your book and research them further. When in doubt, always look it up and add more facts to the story, not to impress readers but to convince them you know what you're writing about.

★ ★ ★

Now that you have:

- written hooks into your book
- hit the ground running
- chosen your words wisely
- shown rather than told
- added depth, colour and sense
- turned factoids into facts

Your book can now be proofread, formatted and uploaded as an ebook.

Have Your Manuscript Proofed

If you have written a short story, novella, full-length non-fiction book or novel, then your document's word count will run into the thousands. You will have spent months staring at the written pages, creating, developing, expanding and then editing your precious work. The problem is that, as writers, at the final stage when we want to make sure that our book is the very best it can be, we are often too close to it. We tend to read *what we think we have written, not exactly what we have written*, and this applies to both the storyline and the grammar. No matter how many times you have read through your book, there will be room for improvement.

Before you convert your document into an ebook, you need readers to content edit the storyline, and not just for punctuation, spelling and grammar. There are few things more frustrating for authors than spending hours and hours writing and proofreading their own work, only for reviewers to point out poor phrasing or wording, anachronisms, inconsistencies and overlooked grammatical and spelling mistakes. You want readers to positively review your book based on its literary merits, not adversely review it based on deficient formatting or grammar. Regardless of how many times you have read over it yourself, fresh eyes will find mistakes in it.

How many times have you seen poor reviews because of the production of the book? Add to that the number of negative reviews because of "wooden dialogue" or "cardboard characters" even if the reviewer thinks that the premise of the book was good? Pick any fictional novel from the top 100 sellers and click on the reviews. Check the one-star reviews and you will see that there are consistent themes that reviewers pick up on and they are listed in the pages below. To help avoid this happening to your ebook and give it the very best chance of commercial success, before you convert your book into ebook format or e-publish your book, you need to have it content edited in the following ways:

1. Make sure that you have spellchecked the document in its entirety without ever clicking on the "ignore rule" tab, otherwise the programme will skip over some basic mistakes. Sometimes the grammar checks miss obvious mistakes on the first check, so having it repeated by someone else is always worthwhile.

2. Make sure at least one other person other than a friend or family member has spellchecked the document as above, and read the story as a reader would. Friends and family may tell you what you want hear and that may not always be a true reflection of the quality of your work. Protecting your feelings may be their primary concern rather than giving you an honest critique.

3. There are many simple mistakes that the spellcheck does not always find. Checking them using the Find function can save you some heartache later on. Using the Find function, check the use of the following words.

   Exercise 7. Take a half hour to spellcheck your manuscript and check out the following commonly misspelled words and their context:

   there, their, they're

   were, where, we're

   your, you're

   its, it's

   quit, quite, quiet

   to, too

   whose, who's

   rain, reign, rein

   fair, fare

   fro, for, from

   desert, dessert

   affect, effect

   than, then

   chose, choose

   lose, loose

   Make sure your spellcheck is using United Kingdom English and not United States. Although differences are subtle, if you are inconsistent through the work, then it will annoy your readers.

UK Standard Style and Grammar Guide

Proofreading your own manuscript is not an easy task, and if you can afford to have your book professionally edited instead, that is certainly preferable. As a general rule of thumb, expect to pay £3–5 for each 1,000 words.

If, on the other hand, you do have an eye for detail and you would like to take on the arduous task of proofreading your own book, then you can follow these grammatical rules:

Abbreviations and contractions

Use the full stop after abbreviations and contractions only where the last letter is not the final letter of the word: No., Capt., a.m., p.m., i.e., e.g. (upper- and lower-case), and for personal initials, e.g. W.B. Yeats.

The full stop is omitted thus: Mr, Dr, St, Ltd; after sets of initials: BBC, NATO, MP and after abbreviated units of measurement (ft, in, m, km, lb).

Capitalisation

Aim for minimum use of capitalisation. Generally, however, the following are capped:

Specific organisations and groups, institutions and religious bodies: the Labour Party, the Church, Hinduism, Buddhism, Jews, Islam and Muslim.

Titles and ranks where a specific individual is named: Queen Charlotte, but a queen, all lords, no bishops, kings of England.

Historical periods, wars and economic or political periods: Neolithic, Stone Age, the Second World War, the Depression.

Geographical locations recognised as social/political regions: the Midlands, the West Country, but the north, the south-west.

Figures and numbers

Write numbers below 100 in words (except where the author is comparing numbers or recording a unit of measurement); 100 and above as numerals: 2 cats and 144 dogs, six dogs and eighty-six cats; I could see for 6 miles.

For collective numbers use the least number of figures possible: 1944–5, 1986–93, 1997–2003. But note: 1990–95, 16–17, 116–17.

Set dates: 1 February 1950, in the late nineteenth century (but late-nineteenth century war), the eighties, the 1980s, but in the 1970s and '80s. AD (preceding date) and BC (following date).

Set times of the day: four o'clock, 11.15 a.m., 7.45 p.m., a quarter to eight, half past nine.

Italics

Use italics for the titles of books, book-length poems, newspapers and magazines; works of performed art, television and radio programmes; names of ships.

Follow the *Oxford Guide to Style* for foreign and anglicised words and use italics for emphasis sparingly.

Layout

The first line of a chapter should normally be set full out. A new section, following a one-line space, also should be set full out. Text which follows an extract or verse quote, also full out, unless this impairs the sense, in which case it should be indented as a new paragraph.

However, the layout of headings, quotations and lists, order and content of preliminary matter and the construction of notes and references must be retained.

Punctuation

Some points that may cause difficulty are:

Possessives: The inclusion or omission of the possessive s should be decided on the grounds of euphony; this means that some possessives will have an s and some will not, but there should be some system. The *Oxford Guide* recommends that (except in ancient names) 's should be used in all monosyllables and disyllables, and in longer words accented on the penultimate syllable. Also, 's should be used except when the last syllable of the word is pronounced *iz*: Bridges', Moses', but James's, Thomas's.

Watch out for the incorrect apostrophe in its, yours, ours, theirs, hers.

Plurals: Do not use the apostrophe when creating plurals: the Joneses (not the Jones's); the 1990s (not the 1990's); QCs (not QC's). Do not employ what is sometimes known as the "greengrocer's apostrophe": orange's for oranges and cauli's for cauliflowers.

No apostrophe in phone, plane, bus, flu, etc.

Dashes and ellipses

The most common versions of the dash are the en dash (–) and the em dash (—).

For parenthetical dashes, use spaced en rules.

For the omission of part of a word, or for abruptly curtailed speech, use a closed-up em rule.

For the omission of a whole word, use a spaced em rule.

Ellipses should be spaced thus… with a full stop at the end of the sentence, if relevant.

Hyphenation

Do not hyphenate unnecessarily.

Use hyphens to avoid ambiguity: a little used car or a little-used car; when employing words attributively: an ill-informed person; in phrasal compounds: jack-in-the-box; in compound adjectives preceding a noun: working-class hero; where part of the compound is a measurement: 9-mile run.

Omit hyphens when employing words predicatively: that person is ill informed; when the first word of the compound is an adverb: widely known facts; or where the compound is a name: Iron Age fort.

Quotations

Use double quotation marks, reserving single quotation marks for a quote within a quote.

Place punctuation marks in relation to quotation marks according to sense. The closing inverted comma precedes all punctuation except an exclamation mark, question mark, dash or ellipsis belonging to the quotation. Where a full sentence, with an initial capital, is quoted at the end of a main (author's) sentence, the full stop should precede the inverted comma.

In dialogue the punctuation is always placed inside the punctuation marks: "It is," he said, "a great album."

Closing parenthesis

A full stop should precede a closing parenthesis only if the parentheses enclose a complete sentence that is not part of a longer sentence. A question mark or exclamation mark may precede or follow a closing parenthesis as the sense demands. A comma, colon, semicolon or a parenthetical dash should never precede a closing parenthesis.

Spelling

Collective nouns are singular, e.g. company, government. Verbs used with them must also be singular.

Optional endings: -ise or -ize (author's choice, but be consistent).

Retain American spelling for proper names: Pearl Harbor, Rockefeller Center.

> *Exercise 8. Take a half hour to familiarise yourself with the grammatical rules outlined above. Whether you proofread your manuscript or pay a professional to edit it, applying these rules will improve your writing.*

Formatting Issues when Typesetting Your Manuscript

If you're proofreading your own manuscript, save your work often as you make new changes to ensure that the changes are recorded. There is nothing worse than getting halfway through a painstaking edit, and then experiencing a computer glitch or becoming distracted unexpectedly and losing all your hard work, and then trying to remember the changes that you made previously.

When converting your book into ebook format, your document must not have any blank or white space, so delete all the page breaks except at the end of a chapter. Enter a page break at the end of each chapter to prevent the text from running together once it's converted into ebook format. To insert a page break in Microsoft Word, click "Insert" at the top menu bar and select "Page Break."

Once the page breaks have been added, you need to make sure that there are no "hard returns" in your manuscript which could throw out the spacing and paragraphs when the book is typeset. Hard returns cause the word processor to start a new line regardless of how margins are set. They tend to be found in manuscripts when authors are used to old-fashioned typewriters and hit the "return" button at the end of each line.

To identify them, go to the top of the menu bar in Word format and click "Home," where you will find this symbol: ¶. If you click on it, it will show you all the manual spaces and returns that occur in your manuscript.

This is the pilcrow, and more commonly referred to as the "paragraph mark" or "blind P." When typesetting your manuscript, the pilcrow is a trusted friend because it tells you where the hidden "space gremlins" are which need to be removed. If you find a ¶ at the end of every line, then you will need to go through and replace them with a space instead.

To manually indent paragraphs, do not use the "Space" or "Tab" bars. This will not convert properly for Kindle. Instead, use the Word-default Paragraph Formatting to indent paragraphs and lists in your manuscript. There are two ways in which you can indent paragraphs:

1. Click on "Page Layout" and specify the amount of indentation in the "Indent" option.
2. Use the ruler at the top of the page to change the indentation. If you do not see a ruler in your Word document, click on "View" and check the ruler option.

You can also follow the online guide:
http://www.ehow.com/how_4477948_set-first-line-indent-microsoft.html

If you have a book with images in it then your images should be inserted in JPEG (or .jpeg) format with centre alignment. Do not copy and paste from another source or it will corrupt when you convert the document. The easiest way to do it is to select "Insert > Picture > [locate and select the file]." If your book has a lot of images, it can be viewed in colour by most e-readers and by readers using applications for PC, Mac, iPad, iPhone and Android.

Similarly, if your book has any graphs or tables in it, they can be inserted using the "Insert" tab at the top of your menu bar and these will then be converted automatically when your book is converted into ebook format.

Fortunately, you can use bold characters, italics and headings, as they will translate into your ebook automatically and directly. Remove bullet points, special fonts, headers and footers as they will not be transferred when you convert it.

Exercise 9. Take time to check your manuscript to avoid spacing issues, indent any new paragraphs and lists and remove "hard returns."

Write a Good Synopsis and Back Cover Blurb

Now that the fundamental issues of increased marketability, professional proofreading and formatting have been addressed (i.e. structural issues), we can turn our attention to the essential information relevant to your book's content (descriptive metadata) which most browsers on Amazon and other e-publishing platforms will read before deciding whether to purchase your book.

First and foremost, make sure you have a catchy synopsis and back cover text for your book. The synopsis should not be more than one page long. If you find this difficult to do, then write a chapter-by-chapter summary of the storyline and then pick out two lines from each chapter and highlight them in a longer, two or three-page version of the synopsis. Leave it for a day, and then take your long synopsis and pare it down to a short, one-page descriptive synopsis. For fiction, you want to make sure the synopsis does not give the plot away; for non-fiction, it should tell the reader what they will be learning by reading your book.

The back cover blurb should not give the plotline away but hook the readers into reading your novel. Talk about the early stages of the book to draw readers in and then give them just enough detail to keep them interested and guessing at the outcome. If you have any reviews or celebrity endorsements then slot short, pithy quotes from them onto the back cover.

Now the difficult part – you need to summarise your book and include any endorsements, all between 80–120 words, in your back cover blurb. That's about the same length as this paragraph, which is exactly 98 words long! Anything shorter is too short and anything longer is too wordy.

A back cover blurb is like a trailer for a movie, and like a first impression in an interview. You only get one chance to make a first impression. Similarly, you only get one chance with your back cover text to inform and entice readers into reading your book.

To write a good synopsis and back cover blurb, you need to recognise what your readers want to know about your book. Put yourself into the mind-set of casual browsers in a bookshop or on Amazon who are spoiled for choice. Why should they purchase *your* book over others in this same genre? How is it going to speak to them and appeal to them in particular? How is it going to improve their lives? How is it going to move them and inspire them?

Make the blurb concise and exciting. So many blurbs start with "This is a story about…" and within a few sentences, they have lost you. It is your shop window for your bookstore. Read some synopses and back cover blurbs from bestselling novels in your genre and copy their style. There is nothing wrong with following other authors' tried and tested formats in drafting suitable back cover copy for your book.

> *Exercise 10. Go to your bookshelf and pull out books in the same genre as yours and read the back cover copy. What did they say in the blurb that made you want to read these books? What clues and buzz words did the authors use to tell you what kind of books they are?*
>
> *Did the language and voice used in the blurb tell you about the tone of the book? If the book is humorous or action-packed, was this obvious in the way the blurb was done? If the book was dark, could you tell? Could you hear the distinctive voice of the author in the blurb? Did you read the blurb and think "Sounds great! I should read this book again"?*

For an example of a book's comic tone caught in the blurb, read the blurbs of Jeff Strand's novels at Fictionwise or on Amazon. Remember your book is *primarily* about people rather than settings, historical locations or scientific facts. With works of non-fiction, tell the reader in a few sentences how they will benefit from reading your book. With works of fiction, bring out the human-interest element in your book or the thrill-seeking aspect to your novel to draw readers in and hold their interest throughout.

You can also edit your book brief or "product description" on Amazon and other publishing platforms to incorporate any new five-star reviews that you receive and keep it updated. The first thing a potential reader will do is read the book's summary and reviews, especially poor ones. From a commercial perspective, think of your book like it was something that you plan to sell on eBay. You have to sum up your book in a pithy description and buyers will leave positive, neutral or negative feedback on your account. These are the first things that "shoppers" or consumers ("end users") will look at when considering whether to buy your product, or, in the case of books, whether to buy into your storyline and decide to purchase and digitally download a copy of your ebook.

Improve Your Book's Frontage

Make sure your Front Matter is professional looking. Front Matter is the beginning pages of a book, which include a Title Page, Copyright Page, Dedication, Acknowledgements, Table of Contents, and possibly a Preface or Prologue.

For a stylish and professional presentation, you should add a Title Page. It is their first impression of you as an author, so you need to get it right. The font of the title of your book should be sized between 24–36 point (depending on the number of words in your title) and centred about one-third of the way down the Title Page with the author's name sized between 14–18 point a few lines below. Insert a page break between your Title Page and the next page of your book, along with page breaks between each front matter page mentioned above and between each chapter. You will see a grey space between each section/chapter, which tells you that you have inserted page breaks properly.

After the Title Page, you need to include a Copyright Page. The most important feature on the copyright page is, of course, the copyright notice itself. It should consist of the following elements:

1. The © symbol, or the word "copyright"
2. The year of first publication of your book
3. Identification of the owner of the copyright – by name, abbreviation, or some other way that it's publically recognisable.

It should look something like the copyright for this book, which looks like this: © Darin Jewell and Conrad Jones 2013.

There is a range of other information that you can add to the Copyright Page, and this is up to the author's discretion. For example, you can include a link to your website or blog, a list of your other publications; you can state which edition of your book it is, provide ordering information, and so on. For more detailed information on what you might want to include on this page, see:

http://www.thebookdesigner.com/2009/10/self-publishing-basics-the-copyright-page/

Most authors like to have a dedication and acknowledgements in the first few pages at the front of their books. These should be on separate, consecutive pages after the Copyright Page. If you have people that you want to mention and thank for their help and support, then you can customise these pages. The Dedication should be short such as "To my son and daughter." You do not need to explain why you dedicated your book to them in particular, especially if your relationship with the person you dedicated your book to should change over time.

For instance, if you put "To my loving wife and life-long partner," it could sound like two persons rather than one which can cause problems in itself, and if the unfortunate should happen and you divorce, you'll regret your detailed dedication. On the other hand, if you put "To my rose," that will suffice. Do tell the person whom you would like to dedicate your book to in advance that you plan to do so. They may say "Thanks, but there's no need," which may be a harbinger of things to come, in which case you'll be glad you asked!

One of my favourite book dedications is from *Winnie the Pooh*, which reads:

To Her

Hand in hand we come
Christopher Robin and I
To lay this book in your lap
Say you're surprised?
Say you like it?
Say it's just what you wanted?
Because it's yours –
Because we love you.

The Acknowledgements page enables you to thank all those who have been instrumental in supporting your literary pursuits and bringing your book to print. Careful thought needs to be given to how many people are mentioned and in what order they're acknowledged. Express your appreciation in a concise manner and avoid strong emotive language. Keep it to one page and avoid the temptation to mention everyone under the sun and keep the acknowledgements under 100 words in length.

Here is a good example of how *not* to do it:

> *I would like to express my deepest, sincere gratitude to the people who have helped & supported me throughout my project. I am grateful to my teacher for her continuous support for the project, from initial advice & contacts in the early stages of conceptual inception & through on-going advice & encouragement to this day.*
>
> *A special thanks of mine goes to my colleague who helped me in completing the book & he exchanged his interesting ideas, thoughts & made this project factually accurate.*
>
> *I wish to thank my parents for their undivided support and interest who inspired me and encouraged me to go my own way, without whom I would be unable to complete my novel which I hope will inspire others. At last but*

not the least I want to thank my friends who appreciated me for my work and motivated me and finally to God who made all the things possible...[1]

This acknowledgement should be revised to read:

I want to thank my parents for all their encouragement over the years, without which this book would not have been written.

I would like to express my sincere gratitude to my teacher, Mrs Evans, for her continuous support and feedback. Thanks for being there for me.

And a special thanks to David Kanute who helped me in completing the book and to Clare Sampson with proofreading and editing.

Finally, I would like to thank God for his daily inspiration.

If you are going to include an Introduction, Preface or Prologue in your book to spell out the benefits to the reader or ease them into the story with some historical context, it should follow the Acknowledgements or, if you'd prefer, the Table of Contents. Follow the same format as above, remembering to insert a page break after each section.

Create an Active Table of Contents (TOC)

For digital books, page numbers don't really apply. This is due to the fact that Amazon Kindle content is resizable, and the number of pages within the book changes as the text scales. Your book should have an active Table of Contents for easy navigation.

On a personal computer, you can use Microsoft Word's built-in Table of Contents creator to generate an active TOC for your book. More details on this feature can be found at:

http://support.microsoft.com/kb/285059

If you're using a Mac computer, you will need to create a Table of Contents manually using the Hyperlink and Bookmark functions.

1 http://wiki.answers.com/Q/How_to_write_acknowledgement (accessed 11 March, 2013).

Converting Your Word Document for Amazon Kindle

When uploading your book to Amazon Kindle, you'll have the option to "Go to" the cover image, beginning and the Table of Contents of your book, anywhere from the content. These are defined by what is known as "Guide Items." If you upload a cover image, the first Guide Item will be set automatically. To define the other Guide Items, you can do the following:

For the beginning

Place the cursor where you want the book to start, click on "Insert > Bookmark." In the "Bookmark name:" field, type "Start" (without the quote marks) and click "Add."

For the Table of Contents

Place the cursor at the beginning of the first entry in the Table of Contents. Click on "Insert > Bookmark." In the "Bookmark name:" field, type "TOC" (without the quote marks) and click "Add."

Creating "Back Matter"

Back Matter consists of the last pages in your book, once the story has ended, which provide additional information that the reader should know such as Bibliographical Info, Appendices, Notes and Glossaries.

There is no specific order in which Back Matter should be presented, so use your own judgment and be sure to insert page breaks after each section.

Saving as Filtered HTML

Once you have inserted your page breaks and you are confident with the layout of your book, save your Word file to your Documents folder or Desktop in Web Page, Filtered (*HTM and *HTML) (for PC) or Web

Page (.htm) (for Mac) format. This format is required to build a successful ebook. Filtered HTML is where the Word-specific functions have been removed from your document. This is useful when you want to display features which are designed specifically for Word, such as "frames" and "text boxes."

To convert a Word file into Filtered HTML, follow these three steps:

1. Open your Word file and click "File," then "Save as."
2. In the "Save" as type box, click "Web Page," then "Filtered."
3. Click "Save."

If you save the file as Filtered HTML and reopen it in Word, its format and appearance may be slightly different as the Word specific-functionality will have been deleted when you saved it. For this reason, save into Filtered HTML only *after* you're finished improving and formatting the document as outlined above and do not plan on making any more changes.

When saving the Word file as HTML, all the images (if any) in the Word file will be extracted, and will be stored in a separate folder. This folder will be saved in the same location where the HTML file is saved.

Uploading an Ebook for Sale on Amazon Kindle: The Technical Part

Once you are fully satisfied with the quality and presentation of your book, upload the converted Word file to Kindle Direct Publishing (KDP) – https://kdp.amazon.com/self-publishing/signin

Within KDP you can firstly add your cover by uploading a product image, which will be added automatically to your book file during publishing.

Once you complete the remaining metadata in KDP and click "Save and publish," your book will appear for sale on the Kindle Store approximately 12 hours later. Within 48 to 72 hours, all other book features should be available on the detail page, such as the product description and links to related physical editions.

Title description

Enter the title of your ebook here. If your ebook is part of a series, you can enter the series title and/or volume number. The title is important to book buyers and new readers. Make sure the title of the book is descriptive of both the genre and content of the book. It's no good writing a crime thriller entitled *Love and Transformation*. The title might mean a lot to you as the author but it will say little and will be confusing to a reader browsing the contemporary thriller charts.

> *Exercise 11. If you had to retitle your book, what would you call it? Is the current title appropriate for the genre, i.e. does it tell you straight away what genre it's in? Does it reflect the tone of your book? Is the title easy to spell and easy to remember? Have you chosen a keyword or phrase from your book? If your book could be summed up in one word, what would it be called? And in two words?*

Description (of your book)

Like the copy on the inside flap of a hardcover book, the description tells readers a bit about your ebook. You can enter a description for your ebook that is between 30 and 4,000 characters in length. At this time, multimedia items such as embedded YouTube videos are not supported in the description. Your book description should appear within 72 hours of the text being uploaded.

Contributors

Enter the names of various people who have contributed to your ebook including authors, editors, illustrators, translators and more. At least one contributor's name is required.

Language

Enter the main language in which your content appears. Kindle currently supports many languages, including English, French, German, Spanish, Italian, Portuguese, Catalan, Galician and Basque.

Publication date

If your title has been previously published in physical or digital format, enter the original publication date. Otherwise, the Kindle Store will automatically enter the date the item is being published once everything has been processed.

Publisher

Enter the publisher's name that you would like listed for your ebook on the book's detail page. This can be an individual or a company name.

ISBN

If you have purchased an ISBN (International Standard Book Number) for your ebook, you should enter it here. ISBNs for print editions should *not* be entered in this field.

Verifying your publishing rights

If your title is intended for the general public, check "This book is in the public domain." If the publishing rights to your book are privately held, check "I hold the rights to this book." Kindle may refuse public domain content already available through their programme.

Categories/genre: The key to understanding your target market

This information will help interested readers find your ebook and is very important. Choose from dozens of categories: Antiques to True Crime and everything in between. Each category also contains subcategories to further classify your content. This section is crucial, as it will pull readers to your book. Don't just pick "Thriller" or "Romance." Think carefully about who your readers will be.

If you are not sure about the precise genre and primary market for your book, or if your book crosses into various genres, it would be useful to go to your local bookshop and identify where you can see your book sitting on the bookshelves if it was in print, i.e. which two books you can see it sitting between. Generally, this is based on your book's genre and your surname, but it is essential for you to know your market if you're going to sell your book to them.

Exercise 12. Spend a half hour observing the people who are casually browsing books in this same section of the bookshop, and take notes. Here is a checklist of questions you might answer in your observational research of book buyers:

Are they primarily male or female?

What is their average age (you should have a ten-year age range)?

What ethnic group do you think they are in?

What is their likely profession?

What does their daily routine involve? (shopping, commuting, planning)

Do you think they are looking to buy a book to read to relax and pass time, or are they looking for guidance and instruction manuals?

What are their interests likely to be (besides reading books)?

This field research will help both in terms of narrowing down the genre (and sub-genre) and positioning your ebook properly within the market.

Once you have listed the types of people, groups and organisations that fall into your target market, you then need to prioritise them in terms of which are most likely to buy your ebook, and do some further research: find out how and where you might contact them to raise awareness of your ebook's publication, and encourage them to buy and download a digital copy of your book.

Keywords and key phrases

It is important to identify and list the keywords that are most likely to sell your ebook. Research other titles in your book's genre among books that are on the top 100 paid in Kindle Store list. To find a Kindle book's sales rank on Amazon – scroll down and look for "Product information." If the book is in the "top 100" it will be given a sales ranking for its categories. If it's not in the top 100, then no sales rank will appear in "Product information."

See whether the top purchased books in your book category or genre contain the same "keyword" or phrase. Use the Amazon "type ahead" feature (the search bar on their site) and type in your keyword or phrase and you'll notice how it "types ahead," suggesting book titles for you. "Type ahead" phrases result from many people searching for a particular title. Incorporate that phrase or keyword into your title and your book will be found more easily on Amazon Kindle.

When you upload your book to Amazon's Kindle Digital Platform (KDP), you are given the option of typing in seven keywords or phrases to help identify your book. Do your homework by researching keywords and phrases that people might search under to find your book as explained above, and do make sure to use all seven! Separate keywords and key phrases using commas.

You can check popular keyword searches on Google Adwords as well, but use these only if necessary, after you've exhausted all the keywords and phrases you found on Amazon first. Remember, Amazon has its own search engine so when you identify a keyword or phrase on Amazon it is showing up because it is a popular search – so use it. You can also go back and change keywords. This allows you to experiment regularly to see which keywords and phrases work best for finding your book.

> *Exercise 12. Take a half hour to identity and "tag" seven keywords or keyword phrases that will help people to find your book on Amazon. For example, if your book is entitled* The Devil's Diary, *you might select*

> *"The Devil's Diary, your name, urban fantasy, horror, paranormal thriller, occult, supernatural thriller," each of which describes your book.*

One of the main benefits of self-publishing is that you can modify the cover, description, pricing, keywords and so on any time you'd like, and this will be implemented quickly in your book's Amazon listing. Take full advantage of this author privilege to keep your book listing current and prominent in the Amazon search engine.

Product image: Cover thumbnail

People do tend to judge a book by the cover. To some extent, it is a matter of personal choice, and no matter how famous you are, it is easy to get it wrong – take, for example, the recent cover design for J.K. Rowling's *A Casual Vacancy*. It is clear they were trying to differentiate the book from the Harry Potter books, and it certainly achieves that end, but if you listen to the critics, it's for all the wrong reasons. If your cover is boring and uninspiring, casual browsers may assume that your book will be the same.

If your book cover isn't eye-catching, particularly as a thumbnail which is a reduced-size version of your cover used to help recognise and organise the book, the potential reader may by-pass it without a second glance. The cover may look brilliant when it is full-sized but in the ebook world it will lose its detail if it is too busy. You will see many thumbnail covers that have been designed on Photoshop and they do stand out and draw you in. If your ebook isn't selling, why not try a new cover?

When *The Child Taker* was published, it had an image of an empty swing which was really effective in conveying the sense of a child being abducted, but when the cover was reduced to thumbnail size for the Amazon listing, the image looked more like a doorway rather than an empty swing, and therefore it lost its intended impact. This did not mean Conrad Jones had to abandon the notion of an empty swing altogether, but he worked with the publisher to select a different image which would convey this sentiment in a thumbnail version as well.

Uploading your cover image

Don't pick a cover which is too detailed or busy. Images must be in TIFF (.tif/.tiff) or JPEG (.jpeg/.jpg) format. You need to size your cover art to at least 1,000 pixels on the longest side. This image will be embedded as the cover inside your book and will appear on the product detail page and in Amazon search results.

Digital Rights Management

You may choose, on a title basis, to apply Digital Rights Management (DRM) technology, which is intended to prevent unauthorised access to or the copying of digital content files for titles. Once your title is published, this setting cannot be changed.

Uploading your book file

After selecting the DRM option that suits you best, the "Browse for book" button will appear. This search facility allows you to browse your computer for digital content and upload it to the Kindle Direct Publishing server. Book files must be less than 50 MB in size, which occasionally can be difficult for books with numerous high-resolution images in them.

Changing your product details

You can change your product details (metadata) anytime you'd like by returning to the "Bookshelf" tab and following the steps below.

1. Return to Bookshelf and click the "Actions" button next to the title for which you would like to update the details.
2. Click "Edit book details" or "Edit rights, royalty, and pricing."
3. Enter the changes you would like published.
4. Click "Save and continue," then click "Save and publish."

Your ebook is now published!

2

HOW TO USE FACEBOOK AND OTHER SOCIAL NETWORKING SITES TO SELL YOUR EBOOK

If you have already published a digital book or you are about to, then you will need to build an Internet marketing platform.

The platform is the foundation from which your author brand will develop and grow. You can easily lay the foundations for an effective marketing foundation in a day. From there you can grow your profile, build your fan base and add followers to each site with minimal effort. As your followers and friends grow, your posts and messages will reach more eyes and if you target your contacts wisely, they will share your links and promotions with their followers, which can reach into the hundreds of thousands. There are a plethora of social networking sites and you cannot work them all to their full advantage so pick the biggest to start with and then you can dabble with the sites on the periphery if you choose to at a later date.

Firstly, what is social media and why is it important? Social media refers to the interaction of people in which they create, share and comment on particular topics or content among themselves in online (or "virtual") communities. For literary purposes, social media channels include "social networking," "social bookmarking" and "social cataloguing."

Social networking sites facilitate the building of social relations among people who might share past history, common interests, activities and daily interactions. Social bookmarking sites enable users to add, annotate, edit, and share bookmarks or "tags" of web documents. Social cataloguing sites are designed to enable readers to catalogue and review books, owned or otherwise, of interest to them, and share their own personal thoughts on various works of literature in this way.

In this section, we will be focusing primarily on social networking sites, in particular the industry leaders including Facebook and LinkedIn, and explaining how to set yourself up on them to promote your book and how to get the most out of them in this regard, as these sites are integral to any successful Internet marketing campaign.

Best Social Media Websites for Books

According to *eBizMBA Rank*, by the end of 2012, the most popular social media sites were as follows:

1.	Facebook	750,000,000 – estimated unique monthly visitors
2.	Twitter	250,000,000 – estimated unique monthly visitors
3.	LinkedIn	110,000,000 – estimated unique monthly visitors
4.	MySpace	70,500,000 – estimated unique monthly visitors
5.	Google Plus+	65,000,000 – estimated unique monthly visitors
6.	DeviantArt	25,500,000 – estimated unique monthly visitors
7.	LiveJournal	20,500,000 – estimated unique monthly visitors
8.	Tagged	19,500,000 – estimated unique monthly visitors
9.	Orkut	17,500,000 – estimated unique monthly visitors

10.	Pinterest	Pinterest	15,500,000 – estimated unique monthly visitors
11.	cafemom	CafeMom	12,500,000 – estimated unique monthly visitors
12.	Ning	Ning	12,000,000 – estimated unique monthly visitors
13.	meetup	Meetup	7,500,000 – estimated unique monthly visitors
14.	mylife	myLife	5,400,000 – estimated unique monthly visitors
15.	badoo	Badoo	2,500,000 – estimated unique monthly visitors

Some of these are social bookmarking sites, like Twitter and Pinterest, but for now we want to concentrate on the following social networking sites which we find are most useful in developing your core marketing foundation for your book – Facebook, LinkedIn, MySpace, Google+, Ning and Bebo.

We will discuss these various sites in their order of importance and utility in promoting your book. Their level of importance will change for you as an author as your marketing develops. Some authors find Facebook the best means to promote their book, while others prefer LinkedIn or Ning.

One of the main strengths of social media is that most of these sites can be linked so once you have an account set up, any post that you make on one site can be shared on the others simply at the click of a button. Remember that we are showing you how to set up your profile on these sites and set yourself up as a published author "in a day." You will not see book sales on day one but if you do it right, you will on day two and your sales will continually grow as your author brand and readership increases, providing your book is good (as explained in Chapter 1).

No marketing campaign on the planet will compensate for a poorly written or poorly presented novel, weak plot or obscure subject matter.

Do not spend money on advertising in the press or with companies who claim to send out press releases for you. *Soft Target* was published as a paperback with one of the biggest self-publishing companies around. They offered some marketing packages, which on paper looked amazing but in reality you can spend £3,000 without seeing any tangible return on your investment. You will be keen and enthusiastic about getting your message to as many people as possible and paying someone to do it for you appears to be the easy option, but we can guarantee that this is a waste of money, especially if you are an independent author. Most blanket press releases don't make it past the spam filters and as we said before, your book is not news yet.

I know a fellow thriller writer who had a friend working in the advertising department at a glossy men's monthly magazine. It is a well-established publication with a huge readership. His friend skilfully secured him a double-page spread advertising his book for free. It sounded like an author's dream come true; two glossy pages in a leading high-street magazine to advertise his book with an editorial spread about the author and the plotline. He ordered hundreds of hard copies of his novel in anticipation of the sales rush for his books.

When the magazine came out, he logged online every hour on the hour to check sales. Nothing happened, in actual fact he sold fewer copies that month than in the month before. The advertising space would have cost him thousands of pounds. He was devastated by the result and if he had bought that advertising space, I think he would have thrown himself under a bus.

When you are preparing your marketing plans, timing is crucial. If you are looking for a magic formula to sell 10,000 copies of your book, then you'll be disappointed. There is no one simple solution. You have to use a targeted strategy rather than shotgun approach to successfully set up a solid marketing foundation for your book, during which you are aiming multiple activities at the same readership and targeting a specific group of people with shared interests.

Ideally you should build up interest in your launch weeks before the actual date but make sure that your book or ebook is uploaded to various retail sites on the Internet and available prior to the launch. If you have the luxury of building foundations before publication, then you are in the perfect position to generate sales from the day your book goes live. If you have already published, then don't worry because you can establish your foundations and then re-launch to your new followers. Remember that careful timing is essential: you should build interest in your launch steadily, peaking just before it goes live. Don't waste a media opportunity by announcing in July that your book will be available from Christmas because, unless you are already a household name, no one will remember.

Develop a Marketing Checklist and Track Your Results

To plan your promotional activities and monitor their success, firstly you need to set up a checklist whereby you can record your activities, set completed-by dates and tick each activity off once it's accomplished. Never throw the checklist away, as you can use it for reference in years to come. This process does require a bit of experimentation, so record as much detail as you can until you have found the format that works for you. As you set up your accounts on Facebook and the other sites, record your passwords and the dates you joined up. Once you have established a foundation, keep a record of when you interacted in each forum or group and that will prompt you to go back and check for any messages sent directly to you that are waiting for a reply.

You can set your accounts so every post in a conversation is sent to your mobile phone and laptop, which is great if you do not want to miss a thing (but a nightmare when your phone is beeping every few minutes). Some readers' and writers' forums are busy places with new posts every few seconds. You cannot be expected to keep your notifications set to receive everything that happens so be sure to set your notifications to the minimum especially as your list of contacts grow.

Keep your checklist up to date, as it will be invaluable to save you time as you develop your author brand and build up a fan base or following. For example:

Activity	When	Completed	Comments/ results
Post a discussion on Ning about thriller writers' forums	1 week before launch	yes	Received invitation to present at an online forum about my biography and new novel. Contact Dave McCann's Facebook page
Contact Carol at Radio Merseyside 0151-487-0000 carol.jones@bbc.radio	1 week after launch	Called Tuesday	Appearing on Carol's show 5/2/2013
Send letters to writing groups in North Wales	2 weeks after launch	Sent out 8 letters	Had 5 replies and 2 invites to present in March

Use a daily, weekly, monthly and six-monthly to-do list to keep yourself organised. For example:

Daily	Weekly	Monthly	6 Monthly
	Check sales reports		
Record any comments on highs and lows	Upload more postings on discussion boards	Update contact lists	Update local radio
Check book reviews; reply to reviewers	Send out bookmarks	Update marketing plan	Update local radio
Check Facebook and update status; reply to any messages	Update book reviews on Goodreads	Update local newspaper	

As a writer, it's all too easy to become totally encapsulated in writing your next book and neglect your marketing plan, which is paramount to the commercial success of your book. I remember asking an author who was published recently what he planned to do to sell and market his book, and he replied, "I think that's the publisher's job." I knew straight away he was not going to be a commercially successful author with that approach. As a general rule of thumb, you should spend as much time promoting your book as you did writing it. Books don't write themselves. They don't sell themselves either.

Until you are disciplined enough to follow a monthly marketing routine automatically, use a "to-do" list daily. Use the power of social media to spread the word about your ebook. The Internet is the key to letting an unknown author place his or her novel next to the biggest names in the literary world. If you use it correctly, you can generate a lot of interest in your books. If you get it wrong, you can become an annoying Internet troll harassing everyone. It is a fine line to cross, so do be careful. Be polite at all times, even when people criticise your work. Remain positive and friendly or you will lose readers when you are trying to gain them and always aim to endear people to you as the author.

> *Exercise 1. Set up a daily, weekly, monthly and six-monthly checklist for your marketing activities. Create a schedule to devoting half of your time to writing your next book and the other half to promoting your last one. Some authors devote the morning to the former and the afternoon to the latter. Some write the first three days of the week and promote the next three days. Develop pattern that works for you, but the important point is that you* actually *devote equal time to both.*

Setting Yourself Up on Facebook

A social network facilitates regular communication between individuals who are connected by friendship or common interest. Most common interest manifests itself as a group. All you have to do is search on Google or other search engines on the Internet for certain keywords linked to your book and you will find groups to join. You can use these networks to enhance your personal network, and increase sales. The key is to use all appropriate functions of a given social network for maximum benefit.

The best place to start is setting up a Facebook (*www.facebook.com*) account and building up a fan base. Facebook allows you to create a profile, join groups of people with similar interests, discuss your personal interests and communicate directly with friends and potential readers. Facebook is massive and is a gift to the unknown author. Every author should be on Facebook regardless of the genre they write in or their literary status, whether they're a first-time author or previously published.

On Facebook, users invite their friends to join their network and send them messages, updating their personal profiles to notify friends about themselves. It is an easy way to stay in touch with friends, and keep them informed of what is happening in your life, *such as publishing a new book.* Users can join relevant networks, which are organised by city, workplace, school, and region. Rather than emailing all your friends individually to tell them about your recently published or forthcoming book, you can tell them all at once this way.

To create a Facebook page, go to http://www.facebook.com/pages and click "Create page" in the upper right-hand corner.

Build your profession into your Facebook name. For example, Conrad Jones's Facebook page is "Conrad Jones bestselling Kindle author." That is not for vanity; it's because he wants people to know they have found the right Conrad Jones and when he requests to join a writing group, it tells them that he might have something useful to offer the group.

Choose the appropriate option from "Local," "Brand or product" or "Artist, band or public figure." You may want to choose the third option and then "Writer" if you are promoting with your name. Otherwise, choose "Brand or product" and then "website" to link to your book promotion blog. Once you are done creating your page, be a fan of it to add it to your personal Facebook profile.

If you have a blog (or "weblog," which we will discuss later), import your blog's feed through the "Notes" feature on the page you just created. You can use your blog's normal RSS ("Rich Site Summary") feed to do this. RSS feeds are often referred to as "really simple syndication" feeds because they benefit authors by letting them syndicate content and distribute information automatically. By posting this feed to "Notes," this enables you to update all your social networking activities to this page and thereby keep your readers constantly informed with relevant links, and anything else you want to tell others about your book. You can also share your book's Amazon link and reviews posted by any other user or website in this way.

Next, you should start building a fan base or following for the page you just created. Share your new page with your friends, and ask them to invite their friends. Make it into an online viral (word-of-mouse) marketing campaign, where anyone who joins invites their friends, and they in turn invite their friends, and so on. That is what social networking is all about!

Resist the temptation to place an advertisement on Facebook for your book, where you agree to "pay for page impressions" or "pay for clicks" to your page. This may bring in some visitors, but there are problems associated with this form of generalised pay-per-click advertising as it is difficult to measure tangible results. Basically, you would be paying for something without having any way of knowing for sure whether you benefited from doing so. You can build up your own, much more tailored network of contacts if you use other applications available to you on the site. And if you did decide to pay for any advertisements on Facebook, focus on the "Sponsored stories" and "Promoting a post" applications on the site, but start by experimenting with a small investment of £5 to £20 and then decide for yourself whether it generated many new visitors and "friends" to your site – not just any visitors, but those interested in you and your writing rather than those trying to sell you something.

You can track your visitor activity using another Facebook application called Facebook Insights. By familiarising yourself and understanding user activity and performance, fans and respondents, and trends and comparisons, you will be better equipped to improve your book's adverts on Facebook and elsewhere. Facebook Insights is a free service for all Facebook pages.

If you already have a Facebook page, hopefully you have established the basics. Go to the "search friend" space at the top of your profile and type in "Kindle." Over 20 groups will appear and you need to join them all. Some of them will be invitation only but you can request an invite. When you have joined a group, make sure that you interact in a positive manner and add the other members as friends. This way your profile as a writer is growing and you are reaching dozens and dozens of people who are interested in books. Do not just join and post a link to your Amazon page and then disappear or you will turn people off you very quickly. Joining a group for shameless self-promotion will not gain you any fans; in fact, it's likely to have the opposite effect.

Using the search bar, type in the names of authors and writers, dozens of groups will appear. Join them and follow the steps above. Add their members to your friends list and remember that the more friends you have and the more interesting your posts are the more people will be interested in you and your books. Introduce yourself to the group and express the desire to talk to other authors and readers about writing and promoting books. Mention that you are looking for reviewers to give you feedback. Do not forget to send speedy replies to any communication you receive.

Once again, do a search, but this time type in "readers." You must be careful with readers' sites. Readers' sites detest self-promotion, especially from unknown self-published authors, and they can be easily offended. Join as many groups as possible and add as many friends from those groups as you can. If you have more time, dedicate time every few days, or if you have less time, every week, to updating and informing people about your book, launch dates, book signings and speaking engagements by regularly updating your profile status.

How to Master Facebook Marketing in One Step Every Day

Watch and learn

Spend some time today exploring other pages on Facebook. Do some searching to find complementary businesses as well as competitors that you can learn from. Look at the Facebook pages of the big brands you admire and the brands your customers have told you they admire.

- Go to www.facebook.com/search to start your research
- Select the pages option to filter your results
- Enter the names of your competitors or keywords in your industry to find pages that may be in your market, although it should be noted that the Facebook search bar is not very robust and sometimes does not find the Facebook page you are looking for – even when you enter the exact name of the page!

If you cannot find the Facebook page of your competitors, go to their websites to see if they have a link to their Facebook page. You can use a third-party search tool called www.FBInstant.net to do some research.

Exercise 2. Spend an hour studying the successful Facebook pages mentioned in these articles:

- *AllFacebook: The 100 Most Engaging Brands on Facebook*
- *HubSpot: 20 Examples of Great Facebook Pages*
- *HubSpot: 7 Awesome B2B Facebook Fan Pages*
- *Social Media Examiner: Top 10 Small Business Facebook Pages: 2011 Winners*

And ask yourself the following questions:

What are you looking for on these pages? You are gathering information about what is working and taking note of these key points:

How often is the page posting? What times are they posting?

What are they posting?

What is getting the most interaction – pictures, links, videos, questions?

Try out the following:

Liking, commenting or sharing one of your page posts (or other content on your page – such as photos, videos, albums)

Answering a question you posted

RSVP-ing to an event created by your page

Tagging your page either in your status or a photo

Checking into your place

Liking or sharing a check-in deal

Does the page have a "welcome tab" or any other custom tabs?

How does the welcome tab showcase the business?

What other tabs do they have? Tabs are located on the left side bar of the Facebook page.

It is also worthwhile to take note of what is not working for these pages and what you can do better. For example, see how Pringles, Nutella, and Reese's do a great job with varying their posts and encouraging engagement on Facebook, while other lesser-known companies have a Facebook presence, but do little to actively post or simply post adverts about their products, which will not build up a fan-following on Facebook and can actually be counterproductive.

Understand Facebook "best practices"

Now that you have spent some time researching the competition and big brands, you may notice some Facebook "rules of thumb" that bubble to the surface. While there are not any hard and fast rules in social media, there are some general "best practices" that are you can start with as a base. Ultimately, you will have to find your own way with what works with your audience and what they need from you, but there are definitely some pitfalls and quicksand that you want to avoid along the way.

You will notice that successful brands on Facebook do not preach or sell to their fan base, they engage with them. Just like in the real world. Customers know when a salesperson is being disingenuous and it turns them off. They also know when a salesperson is genuinely interested in understanding their needs and finding out how best to meet those needs. Facebook is no different.

Here are some good general unwritten rules that should guide your Facebook page posts:

- **Post daily.** This may seem excessive but as people make more friends and Like more pages, your posts may be missed. If you are only posting once or twice a week then it could be a long time between posts if your community misses one or two of them. Studies have shown that posting three to five times a day can be a good amount for pages (make sure you are varying your posts and also watch your statistics to see what works best for your community). You can decide to take the weekend off but also realise that the weekend is when many people are on Facebook.
- **Focus on engagement.** You are trying to connect and get a response from your community. Ask questions, post helpful tips, links to articles that your audience will Like and Share. When you make the posts about your audience and what they need rather than selling, you will develop a richer and deeper relationship with your community. You will sell more as a by-product of that deeper relationship. Set aside time to follow up on posts and respond to questions on your Wall.
- **Have a call to action.** Ask people to click the Like or comment on the post. Have them watch your video or go to your website.
- **Do not oversell or undersell.** No one likes a never-ending sales pitch. By the same token, make sure you do highlight your book from time to time! Use the 80–20 rule for content/connection posts vs. sales messages. So if you decide to post five times a week, one of

the posts should be a subtle sales message and four posts will be other helpful or entertaining content for your community.

- **Make it fun.** Facebook is a social community. People are there to have fun. This is a place where you can let your corporate hair down a little. Stay true to your author brand in terms of your Facebook demeanour, but think of ways to capture and hold the attention of your audience as you do with your writing.

These unwritten rules of best practice on Facebook are a good place to start but you need to see what works best for you. There is no one "right" way to do everything on Facebook.

Learn Facebook lingo

Do you like me or do you Like me? Like, what's that all about?

Learning to "speak Facebook" is simple. Here's what you need to know:

Application (or "app" for short): Applications, apps, or applets are software programs tailored to interact with Facebook users. Apps are used to facilitate any number of content-sharing or interaction functions between your Facebook page, your website or blog, and users, for example to showcase your LinkedIn profile or YouTube channel on your Facebook page.

Fan: When you or another Facebook individual chooses to Like a person's or organisation's page, you become a Fan of that person or enterprise. It is like being a diehard Trekkie or one of those people who seems to live permanently at Starbucks. According to the latest stats, 56% of people are likely to recommend a brand to a friend after becoming a fan, and there is nothing better than a recommendation from a trusted friend to others to sell your book – that is what online (viral) marketing is all about.

In 2010, Facebook changed the vernacular slightly from "fan pages" to "business pages" that users could "Like," but the term fan remains popular and is still commonly used, long after the last real Elvis "fan" has left the building.

Friend: One of the trickier Facebook terms, friend is used as a noun and a verb in Facebook-ese. As a noun, a friend is someone with whom you have established a connection in your social network. The act of making that connection is to "friend" (or befriend) someone. Facebook has been different from Twitter and Google+ (but similar to LinkedIn) in that people have to mutually agree to become connected as friends. This changed slightly in September 2011 with the advent of the subscribe function, which enables you to get the same updates that their friends do if they allow the subscribe function, even if they remain aloof and do not want to befriend you.

Friend list: As the name suggests, this is simply a list of one's Facebook friends. Facebook has enhanced the capabilities of friend lists recently so you can select which of your friends you would like to share certain details or information with. Some may be interested in your book, whereas others might be interested more in your social activities. Posting to a select friend list resolves that problem and Facebook is currently developing a "smart list" application which will automatically identify what information goes out to which of your friends in future.

Group: This is a group of Facebook users organised around a common interest, which is very important for authors wanting to discuss writing in general or their book in particular. Any Facebook user can create his or her own group. Group members can engage in live "group chat" and can receive mailing list notifications.

Like: In the world according to Facebook, "like" can have three different meanings:

- When someone professes their affinity for someone's Facebook page, they can actively "Like" it and thereby become a fan
- When someone on Facebook wants to express their agreement with another person's comments on their Wall (or news feed), they will "Like" the comment
- A "Like" button can be installed on websites outside of Facebook which, when clicked, enables the person to "Like" a page on a website

or a blog post, which will then post a "story" to their news feed that they have liked that post or page on a website; this "Like" button does not translate into someone becoming a "fan;" rather, it posts a one-time story onto the person's Wall (or news feed)

Network: In Facebook parlance, a network is a common association of Facebook users based on a school or employer.

News feed: This is where your friends' wall posts are aggregated for you to view in a select section of your Facebook homepage. It keeps users informed of what their friends (or the enterprise they "Like") are doing.

Social plugins: These are applications that you can install and reside on your website. They help connect your website and your fans to your Facebook page. They can show visitors to your site who in their social network recently engaged with your site and make recommendations to the social network based on interactions between your company and your fans. The Like button is the best-known social-plugin but it is only one of many. A Like box can be added to your site which will allow people to become your fan without leaving your site.

You can see a full list at: http://developers.facebook.com/docs/plugins

Tag: Friends can "tag" their friends in posts, pictures, notes and videos by typing the @ symbol followed by the person's name. Then they select the name from a dropdown list to hyperlink it to the other person's profile. The person will get a notification that they have been tagged. People and other pages can tag your Facebook page as well by using the same method. A Facebook page cannot tag a person unless the administrator of the page is a friend of that person. Use the tagging feature sparingly – too much tagging on one page can be spam-like.

Ticker: This is one of Facebook's features and it is found on the right side bar of the news feed. Ticker posts "activity stories" such as commenting on someone's post or picture, checking in, using apps, Liking a page, and so on. The news feed will contain status updates and posts from friends and pages that you Like.

Timeline: Think of this as the story of your life, Facebook-style. Whereas the news feed drops stories as new ones are added, the timeline feature lets users determine how much, or how little, of their life is shared via this linear view of your life history.

Wall: This is your electronic whiteboard on your Facebook page, the place where you post content and your fans can post their comments. You used to have a Wall on your personal profile, but now your friends can post on your timeline. There is a blank field that allows up to 5,000 characters of comments, which you then publish by hitting the "Share" button. You can also post links, photos, videos or questions to your Wall. Fans and other Facebook pages can tag your page and the post will show up on your Wall.

That is all there is to it. Now you speak, *parlez* and *habla* Facebook.

Add to your page

Now that you are familiar with the lingo, it's time to spruce up your page. Your page should be an inviting place for people to come and should give potential fans a clear picture of your literary achievements and aspirations.

The first thing to add to your book's page is the cover photo. Since Facebook launched the timeline feature for all such pages, you now have the ability to showcase even more of your book's content. There are a number of things you can do to make the cover photo creative and interactive, including:

- Connecting the profile picture to the cover photo
- Highlighting your book's local or regional "hooks"
- Showing fans reading and endorsing your book
- Showing yourself and readers at a book signing

The next thing to consider to brand your page is the profile picture. This is the image that will appear when people search for your book, so you want it to include your logo and name. You can connect your profile picture to your cover photo if you wish for an interesting first impression.

Once you have your new profile picture, you can upload it and adjust it by following these steps:

1. Click the "Edit profile picture" button as you hover over the picture.
2. Select "Upload a new photo."
3. Click the "Choose file" button to find your new profile picture.
4. Once uploaded, underneath the picture, click the "Edit thumbnail" link to select the portion of the picture you would like displayed next to your posts.

You may want to add some additional apps to spice up your Facebook page. Here is a list of some of the more commonly used apps. Select the ones that will be useful for your book:

Networked Blogs: http://apps.facebook.com/blognetworks

This will import your blog (if you have one) automatically into your Wall whenever you have a new post.

RSS Graffiti: http://apps.facebook.com/rssgraffiti

This will import any RSS feed into your wall.

Payment: http://apps.facebook.com/payment

Use this application to create a storefront on your fan page. This is useful because you can sell your book directly from your fan page. You can set it so that your fans get special discounts available only to them.

Causes: http://apps.facebook.com/causes

If you want your book to raise money for a special cause or concern, this application enables you to do so.

Booshaka: http://www.booshaka.com/

This shows a list of your top fans by how much they interact with you.

Fan of the Week: https://apps.facebook.com/fanofthe/

This automatically picks your "fan of the week" based on interaction and posts the message about the new fan each week.

Another website called Involver (www.involver.com) lists further useful apps that you can incorporate into your book's marketing plans. There is a YouTube application and a Twitter application that will import information from those social media sites into tabs on your Facebook page.

Understanding EdgeRank and the art of engagement

Remember first and foremost that Facebook is a business and it makes money by serving up readers to advertisers, just like any other content-driven journalistic enterprise. Like any good content provider, Facebook thrives on giving its audience content that is popular, relevant and timely.

These three attributes, which Facebook refers to as weight (relevance), affinity (popularity), and time decay (timely), comprise the "EdgeRank." These three things are the "edges" that determine what content is likely to be most interesting to you, the audience, and drives its "rankings."

"Affinity" is the score between the viewer and the "edge" creator. How closely you are tied to the person creating the content determines this score. "Weight" is the value given to the comments and actions any given post receives from your Facebook community. As they "Like" it, comment on it and tag it, it gains in relevance to the community at large.

"Time decay" is just the lessening value of the content as time passes. Today's news is news. Yesterday's news is history.

The more often others comment on, click, Like and tag your content, the sharper your "edges" and the more likely your content will display in their news feeds. Gaining a high EdgeRank is contingent on creating content that gets people to click on it and do so consistently.

Give people content they find interesting and they will take Facebook action that raises your EdgeRank scores and leads to more "face time" in the literal sense on Facebook. You can use the independent third-party website www.edgerankchecker.com to gauge your score.

This site only provides an estimate of how well you are engaging your audience and is not an actual Facebook score. The site also tells you what days your page tends to get the best engagement. Do not assume people will respond just because you gave them great content. It is still best to come out and ask for a response. If you look at the posts from successful Facebook sites you will notice that they almost always ask for some type of input at the end. What do you think? Do you agree? Can you think of other ways to encourage people to provide input? Using these questions will help illicit a response from your audience, and thus move you up the EdgeRankings.

With the latest changes in Facebook, it is even more important to get that coveted interaction because your post will be more prominently featured as a top story. This top story shows more prominently even though it may have been posted an hour ago and there are other more "recent stories."

One of Facebook's newest metrics that measures your engagement is the "People are talking about this" statistic. This number will give you a good sense of your interaction levels. Watch the trend of this number in your "insights" by watching the "Weekly talking about this" graph.

Put on a show

Facebook, like most social networking websites, is all about community. Leverage Facebook to bring the community together in real time (albeit virtually) and foster that sense of togetherness – just you, your book and your closest fans and friends.

Exercise 3. Spend some time brainstorming and planning the types of events you can host on Facebook.

Some ideas include:

- Formally launch or announce the publication of your book
- Host a panel webinar regarding recent developments on Facebook or changes in the publishing industry in response to the digital revolution
- Host a live chat on your Wall with an expert in your book's genre

You will need an application or plug-in for video such as:

http://www.facebook.com/ustream or http://www.linqto.com/

Live events on Facebook let you speak directly to your potential fans and vice versa. They provide you with an opportunity for you to engage readers in real-time while highlighting your books, explaining details about relevant "hooks" in your books, or just showing your appreciation to your fans by giving them an experience that is unique to your author brand, something which they can then share with their social network and help spread the word and recommend your work to others.

Using video adds a slight layer of complexity insofar as you will need an app or plugin, but hosting a live chat on your Wall can be the easiest way to do something special for your audience. You can act as moderator and post questions directly to the Wall and have the expert answer or you can have your Facebook community post questions directly on your Wall and get a direct answer and as an added bonus, this activity helps your EdgeRankings.

And the winner is... your book

> *Exercise 4. Take 20 minutes to look at the Cathedral City Facebook page and see what they have done to generate interest in their product on their Facebook page.*

Sales of Cathedral City cheese topped £230 million in 2011, accounting for about ten per cent of the nation's cheese market. The brand has successfully used social media to further its appeal and now has over 15,000 followers ("Likes") on its Facebook page. The value of Cathedral

City sales have risen by eighty per cent over the past four years and the cheese is now stocked in one in every three British households. *What have they done to drive sales through their social media campaigns?*

On a smaller scale, take a look at various literary contests on Facebook. Put "book contest Facebook" into any search engine for a current list. For example, Bookshare (www.bookshare.org) uploaded a Facebook contest page asking "How has Bookshare made a difference in your life? Tell us in 150 words or less how Bookshare has helped you, your child, or your students and inspire other people with print disabilities to read and open up the world of books." In the contest details, it states that "Bookshare is the world's largest online accessible library of copyrighted content for people with print disabilities... The library has tens of thousands of books including fiction, non-fiction, textbooks, educational reading, newspapers and magazines, plus software applications that read digital content." *What can you do to mirror Bookshare's marketing campaign?*

There is a difference between a sweepstakes and a contest and that difference is significant in Facebook terms. In a sweepstakes, people drop their entry in a box, real or virtual, and wait to see whose lucky ticket is drawn. But a contest requires entrants to get creative. It requires participants to get engaged and that engagement drives relevance, something Facebook and Facebook relationships thrive on.

If you want to run your own Facebook contest centred on your book, keep the following tips in mind:

1. Integrate and cross-promote your contest across your marketing media.

2. Award prizes relevant to your author brand and your books, prizes that will keep telling your story long after the contest is over.

3. Read Facebook's contest rules carefully. They will shut you down if they find you breaking their rules. Spend some time studying http://www.facebook.com/promotions_guidelines.php

Gaining further insights

You may think you are doing everything you can to build an engaged Facebook audience, but just to be sure you can check on Facebook's analytic package called "insights." To see the Insights for your page, click the "Edit page" button on the upper right of the page (assuming that you are logged in as one of the page administrators). Select "Insights" from the left-hand navigation. This will take you to the "Overview" page, which has two sections. You will see graphs showing users, which represent the counts of people who have viewed or interacted with your page (even if they have not "Liked" it).

Right underneath that is the overview for interactions, which counts the number of people who have Liked or commented on your posts. You can click "See details" for either users or interactions to see what is behind the totals. Importantly, the user details include the "Like sources" so you can get a feel for where your audience is coming from. The user details have standard demographics for the people who Like your page. If you click on "See details" for interactions, it will take you to a page showing how many times each of your page posts has been viewed. It will also show you the feedback for each day – how many people Liked, commented or unsubscribed (perhaps it was something you said?). Underneath that is one of the gems of insights, a listing of every one of your posts with counts for impressions and feedback. This gives you a good sense of what "works," i.e. which of your postings are engaging readers. Facebook is rolling out new insights and metrics all the time, so it would be useful to log onto this section and see the latest they have to offer.

The overview page displays a graph of your weekly total reach as well as the viral reach of each of your posts. You can filter this by post type to see which posts work best for you. If you drag the pointer over the question marks, Facebook will give you a tutorial to help you along.

Insights can tell you about those plug-ins that you've been putting on your website, including the "Like" button. You will be able to see which content from your website is generating the most "Shares," which of the plug-ins that you have installed are getting the most clicks and what are the most active times for sharing on your site. Whether the details are about your website or your Facebook page, insights provide you with useful information about your readership and contributes to the author brand that you are building. The more you know about your readers the more you can tailor your marketing campaign to suit them.

Besides insights on your Facebook page, you can monitor what is being said about you or your book on social networks in general. There are a number of free online tools that enable you to do this including:

- Kurrently (www.kurrently.com) – monitors Facebook and Twitter activity
- Social Mention (www.socialmention.com) – searches user-generated content such as blogs, comments, bookmarks, events, news and videos, and monitors more than 100 social media sources including Twitter, Facebook, FriendFeed, YouTube, Digg, Google, etc.
- Topsy (www.topsy.com) – social analysis and search tool powered by tweets and sorted by relevance or date
- HowSociable (www.howsociable.com) – analyses activity on thirty-six popular social media sites; allows you to identify your author brand's strengths and weaknesses, set goals and measure improvements
- Tinker (www.tinker.com) – searches for the top news events, topics and places people are talking about

There are aspects of Facebook marketing that seem complicated at first, but you can substantially improve the metrics that matter in terms of tailoring your book's marketing campaigns to reach millions of potential readers in a relatively short period of time. The time invested in learning more about Facebook marketing will help you generate more traffic to your website, more sales, and more and better ways to connect with your readers so they can provide useful feedback on your books and tell you what they want and expect from your writing.

"Must-dos" when Tailoring Facebook for Your Book's Promotion

Facebook is the quickest and most effective way to connect with friends and family and can be an effective way to promote your book and yourself, but you may be wasting your time (or worse) if you do not learn how to use it effectively. Here are the steps on how to set up an account and the tips and common mistakes authors make on Facebook, along with ways on how to avoid them.

Use your to-do list to set out goals and objectives

> *Exercise 5. Before you start using Facebook on a daily basis to promote your book (or any other social network), think through your goals first. Are you using it primarily for business? Should you separate your business and personal identities? What are you hoping to achieve through social networking? How will you measure your success? How can you measure your efforts? How can you link Facebook to your other networks? How much time will you budget for promoting your book on Facebook? The answers to these questions will determine how you use it and how often you log into Facebook to promote yourself and your book.*

Set up a personal profile before you set up a fan page

There is nothing wrong with using your personal Facebook profile to promote your book, but Facebook's rules require that profiles be set up in the name of a real person and they limit each person to one profile. If you set up your profile under a pen name or as one of the main characters in your book, you risk having your account cancelled by Facebook. To create a presence for the title of your book, you need to set up a fan page.

Use a professional image such as your book cover

You may want to use your book cover as your Facebook image sometimes – for example, during your book launch. But most of the time you should use a photo of yourself. Facebook is a social network and people want to befriend a person, not a book. Do not undermine your credibility by using a picture of yourself with a group of friends at a party. Make it personal and professional. On all your networks you should use your standard author publicity photo or your book cover.

Always be polite and professional

We have all seen people who use social networks to solely promote themselves. They post a constant stream of promotional messages and even make purely promotional posts on other people's profiles and pages. Do not forget that Facebook is a *social* network – you need to develop relationships with people first. If you interact with others, post useful comments, help others out and participate in the community, most people will not mind if you make some promotional posts. Just be somewhat subtle about it and do not overdo it.

Remember that bad news travels faster than good news so be careful when interacting with readers/fans. We have all witnessed some long-winded exchanges on book review sites that would make you cringe. Eventually the argument becomes the focus rather than the book or the review. Social networking sites precipitate word-of-mouse (*viral*) marketing, adding value to your book, so do not underestimate the damage you could do by being crass or obtuse.

Third-party endorsements are the best recommendation that you can hope for and readers love it when you comment on their review of your book, even if it is a mediocre or poor review. Remember that they have spent their money buying your book, invested their time reading it and then taken the time to sit down and share their thoughts with you or write a review. They are entitled to their opinion and listening to your readers is one of the best ways to improve your writing and increase your marketing reach.

Make sure that you interact

Some authors never mention their book anywhere, even on their own profile! Writing and publishing a book *is* a major accomplishment – list it prominently in your profile. Mention it in the info box beneath your photo and include a link to your book's website or Amazon page on your information tab. Mention your book promotion activities or articles regularly in your status updates. If you're still working on your book, say so in your profile and talk about your progress in your status updates.

Make sure that you join groups

Facebook groups are one of the most important ways to promote a book on Facebook. Use the search box at the top of the screen to find groups that cater to your book's topic, genre or target audience and become active in those groups. Do not forget groups geared towards authors and publishing. Join in the discussions, comment on wall posts, post your own discussion question or send a message to the group leader with a suggestion. You can even start your own group.

Follow other fan pages

In addition to setting up a fan page for your book or business, it is a good idea to join (or "Like") other relevant pages. Some fan pages have discussions or allow fans to make wall posts. Drop by occasionally to make a comment, without appearing too promotion-oriented. Check out the fan pages of well-known authors who write books similar to yours.

Do not wait for people to find you, go and find them

Once you become active on Facebook, you will start to receive friend requests and fans. But do not just sit and wait for people to find you. Include a prominent link to your Facebook profile and other pages on your own website, blog and email signature. As you visit other blogs and websites, actively look for the Facebook icon on those sites so you can connect with them on Facebook. Also, look for new friends in the Facebook groups that you join – the people in relevant groups probably share some of your interests.

Make sure you change your privacy settings

In their efforts to generate revenue, Facebook continues to look for ways to use the personal data on their site. As a result, Facebook has made a number of changes to their privacy policies and default privacy settings over the past few years. Make time today to review your privacy settings on a fortnightly basis.

Exercise 6. Click on the "Account" link in the upper right corner of your Facebook screen and select "Privacy settings." Review each of the privacy pages and think about how to best adjust the settings to protect your personal information, while still making information accessible for promotion purposes. And be careful about revealing too much personal information anywhere online.

Spending too much time on Facebook

Social networks like Facebook can be addictive, and it is easy to spend way too much time on the site. Schedule a set amount of time each week for networking. Facebook can be an enjoyable and effective way to promote your book and yourself. Have fun with it but keep in mind that there are other social media sites that require similar time and attention.

LinkedIn Can Sell and Market Your Book

Join LinkedIn and follow the same basic rules as the Facebook tips. Remember that LinkedIn is a professional site for executives and senior management from every industry. There are a multitude of author groups, publishers groups, self-publishers, agents and marketing forums. The site gives you the facility to invite everyone in your email address book to join your network by clicking one button. The author groups and marketing forums are extremely vibrant and useful.

Join marketing groups and as many book-related forums as you can. Set aside half an hour every day to participate in the forums. Read the discussions in the marketing forums as there are hundreds of people asking the same questions as you are. There is a plethora of information to be learned on this site and people are very quick to point out any pitfalls that they have fallen into. Learning from other authors' mistakes and helping them to avoid the ones you've made is a valuable exercise.

Link your LinkedIn account to your Twitter and Facebook accounts. They will syncronise at the click of an icon, saving you a lot of time and effort. These channels thrive on authentic social interactions, so be careful not to overtly sell yourself or your ebook to avoid alienating the connections that you make. For example, rather than posting multiple messages about your ebook being available for sale, try to contribute meaningful dialogue in conversations about relevant and related topics. This will position you as an intelligent writer whose advice people follow, which will help build your author brand.

Be careful not to hassle or annoy literary agents and publishers. You will find some cringe-worthy conversations between disparaging, know-it-all writers and not-so-desperate agents on the site. They tend to be short, one-sided affairs with abrupt endings! While you might be tempted to tell them what you think about the publishing industry's exclusivity and their representation and publication of celebrity authors writing dross or those who have their books ghost-written and put their names to them, it's better to only offer constructive, positive information that may help other writers. Always be mindful not to say anything which might offend and alienate *anyone* on discussion boards, writings forums, at writing groups or in any of your marketing channels.

Talk about your ebook in an open forum intelligently and realistically. Don't claim to have sold 10,000 copies of your ebook when your Amazon ranking proves you have sold ten. You can share any genuine reviews that you receive and post links to your ebook, which gives your target audience the chance to glance at your work and make up their own minds as to its merits and its commercial success.

LinkedIn is a useful tool also for making business connections and meeting other authors, but remember that it is just another tool in the box. Even the most active users miss out on some simple ways to optimise the way they use LinkedIn. Below are a few tips on how to make the most of your LinkedIn presence.

- **Think about your goals.** Why are you on LinkedIn? Is it to find new readers and other authors? To be discovered as an aspiring new author by an agent or publisher? A mix of the two? Your goals should drive your entire presence on the site.
- **Post a picture of your face.** You should have a professional looking headshot as your LinkedIn photo so people can put a name to a face. If you're uncomfortable with readers or prospective agents seeing your picture next to your professional credentials, you can change your privacy settings so only your connections can see your photo.
- **Use LinkedIn to remember names.** LinkedIn can also help with offline networking. Simply checking on someone's profile after meeting them at a networking event, even if you do not connect, can help you remember their name and what they do. This is another reason why having a picture is important – it will help people remember you.
- **Make the most of your LinkedIn headline.** Your headline does not have to be your job title alone. Keep it concise, but make sure that it conveys what you do and what your skills are.
- **Post status.** Updating your status gives you visibility on your connections' LinkedIn home page. If you have found something online you think your business connections would like, or you have good news to share about your work, spread the word by posting it on LinkedIn.
- **Write a content-rich but concise summary about yourself.** Your summary should be about you as a writing professional, not your book.

Use concrete details like results you have generated and the work you do on a daily basis to *show* people how professional you are, not *tell* them. It is important to strike the right balance between self-promotion and self-aggrandisement. Just stick to the facts, and be subtle in your approach. You want to use your profile and summary to endear readers to you, not alienate them by talking solely about me, myself and I.

- **Explore various LinkedIn applications.** Add Amazon's Reading List application to your LinkedIn profiles and find out what other people in your industry are reading. It's simple! Start by adding the books you are planning to read, reading right now and have read already to the list. You can then discover a world of books that your peers in your current industry and in your network are reading. You can also follow specific like-minded people and share your love of books with each other. If you are not sure how the fiction you read is relevant to your professional connections, think again. Authors often get more comments on this list than anything else in their profile.
- **Add further sections.** This will give readers a better view of who you are and what you are interested in. This will help link them to you. LinkedIn offers several sections beyond the standard so users can showcase their volunteer experience, book projects, foreign languages and hobbies. This is especially helpful for new networkers who may not have extensive work experience outside of writing a book. Adding more sections can add weight to any profile and will help others to identify you as someone they would like to get to know or follow because of shared history, experiences, pursuits and interests.
- **Connect with care.** Your network is only as valuable as the strength of your connections. For some professionals, it is advantageous to connect generally, but often authors tend to favour smaller useful lists. If you would like to connect with someone and think it might be a stretch, be sure to personalise the message you send with the invite to explain why you want to connect with them in particular (for their benefit, not necessarily your own) and why this person should want to connect with you.

- **Join and participate in discussion groups.** Some groups are full of spam, drivel and dross, but many others are generally valuable. For example, book marketing groups are great places to get and give useful writing tips and advice on contacts, upcoming events and so on. Do a little research, think back to your goals and you will likely find groups that will help you reach them. If you cannot find a suitable group to marry up with your specialist writing and unique interests, start one!

Writers are creative. That's what they do day in and day out in their writing, create captivating scenes and characters. Think about creating an account for your protagonist and hold conversations in the voice of that character. The Jack Reacher (Lee Child) forums are constantly busy with readers and avid fans discussing the fictional hero as if he's real. It is not everyone's cup of tea but it works for several authors.

There are networks designed to connect business professionals such as Plaxo, Ryze and most recently BranchOut (a Facebook/LinkedIn hybrid). Explore and perhaps target some of these other social networks based on the content of your book. Follow the same steps in setting up your profiles on those sites as you did for your Facebook and LinkedIn profile. Again, the sites are linked so you might as well take full advantage of the exposure they can offer.

MySpace as a Means to Promote Your Book

myspace.com expands your contact network and increases the number of people you know by enabling you to meet your friends' friends, their friends' friends and their friends' friends' friends. This is how it works:

1. You join MySpace and create a profile.
2. You invite your friends to join MySpace and search MySpace for friends who are already members. These people become part of your initial "Friend Space."

3. All of the people in your friends' Friend Space become part of your network, and so on. You then have connections to more people than you did 15 minutes ago.

You can request to add anyone to your Friend Space, and if your invitation is accepted, you can send that person a general email, text messages or link to your book.

In your profile, you can write about your book, as well as your literary inspirations and aspirations. You might mention your goals as a writer, your next book project, your literary achievements and any reviews that have been written about your book. You can provide links to online websites where your books are available for purchase, including your own website or blog. The more content-rich your profile is on your MySpace the more likely you are to draw in interest from others.

Add pictures of the front and back covers of your book. If you are going on any book festivals, writing groups, networking functions or talks, to someone else's book launch or having any book signings of your own, provide dates for those as well, and make sure that you keep your MySpace profile up to date. Include contact information for those who may want to contact you for book signings and appearances, especially if you would like to speak to libraries, schools, societies or peer groups about your books or your literary pursuits.

> *Exercise 7. Browse for groups that have writers in your particular genre or those that have authors who are promoting their own books and support them as best you can. Add others within the publishing industry as "friends" and contact them for practical tips and ideas for publishing and promoting your book.*

Here are some interesting and useful groups on MySpace for authors:

Authors of MySpace (www.myspace.com/myspace_authors) showcases the talents of authors and promotes new releases across its network to other writers. A new book is spotlighted for a week with a trailer in the new books section, where interviews, upcoming events and calendars are posted.

Writers Together (www.myspace.com/writerstogether) is another useful resources for writers. It features authors and their work with links to where their books can be purchased. It provides hundreds of links on writing in general and others that are genre-specific, or related to short fiction and interviews. It explains how to subtly self-promote your book as well as self-promote by promoting and reviewing others' books.

Wordplay Workshop (www.myspace.com/wordplayworkshop) aims to bring together a diverse range of aspiring writers and artists in an interactive MySpace community, where writers can offer constructive criticism, workshops can be hosted, improvisational poetry games, fun challenges and literary competitions. It provides a comfortable writing community designed for this generation, without any dictate or literary dictator presiding over everything. It's like an open mic with rappers, lyricists, poetry podcasts, wordsmiths and wordplays.

The Writer's Services (www.myspace.com/writersservices) specialises in proofreading works of fiction and non-fiction, magazine coverage, and writing blogs. According to their MySpace page, they have specialist knowledge of criminal justice, criminology and forensic psychology, cryptozoology, the paranormal and the horror genre. Obviously, this is genre-specific, but the point is there are similar pages and resources for all types of writers and genres on MySpace's millions of pages, with new ones being added every day.

The Writers Mafia Organization (http://www.myspace.com/writersmafia) provides opportunities for young writers to become published authors. The organisation provides information, support and general community, and regularly hosts writing seminars and participates in publishing projects. Their slogan is "Create. Influence. Change." They believe that "immortal words can help change the world." One of their projects is blurbings.com, which enables new talent to reach a multitude of readers by promoting their name and book on other authors' books, websites and profiles.

If you are a frequent user of MySpace, here are various applications you might find useful both in terms of general interest and in linking to other networking sites:

- Places to Find Me

  http://www.myspace.com/games/play/108953
  This conveniently links your MySpace account to your other social networking profiles on Facebook, Bebo, etc.

- Custom Countdown

  www.myspace.com/games/play/102985
  Counts down to your next big event. Alternatively, try Countup to special events. You can showcase them and use it as a means to add friends.

- iTwitter

  www.myspace.com/games/play/132248
  Displays your latest Twitter updates on your profile page and enables you to post directly to Twitter via your MySpace account.

- Twitter Follow Me

  www.myspace.com/games/play/158397
  Display your own customised Twitter "Follow me" button on your MySpace profile page.

- FriendFeed

  http://www.myspace.com/games/play/110530
  Allows you to enter your FriendFeed nickname and it will show on your profile/home page.

- Profile Photo Album

  http://www.myspace.com/games/play/115953
  You can add your book covers, front and back, if you would like. Browse photos and albums on your MySpace page.

- weRead – Books iRead

  http://www.myspace.com/games/play/103575
  Create your own virtual bookshelf and discover what your friends are reading.

- RSS Reader

  http://www.myspace.com/games/play/107266
  Display your blog, news, or other customised Rich Site Summary feed, perhaps in concert with Google's Feedburner.

- Create Free Polls

  http://www.myspace.com/games/play/109320
  Make an animated flash poll within seconds, share it with friends, and drive visitors to your MySpace page.

- YouTubePost

  http://www.myspace.com/games/play/122774
  You can share any YouTube videos about your book with your MySpace friends.

As you can see from the list above, there are several options available to connect your MySpace account with your other social media sites. Once you have those set up you won't need to log onto each of them each time to keep your profile updated.

MySpace is another instrument in your marketing toolkit, another useful channel to market for your book. Some writers prefer it to LinkedIn, and others prefer Facebook. Just as you use different tools for different jobs, it depends on what you want to achieve from your marketing campaign – to raise your literary profile? Build up a following? Establish yourself as a credible author or an expert in a certain field? Make money from your writing? See it as a self-publishing means to a traditional-published end? All of the above?

Exercise 8. Ask yourself again why you want to sell and market your book. List the reasons in order of priority to you. Tailor your marketing campaign around your priorities. For example, some social networks like Facebook will enable you to establish a "Fan base;" others will facilitate discussion on areas of common interest; some will offer advice to improve your writing; and yet others will help you primarily to sell your book by showcasing it on the site and allow you to upload retail links.

It also depends on what works for you and the amount of time and effort you want to devote to them, and often the usefulness of these social networking sites will change in a relatively short period of time. In fact, considering the dynamic nature of the digital revolution, it is likely that the status and visitor numbers of some social networking sites will have changed considerably, and new networking sites aimed at self-published authors will have sprung up with innovative ways of helping authors to promote themselves and their books on the Internet; bebo.com is a good case in point, which we will come to shortly – it is difficult to know whether it will be out of business or rising up the search engine rankings again – but first, let us turn to another one of the most popular social media channels currently on the Internet for book promotion, Google+.

Your Book Needs Its Own Google+ Page

Google+ (also called Google Plus) was launched in Summer 2011. By December 2012, it had 500 million registered users of whom 235 million were active on a monthly basis. Unlike other social networking sites which are generally accessed through a single website, Google+ is described as a "social layer" on top of the wider Google network of services, and the opportunities it presents are too great to ignore.

For authors, your book should have a Google+ page of its own, which you can use as a hub for all your other social networking activities. Google+ pages allows entities that are not individuals (such as a book) to set up profiles, or "pages," for the posting and syndication of posts.

Google+ requires you to have a profile *before* you create a page. So, you must be active. You must be engaging. You must present yourself as an author on Google+. Google Search prioritises content shared on Google+. So if you create a Google+ page for your book, there's a very good chance it will rank high – very high – in search results, even higher than your amazon.co.uk page. That's actually good because Amazon gives you limited control over the look and feel of your book. Amazon is designed to sell, not to market your book. With Google+, you have more control over the presentation of your book.

Through the creative use of the photos and video tab, you can really give people a taste of what your book is about, a real flavour for your book. By making relevant posts about your book and what it is all about, you can create your own "director's cut" that helps people understand why they should buy it. *You* determine which books go into the shop window of your bookstore, and how they will look in your window display on Google+. And by astutely filling out the "About" section, you can lead people to other places that you want them to go (rather than Amazon determining which books link to yours based on searches and commercial sales). Go ahead and add a link to Amazon, and every other marketplace carrying your book. Add a link to your personal (and most appropriate) social channels to give them a better sense of who you are, as the author. Put in links to extra resources and researched material.

You do not have to post every day. Not even every week. When you do post, make sure it is about *your book*, not about you. Use your Google+ profile for those sorts of posts. That is not to say make it impersonal. Just make sure you keep the page all about your book. The three things to remember when organising a Google+ page for your book are:

- **Make sure it *looks* good.** That means get a great-looking image (maybe your book cover, maybe not) as well as a great-looking banner (maybe previous versions of your cover, maybe images from inside).
- **Make sure it *sounds* good.** This means spending *a lot* of time on your About page. Go beyond posting the blurb for your book. *Sell it!* You can have as many paragraphs as you want. Keep the good at the top.

Always make it easy for would-be readers to link to retail sites to buy your book.

- **Make sure *you're in the loop*.** Go to your settings and set up an email address so that you are getting notified every time someone interacts with your page. Engage in a friendly manner with people who comment or mention your book page.

  Exercise 9. Using the network you've already built with your Google+ personal profile, start telling people about your book's page. Remember they have to "Circle" your book's page before your page can Circle them back. Your book page should Circle almost everyone who Circles it. You will come across the occasional spammer and obsolete profiles/pages, which can be ignored, but make the default assumption that everyone is a fan, unless they prove otherwise.

Google+ cleverly integrates social services such as Google Profiles, and introduces services identified as "Stream," "Circles," "Hangouts" and "Sparks" to provide you with most all the benefits found on other social networking sites, and it often does them better. Here is what they do:

- In the "Stream," which occupies the middle of three columns on the page, users see updates from those in their Circles. There is an input box that allows users to enter a post. Along with the text entry field, there are icons to upload and share photos and videos. The Stream can be filtered and tailored to show only posts from specific Circles.
- "Circles" enable you to organise people into groups for sharing across various Google products and services. Although other users may be able to view a list of people in a user's collection of Circles, they cannot view the names of those Circles. The privacy settings also allow users to hide the users in their Circles, as well as who has them in their Circle. Organisation is done through a drag-and-drop interface. This system replaces the typical friends list function found on other sites such as Facebook. After adding a user to a Circle, it isn't until they are notified and have manually drag-and-dropped the other user to one of their Circles that they are mutually in each

other's Circles. You can share Circles; it's a one-time share, so if the creator of a Circle updates the members, people's shared copies will not be updated.

Another function of Circles is to control the content of one's Stream. You can click on a Circle on the left side of the page and the Stream portion of the page (the centre) will contain only posts shared by users in that Circle. For the unsegmented Stream (includes content from all of a user's Circles), each Circle has a "slider" configuration item with four positions: nothing, some things, most things and everything. The "nothing" position requires you to select (click on) the Circle name to see content from users in that Circle. The "everything" setting, as its name implies, filters nothing out from people in that Circle. The remaining two positions control the quantity of posts that appear in one's main Stream.

The default "Circles" designates friends, family, acquaintances and following, and can be renamed at any time.

The "following" Circle is described as "people you do not know personally, but whose posts you find interesting."

- "Hangouts" are places used to facilitate group video chat (with a maximum of ten people participating in a single Hangout at any point in time). Only Google+ users can join the "Hangout" if they happen to possess the unique URL of the Hangout. Clicking on the "Share" button under any YouTube video reveals an icon that suggests watching the video with friends in a Google+ hangout.
    - If you are also technologically savvy, mobile Hangouts are available and some Google+ users are able to use Hangouts on iPhone and iPad.
    - "Hangouts On-Air" gives you the ability to organise instant webcasts over Google+. The broadcasts can also be recorded for later retrieval.
    - "Hangouts with Extras" will allow users to share documents, share a scratchpad and share their screens with other users.

There are a few ways you can start your own Hangout:

- Go to plus.google.com/hangouts and click the "Start a Hangout" button on the top right side of your screen.
- Click the "Hangouts" icon underneath an interesting post on your Home page to start a hangout about the post.
- Click the "Hangouts" icon on the left side of the page and click "Start a Hangout" under the "Hangout invite" section.
- You can also start a Hangout and send and receive Hangout invites from other Google properties including:
    - o Google Chat properties (i.e. Gmail, Google+, iGoogle, orkut)
    - o Google Calendar

You'll be taken to an invite screen where you'll be able to:

1. Make sure your mic and camera are working correctly by looking at your video feed at the bottom of the page. You should be able to see yourself in the video feed and when you talk, you should see a green bar appear at the bottom of your video.
2. Invite entire Google+ Circles or specific individuals to join you in your Hangout.
3. You can restrict unwelcome individuals from joining your hangout by clicking "Hangout options".

There is also a Google+ Book Club Hangout at:
https://plus.google.com/107103909655175004746/about

Exercise 10. Once you have your Google+ profile in place and G+ page tailored to your book, set up you own literary "Hangout" around you and your book.

Other useful applications for authors on Google+ include:

- "Sparks," a front-end to Google search, enables you to identify topics you might be interested in sharing with others. "Featured interests"

Sparks are also available, based on topics others globally are finding interesting. Sparks is accessed as a pull-down from search results and helps to keep users informed of the latest updates on the topics of their interest.

- "Google+ events" enables you to add events, invite people and share photos and media in real-time from the event.
- "Google+ communities" allow you to have on-going conversations about particular topics.
- "+1 button" which allows you to recommend sites and parts of sites, similar in use to Facebook's "Like" button.
- "Ripples" is a visual tool, showing how re-sharing activity happens regarding a public post. One can replay the public share's activity, zoom in on certain events, identify top contributors, view statistics about average chain length, the most influential people in the chain, the language of the sharers, etc.

Google+ is seen as an alternative and an emerging competitor within the social network industry to Facebook. It will be interesting to see how quickly it climbs up the visitor rankings over the next few years. Will it overtake Facebook and other rival networking sites? It has about one-tenth as many unique monthly visitors as Facebook, so it still has some way to go, but it is catching up quickly.

Use Ning as a Subscription-Based Channel to Market Your Book

Ning was one of the first sites that enabled you to create your *own* social networking site based on a particular subject. The site you create can be about anything you want it to be. Let us say your book is based around a local legend. You can initiate your own social network of people who are interested in that particular legendary place or story.

The weblog facility on Ning is simple to use. Just click on "Create a new blog post" from your profile page and write your blog entries. Friends are easy to make on your own network because you are all there for the same reason, because you are interested in the same subject matter. If you would like, you can have all the activity from the group listed on your profile so you can see how others are socialising on Ning.

You can also upload your own YouTube video to your profile, as well as samples of your writing, copies of reviews and links to your book.

Ning also has forums and groups features. Forums are useful for getting opinions from members or telling them about upcoming events such as your book launch or book signings. Groups add depth to your social networking site. When your members create groups, they are saying that they have particular interests and they want to know who else shares their interests. Then they can all talk about it on the forum.

To use Ning, go to the Ning homepage and click "Try it for free" in the upper right, which will take you to another page where you will be advised of their subscription service. Click "Try it for free" again and you will be asked to enter your name, email address (twice) and password. You need to name your new social network and give it a website address which will end with .ning.com

Think of a descriptive, creative name for your new social network and type it in the name box. Then type a shortened version of that name into the web address box. Click on "Create."

On the next page you will have to choose several options for your social networking site:

- **Privacy:** First, you need to decide whether you want to open your network to the public, or make it accessible by invitation only.
- **Tagline:** Give your social networking site a subtitle or add a catchphrase for your site.

- **Describe:** Tell everyone what your social networking site is about, what they can find there and what they can expect to get out of joining it.
- **Keywords:** These are so people can find your social networking site when they are searching for certain keywords and phrases. Use words and phrases that describe your site, and words that are concise and phrases that you think people will use to find it if they were doing a search.
- **Language:** Choose a language for your site.
- **Icon:** Every site has a picture, photo or other type of graphic to help people see what it is about and to catch people's attention. If the subject is your book, then the front cover would suit.
- **Features:** Decide what features you need and want your members to be able to use. Drag and drop the features you want onto the page, placing them where you want them.
- **Appearance:** Choose a theme for your own social network. These come in different colours and with different designs on them. There are quite a few different themes to choose from. Alternatively, you can use the advanced colour boxes to change the theme or create your own.
- **Questions:** Choose questions you want your members to answer when they sign up for your social network. There are a few sample questions already there you can use. Make up the rest yourself. What do you think your members will want to know about the other members? Do not be intrusive.
- **Launch:** Once you click on the "Launch!" button your social network will be up and running. You can then invite people to join your network and submit the address of your Ning site to members of your other social networking sites inviting them to join.

One of the literary-related groups that is worth joining on Ning is Book Blogs (http://bookblogs.ning.com) which is populated by those who read books, blog about books, write books and publicise books. If you would like to publicise your book in particular within the group, you can do so at http://bookblogs.ning.com/group/promoteyourbooks and advertise your book at http://bookblogs.ning.com/group/advertiseyourwork

Ning formerly had both free and paid options but switched solely to paid subscription services a few years ago. Each pay level allows for different degrees of features, tools, customisation and customer support. More recently, Ning introduced a new way for subscribers to customise and change the appearance of their Ning networks by launching the Ning Design Studio which allows users to choose from pre-made templates which vary in colour, font, background and foreground images, and layout design. You can easily modify and fine-tune the templates, and custom visual changes on your community. The Design Studio makes it possible for you to change the column layout and widths, adjusting the layout on their Ning Network to suit you. The more control that you have over your book's appearance and presentation the better.

Exercise 11. Go to the Ning website and trial the service (30 days for free) to see whether it's for you, whether you feel it meets the marketing aims that you hope to achieve for your book.

Using Bebo to Market Your Book

Bebo is not currently listed on the top 15 social media websites in terms of unique monthly users, but does seem to be phoenix-like in that it is slowly rising from the ashes of what appeared to be its pyre. It was purchased by AOL for $850 million in 2008 and sold two years later to a hedge fund for a sum reportedly to be $10 million. However, in early 2012, Bebo was relaunched with a brand-new design which included a new profile layout option. Further, users can now see who has visited their profiles. A new notification system, similar to Facebook's, notifies users of new inbox messages, lifestream activity and more.

The website, at its height of popularity, overtook MySpace to become the most widely used social networking website in the United Kingdom, eventually registering at least 10.7 million unique users. The website became mired in similar controversies in the UK as those which beset MySpace in the United States and other countries at the time. The site was particularly popular with Irish users – at one point it claimed to have over a million Irish users, ranking it as Ireland's most-visited site.

Bebo is an acronym for "Blog Early, Blog Often." Bebo (www.bebo.com) is different from other social networking sites in that it has a section dedicated to authors. In the Bebo Authors section of the site, also known as Bebo Books (www.bebo.com/Books.jsp), writers are provided with a platform to upload YouTube clips, writing tips and chapter extracts, while allowing them to showcase forthcoming books linked to their personal pages. Friends' updates to Facebook, Twitter, Flickr and other services can be viewed if those friends have linked those accounts to their Bebo profile.

If you click the "Authors" tab on bebo.com, you can browse published and unpublished works either by genre or through Bebo's book charts. Visiting a book's profile will allow you to read an extract, or if you are signed into your Bebo account, you can leave comments, write a review, or add yourself as the book's "fan."

To set up a profile on Bebo for your book, click on the "Authors – register your book" link in the authors section of the site. If you do not have a personal Bebo profile, you will need to register for one; and if you like, you can change the privacy settings so your personal profile can only be seen by those you have added as friends.

Once your personal profile has been configured, you can register your book on the site, entering the title, tagline, assigning it a category and entering a 1,000-word description. For published books, you can also add the publisher and the book's ISBN number.

You then have a profile which you can customise with the cover of your book (click on "Upload profile photo"). You can also add an extract ("Add a chapter" under the "Read" tab), set up a blog or a poll, and pick a more appropriate design for your profile ("Change skins"). And again, the more control you as the author have over your book's online presentation, the better success you will have at raising your literary profile and building up a readership for your writing.

Exercise 12. Consider whether Bebo offers you what you are looking for in terms of possibly serving as a useful platform for getting the most out of your marketing campaign.

Promoting your book on social networking sites eliminates geographical barriers; it is more convenient and cost-effective, and records your marketing success with reviews, recommendations and articles, which will be published online for some time to come. It will not replace the benefit of getting your book into bookstores, but it gives you more control over your book's marketing reach and enables you to tell others around the world who might be interested in reading your book about it once it has been published.

You will probably not have time "in a day" to sample all the social networking sites mentioned here, but if you think carefully about which ones are likely to match up with your own personal aims for your book, you will begin to build a solid marketing foundation from which to work. When you are planning your marketing campaign, you need to decide which tools are most likely to accomplish the task based on your own individual skillset and goals. Facebook, LinkedIn, MySpace, Google+, Ning and Bebo are Internet marketing tools at your disposal, and the aim of this chapter was to explain how you can use them to best effect.

3

BUILD AN AUTHOR BRAND, DEVELOP YOUR AMAZON PROFILE AND PARTICIPATE ON KINDLE BOARDS

Once your book is on sale, it's time to build up a profile platform about you and your work. There are many ways to do this but our advice would be to start with the biggest shop fronts and then work outwards from there. The more profiles you have the easier it will be for people to search for you or stumble across you by chance. Whichever it is, it sells books.

Set Up Your Author Profile on Amazon's Author Central

The Author Central page on Amazon.co.uk provides a useful place for readers to learn about you. Helping readers get to know you is an effective way to introduce them to, or better educate them about, your books. On the author page, essential information is displayed about authors including their bibliography, biography, videos and author photos. You can use Author Central to personalise the contents of the author page dedicated to your books and connect it to your Twitter account.

Here's how to start:

Set up your Author Central account if you have not already done so. If you are uncertain how to do this, then go to any Zadie Smith book and scroll down until you see the "Amazon's Zadie Smith page" link. It will allow you to go to her author profile page. Once you are on this page, scroll down the right hand side of the page. There you will see the "Are you an author" link. Click on the link and it will take you to the set-up page where you can begin to build your own author page. Make sure you have all your information to hand (see below). Amazon starts the creation process for your author page as soon as you sign up for Author Central but it can take three to five days for the author page to appear on the Amazon.co.uk site. You can begin adding content to an author page as soon as you sign up. Once your Author Central account is set up and approved by a publisher (if you have one; if not, you are the publisher), you can add more content and changes will appear on the author page within twenty-four hours of the time you add them in Author Central. In terms of adding information to your author page:

- Once you are in Author Central, click the "Profile" tab and you'll see sections for adding or changing your biography, photos, videos, etc. as well as a section to diarise dates for speaking or other events.
- Click on the "Add" or "Edit" link next to the section, which you want to work on and the instructions will appear, along with space to add information.

If you do not have all the information to hand, do not worry. You can go back and edit the page at any time. Any section that is left blank will not appear on the author page. Sections are always available in Author Central so you can add or change the information later when you have prepared it properly. It is better to leave a section blank than waffle or post an unprofessional biography (see biography section below).

Managing your biography

How to create an author bio in a day

When writers set up a profile page, one part of the setup, which often seems to present problems, is the field asking for an author bio. This section is designed to tell the reader who the writer is, what kind of publications they have had in the past and sometimes, what credentials they have relating to the material they are publishing. It works exactly like the biographical paragraph in a cover letter, which you may have sent to an agent or publisher, but it can be less formal.

People often feel uncomfortable or don't know what to say when called upon to describe themselves like this, and the bio section of the page is often one of the weak points of an author's profile and they end up coming across badly or miss opportunities to hook a new reader. Here are ten tips on writing a good author biography on your Amazon author page:

Do not be embarrassed about being unpublished. Everybody has to make their debut sooner or later. Remember, J.K. Rowling was a first-time author at one time. Moreover, many readers love to discover new authors.

Conversely, do not make a big deal about being unpublished either. Writing may be your lifelong passion, and seeing your work in print may be your life's ambition, but this is a professional communication, and pouring your heart out or waffling looks unprofessional, which will reflect poorly on your writing in general. Do not harp on about the years you have been writing and all the rejections that you have had, as this will not instil confidence in potential readers.

> **Good:** "I have no previous publications."
>
> **Bad:** "I have been writing for ten years and my family love my books but I have never been published. I decided to publish myself because traditional publishers only seem interested in publishing celebrity dross. It's my lifelong dream so please be kind if you review my book."

This example may seem obvious but we have seen many biographies that contain snippets like this. If a reader is taking the time to look at your author page, then they are interested in reading your book. What they read on your page could tip the balance one way or the other.

Listing previous publications

Only list relevant publications. You may have worked on the school magazine in the 1990s, or have written greetings cards, or Internet reviews for a pair of shoes you bought from eBay, but none of that has any bearing on your abilities as a writer. There is no need to "pad out" your personal or professional history either. You do not want to give the impression that you cannot distinguish between different forms or genres of writing, so if you mention your amateurish writings at all, only do so in passing. Feature writing and journalism may be more relevant, as it will lend credibility to your storytelling.

If you have a lot of publications, only list highlights. Some debut authors' profiles feature a long list of publications in all sorts of magazines few of us have ever heard of. Readers may think, "Is the writer making some of these up?" or "If they have had so many publications, why is it that I have never heard of them before?" Be proud of your credits, but pick the highlights when you're trying to generate interest from other people. Sometimes, less is more. Also, choose your highlights carefully based on what you are currently publishing and tailor them accordingly.

> **Good:** My short stories have featured in several publications, including *Martial Arts Magazine* and *Tactical Weapons Monthly*.
>
> **Bad:** I have been published in my company's *Top Shop Staff Magazine*, *Spade Fun Magazine*, *Short Shorts and Erotic Tales*, *Photocopied Weekly*, *Staples in the Middle*, *Fictional Facts*, *My Telescopic Weekly*, *Hairy Tales for Hairy Bikers, Vampire Tales and Frightened Youths*.

Grinding an axe

Do not do it. Writing, like publishing, is personal, and we all have things that frustrate us, whether it is agents who will not take your calls, publishers who will not look at unsolicited or unagented work, or Internet trolls and sockpuppets who seem to get a thrill or benefit by putting down others. But your profile page is not the place to air any grievances.

Remember, you are a creative person who has spent time and effort to write your book. Do not put your valuable creative time to waste.

> **Good:** [nothing, don't do it]
>
> **Bad:** "I wanted to self-publish to prove to publishers that I can be a best-seller without them. Who needs them anyway when you can take your book directly to readers with Amazon? I am glad publishers are struggling to adapt to the digital revolution and I hope Amazon puts them all out of business."

Again this may seem like an obvious "don't" but there are thousands of examples of this on the Internet. Sounding bitter or arrogant will turn readers off before they have read the first line of your book.

> *Exercise 1. Write down your biography, leave it for a day, and then look at it again and think carefully about how you can improve and update it to make it more appealing and interesting to your reader. This section of your Author Central page is not a* Who's Who *entry, listing all of your accomplishments with the intent to impress. Rather, it is intended to endear potential readers to you and your writing.*

Personal experience and credentials

List anything relevant to the specific work. For a new reader who doesn't know you from Adam, it is reassuring to hear that you have written several books which have genuine five-star reviews. If you have credentials or experience relevant to the subject matter of the story that you are publishing, put it in your biography. If the story is about a meteorologist, and you are a weatherman, a pilot, or a sailor, say so. If the story is set in some remote African village and you have worked in that area, that is important to convey in your bio. If you write historical fiction, mentioning your particular expertise in that area will give the reader confidence that your writing will be authentic.

Do not panic if there is nothing relevant to mention. You can still say something interesting about yourself and your writing, such as mentioning your literary inspirations, in other words, those books that inspired and motivated you to write your book. Still, remember not to talk *too* much about others' books – after all, your bio is about you!

Say something about who you are. A few words (and no more) to say where you live and what you do can really make a good impression. If it is not relevant to the story, then certainly mention it but do not dwell on it.

Mention academic qualifications, but do not dwell on them. If you have an English writing qualification or certificate, again this is something that you should mention, but do not give the impression that you think it is all you need. A Master's degree in Creative Writing does not necessarily make you a good storyteller, but it does show that you know how to present your story.

> **Good:** "I run a small holding in Wales" (e.g. when publishing a children's story about Farmer John).

> **Bad:** "I have an MFA in Creative Writing from the University of East Cuffley" (and little else to say about or show for myself).

Make it brief and professional. Your biography really just needs to be anything from two or three lines (brief bio) to three or four paragraphs (e.g. Conrad includes his experiences of witnessing the IRA bombings in Warrington in 1993, which inspired his early books). Stick to the point, do not repeat yourself and try to avoid spelling mistakes. Remember this is for publication. It does not have to be entertaining, but if it is interesting readers may choose to read your work. You are essentially introducing yourself to a prospective new reader.

Make it targeted. Although it is good to have a couple of basic bios ready to go, take a few moments to make sure that they are relevant to the individual sites or publication in question and of interest to your primary readership.

> **Good:** "For the last three years, I have been living in Hackney with my family. My novel draws on my personal experiences driving a taxi in London. I have had stories published in *Time Out* and several other London-based magazines."

Short, to the point and shows that the writer is drawing on his personal experience for his writing.

Exercise 2. Take ten minutes to look once more at improving your author profile. List relevant work, keep it brief and target it to your readers.

Setting up the profile sections

The other sections are simple and easy to use if you follow the links and tips. They will allow you to add images, which should be book covers or relevant photographs of book signings. Do not post pictures of your children or other personal but irrelevant subjects. The bibliography section is automated so that you can search for your books and ebooks using the Amazon database. Once you find them, a simple click adds them to your profile page once they have been verified. Do not add *50 Shades of Grey* to your bibliography!

Using Video Trailers, Uploading to YouTube and Your Profile Pages

Videos are a quick and fun way to add content to your profile pages. YouTube is one of the best ways to do that. This guide provides a walk-through to help newcomers register for a YouTube account and upload their first video. Uploading videos to YouTube might seem a little intimidating if you have not done it before, but once you have done it you will find that it is very quick and easy.

To get started, you will need to set up a YouTube account. If you have already signed up for one, skip this section. If not, here are the steps you need to take[1]:

1. Go to youtube.com
2. Click the large blue "Create account" button, or the smaller link of the same name at the top right of the page.

1 http://lifehacker.com/5804501/how-to-upload-videos-to-youtube-for-beginners

3. Fill out the form with your personal information. If you have a Gmail address, enter it as your email address in this form, as this will save you some time later. When you are done filling out the form, click the "I accept" button.

4. If you used your Gmail account when creating a YouTube account, you will be asked to link them together on the next page. If this is the case, link the accounts. If you *did not* use a Gmail account (because you do not have one) you will be asked to create one on the next page. If this is the case, create a Gmail account and it will be linked to your new YouTube account.

5. Now you are signed up and should be automatically signed in. You will know if you are signed in if you see your YouTube account name in the upper right corner of the screen. If you do not, you should see a "Sign in" link there. Click that, then sign in with your new YouTube username and password.

Now that you have a YouTube account, uploading a video is really easy. Here are the steps you need to follow:

a. Make sure you are signed into your account. To the left of your username, you'll find a link called "Upload." Click on this link.

b. A new page will load and you will be presented with two options. The first is a yellow button labelled "Upload video" and a link titled "Record from webcam." Click the "Upload video" button.

c. Once you have clicked the "Upload video" button, a new window will pop up that will let you select a file from your hard drive. Select the video you want to upload and click the "Choose" button.

d. The video will start to upload and you will see its progress as well as a range of other options. Make sure you *do not* close this page until the video has finished uploading or it will not finish. While the video is uploading you can change the name, add a description, set your privacy options and fill out other relevant information.

e. Once the video has finished uploading, it will need to spend some time processing on YouTube's servers before it is ready for viewing online. You will be able to watch it process at the top of the page. Once it reaches 100 per cent, you'll see a link at the top of the screen that you can click to view your video. Alternatively, you can always find your videos by clicking on your username at the top left of the page and then choosing "Videos" (which may be labelled as "My videos" for some accounts). This will let you access all the videos you have uploaded.

f. When you are on your video's page, you'll be able to watch it and share it. You'll find a button labelled "Share" underneath the video, which will provide you with a link to send to other people and a few other sharing options, such as email and Facebook.

Take a look at a few examples below to get some ideas on how others have used YouTube to promote their books:

http://www.youtube.com/watch?v=F7oUrnWiZRk

http://youtube/1UJzW8rbV7o

http://www.youtube.com/watch?v=B0bMX_hMuTU

http://www.youtube.com/watch?v=Mn8K631A_j8

http://www.youtube.com/watch?v=uRsEb5DYVME

Exercise 3. Take a half hour to set up a YouTube account and do a YouTube trailer for your book. Think carefully in advance what you want to say and script it. Keep it short – a few minutes at most will suffice as an effective video trailer.

Set Up on Kindle Boards

Amazon is the biggest seller of both ebooks and e-readers. Their Kindle reader is one of the most popular handheld devices on the planet at the moment and the increase of independent authors and publishers has given rise to a community of readers and writers using digital platforms for publishing and promoting their books. Amazon recognised the need for their own networking site as the Amazon forums were becoming viral. With this in mind, they created Kindle Boards. This is a massive forum where authors can interact directly and engage with their readers. As most readers frown upon self-promotion, discussion boards of this kind are becoming increasingly useful for more subtle author promotion. Once you have signed up, there are a wide variety of forums to join and interact with readers and writers.

It is important to talk about your book and writing books without being annoying or offensive. So besides linking all your social networking sites to Kindle Boards, what other marketing techniques can you use on these Boards to help readers "find" you and your books without proclaiming "Buy my book, it is brilliant"?

Marketing tips for using Kindle Boards

1. Once you have set up your profile, start a thread in the Kindle Board Book Bazaar for each book you have out, as well as threads in the Kindle Board Writer's Café for topics related to your book and writing, and around the genre you tend to write in.

2. Make use of the Kindle Board image maker to create book cover images of all your Kindle books, then use those cover images, which can be clicked on to take a reader to your Kindle book's page. You can also use the images and links as your signature line.

3. Participate on a discussion thread where you have something useful to contribute, whether it is sharing details about writing or some current or upcoming events in publishing, or because you might have a relevant question about the platform, pricing or promotion of your book. There is a wealth of detail about writing and marketing on the Kindle Boards.

4. Compliment other writers and readers on their achievements. Let them know you are grateful for whatever it is that they are sharing, endearing yourself to other participants on the boards. The more

they like you the more likely they are to become fans and readers of your books or ebooks.

5. You can only post to your own Kindle Board thread once a week, so put a note on your weekly "to do" list. Each time a comment is posted on a thread, it "bumps" that thread back to page one of the boards, so it will be read by many more people at that time. Although only being allowed to make weekly posts to your own threads, it actually means that your threads can benefit from a good rotation of prime realty on the boards.

6. The more threads that you start on different days throughout the week the better chances you will have to attain that prime location. If you have different threads on different days, you can "bump" them up yourself each day with new posts. On Sundays, you can bump certain threads. On Mondays, you can "bump" other threads. Tuesdays, still other threads. And so on.

Forum decorum for the best use of Kindle Boards

Kindle Boards are an excellent place for authors to promote themselves and their work in a subtle way, and before you post on them, you should familiarise yourself with the general tone and culture of these boards. For an excellent summary, see:

http://www.kindleboards.com/index.php/topic,36.0.html

Exercise 4. Take a half hour to set up an account on Kindle Boards. Before making a posting yourself, read other discussions and posts and get the general feel of which effectively contribute to the topic being discussed without overtly engaging in self-promotion.

How do I connect with Kindle Boards social pages?

Check out the Kindle Boards blog (http://www.kboards.blogspot.com) with its email mailing list, the Kindle Boards Facebook page (http://facebook.com/kindleboards), Kindle Boards on Twitter (http://www.twitter.com/kboards1) and Kindle Boards on Pinterest (http://www.pinterest.com/kindleboards).

"Like" or "follow" each of these to ensure you stay connected with Kindle Board updates and promotional opportunities for you and your books.

How do I link to my book's cover in your post?

Linking to Amazon items in your forum posts is simple through this page: http://www.kindleboards.com/link

There is a UK version: http://www.kindleboards.com/uklink

Search for the item you would like to link to, such as your book cover. Click on the item in the search results. Select the link code on the right side of the screen and copy/paste it into your forum post.

You can use this link for items other than books as well – you can make image links for almost anything available on Amazon, and it works for text links, too.

How do I make a signature that includes clickable images of my book covers?

To change your signature, click "Profile" near the top of any Kindle Boards page. On the left side of the window you will see a series of options, click "Forum profile information." Scrolling down, you will see a field labelled "Signature." This is where the code that is created by the following instructions will go. You can also add any text you like as well. There is a character limit of 1,000 for this field, and the code takes up a lot of characters.

At the top of the board's page, there is a link to the "Link-maker 2.0" (third option from the left). Click on that, and you can easily make a link of any Amazon product page. Make sure the drop-down menu option is set to "Kindle store" and enter your ASIN number which looks similar to this – B00A6DCZWW – and can be found below the "Product details" in the Amazon ebook listing page for your book.

Click the "Search" button, and your book will appear. You then need to click "Make a link," which appears below the retail price. Various options will appear on the right. The necessary code will appear in the "To make an image link" field. Click the select link to the right of that field to highlight all of the text, and copy/paste it into your post/signature and you are done. If you are changing your signature, you must click the "Change profile" button to save your changes. We recommend you use the maximum 125-pixel height for your signature.

If you add more than one book, do not add a carriage return (the button on your keyboard you press to make a new paragraph) between each set of code or you'll end up with your images stacked instead of in a row.

If you need more help, you can post a question in the Writer's Café.

> *Exercise 5. Copy and paste or type this URL into your Internet browser for a tutorial on how to link text and add book cover graphics in your forum signature:*
>
> *http://www.kindleboards.com/index.php/topic,46766.0.html*

How do I let readers open an online sample of my book?

To show Kindle Board participants a sample of your work, you can link to any web page, as well as from within your Kindle Boards posts.

Simply use a link that looks like this: http://www.kindleboards.com/sample/?asin=XXXXXXXXXX... and replace those X's with the ten-character ASIN for your book.

Here's an example showing how you might format it for a forum post:

[url=http://www.kindleboards.com/sample/?asin=XXXXXXXXXX]Read a sample of my book![/url]

How do I get a profile page for my book?

A profile page is a clean web page for your book with no distracting links or menu options. Everything on the page is about your book. You can customise it with an author control panel, to add other links to your book, video trailers, and more.

Exercise 6. Copy and paste or type this URL into your Internet browser, a tutorial explaining how to do this:

http://www.kindleboards.com/index.php/topic,40577.0.html

How do I get my book to appear on the Kindle Boards books page?

This is easy... you need to customise your book's profile page using the author control panel. The thread in the URL above has more info on how to do so.

How can I advertise my book on Kindle Boards?

There are several ways to do so and links to the sign-up forms for each are at the bottom of any forum page. Some are free, some are paid, and they include forum banner ads: Forum Featured Book, Facebook/Blog Free Book, Facebook/Blog Bargain Book, and Facebook/Blog Spotlight Book.

If I am offering my ebook for free, can I promote it on KB?

Kindle Boards promotional opportunities for free books are discussed at: http://www.kindleboards.com/free-book-promo/

Is there an easy way for either me or my readers to recommend my book through a Kindle Boards link on Facebook and Twitter?

To recommend a book, use the "Like it!" page: http://www.kindleboards.com/like

You can use one of the badges below to post in your website or your Facebook page, and to highlight your Book Bazaar post or your author profile. See:

http://www.kindleboards.com/graphics/blog/kb-featured-me-button-v3-256x256.png

Kindle Boards is a useful online promotional channel for your book, and there are others. The more profiles you have the better.

Get Your Book Profiled on as Many Sites as You Can… In a Day

Participating in forums and discussion boards

Along with Goodreads and Shelfari, which are covered at length in the next chapter, the following is a shortlist of twenty useful discussion boards on which you can register your author profile to promote your book:

1. Wattpad (www.wattpad.com)

   Wattpad has experienced explosive growth since its inception and has become one of the world's most popular destinations to publish and read ebooks. Wattpad delivers billions of pages from its library of works created and published by the Wattpad community.

2. BookTalk (www.booktalk.org)

   Here you will find an online reading group and book discussion forum that can help you discover new books. You can use BookTalk as a tool to reach a vast audience of book lovers. They have a Google Page Rank of 5, over 14,000 members and close to 700,000 site views per month. Book discussion forums are free and open to anyone including authors and publishers. Create a free account and write about your books in either the fiction book forum or nonfiction book forum. Mail a few copies of your print book and it will be advertised. They will advertise your book on the home page for fifteen to thirty days and on the Featured Book Suggestions page permanently.

3. BookTalk (www.booktalk.com)

   This is another BookTalk site with a .com suffix, which is an online book-lovers' community composed of many of today's bestselling and popular authors. Personalised author home pages contain excerpts from bestselling novels, as well as information about upcoming releases, author notes and personal hobbies and interests, and publisher, literary agent and book industry information. Related articles by BookTalk authors and others in the writing community and upcoming literary events are also included.

4. Library Thing (www.librarything.com)

   This is a social networking site and forum for book aficionados. You can upload a free profile where each book contains tags, reviews and links to conversations about the book.

5. Authonomy (www.authonomy)

   This is an online writing community that features weekly top-rated books and top talent spotters. You can join the forum, upload books and post reviews.

6. WritersNet (www.writersnet.net)

   List yourself at this writers and authors directory, sorted by genre or location. There are also various resources for writers, agents and publishers.

7. Global Writers (www.globalwriters.net)

   Another free website where writers and readers are encouraged to meet, discuss and support each other.

8. Bibliophilia (www.bibliophilia.org)

   This is an online forum for creative writing, fiction writing, story writing, poetry writing, writing contests, writing portfolios and writing help. It offers profiles with books appearing in signature, and lists of favourite and wished books.

9. Booksie (www.booksie.com)

   You can share your poems, short stories, novels and more with the rest of the world on this site. Registration is free.

10. BookBrowse (www.bookbrowse.com)

    Here you will find selected book listings, authors' interviews and useful links to authors' websites.

11. Nothing Binding (www.nothingbinding.com)

    Upload and manage your book cover image and book promotion materials. You can showcase your literary work for free be they books, articles, short stories, essays or poems.

12. Book Buzzr (www.bookbuzzr.com)

    This site has a thirty-day free trial listing and also offers a paid listing with monthly payment of under $5.

13. FiledBy (www.filedby.com)

    This is a kind of "Twitter" for authors, with a platform for books, giving authors their own author site and the capacity to post short blogs.

14. Bookhitch (www.bookhitch.com)

    If you would like a free listing, you can publish a sixty-word description and five keywords on this site. For a premium listing, it costs $19.95 per year for a 120-word description and further space for book reviews.

15. Jacket Flap (www.jacketflap.com)

    This site is for children's and young adult books only. There is a general directory of children's books, publishers and professionals related to children's book publishing. You can create your own profile to add your book and blog for free on the site.

16. Scribd (www.scribd.com)

    This is a digital library that allows users to publish, discover and discuss original writings and books in different languages. You can find out what others are reading on Scribd. This service is somewhat comparable with Wattpad. Authors can upload their PDF, Word and PowerPoint docs to share them with Scribd's large community of readers.

17. Who Wrote What (www.whowrotewhat.net)

    You can advertise free for thirty days on this site, uploading fifty words inviting readers to your website and Amazon Kindle ebook listing where your book is for sale. After thirty days it costs about £5 per month to stay on the site.

18. Savvy Book Writers Blog (www.savvybookwriters.wordpress.com)

    You can submit your book's cover, description and author information and this site will promote your book for free.

19. Book Report Radio (www.bookreportradio.com)

    On this site, you'll find a lively mix of author interviews, audio book previews and chats with influential people in the literary world. The Book Report has become a stable following for bibliophiles and book clubs alike.

20. Figment (www.figment.com)

    Figment is a US-driven book community website where you can share your writing, connect with other people who love to read, and discover new stories and authors.

Many authors participate on forums and discussions boards on various author-related websites, and include a picture of their book cover and a tagline about their book on their postings to promote themselves and their book. Besides those listed above, there is also:

abctales.com

absolutewrite.com

authorsden.com

firstwriter.com

sffchronicles.co.uk (for Sci-fi writers)

writersandartists.co.uk

writersnews.com

writewords.org.uk

Exercise 7. Take an hour to look over these various discussion boards to get a general feel of how they can help you to promote your book by participating in them.

For your book to sell, you need to create a demand for it. You need an audience, a platform – which you will get when your book is showing up on many different websites, visible to a wide variety of readers.

Free Sites to Promote Ebooks in Particular

Here is some information about review sites that are au fait with the digital revolution, where you can list reviews for your ebook for free, in alphabetical order and as described in their own promotional words. If you are a book reader or writer, these sites are great for finding new, interesting books to read as well.

1. Addicted to eBooks (www.addictedtoebooks.com):

   "This website is perfect for readers who want to watch their book budget. This site also allows the author to rate some of the content of their book for those who want to know before they buy a book the level of profanity, violence or sex in a book."

2. AskDavid (www.askdavid.com):

   "This site promotes ebooks and publishes reviews … Only reviews are accepted which cannot be found elsewhere on the web."

3. Author Marketing Club (www.authormarketingclub.com):

   "No longer do you have to dig up your links to the best places to submit your books. We've put them all together here for you in one spot. Just click on the logos below to load each site's form, fill in your details, and you're done."

4. Bargain eBook Hunter (www.bargainebookhunter.com):

"If your title is currently free on Amazon, we want to know about it! Simply use the Contact Form to let us know about your free title and we will consider listing it on our site. There is no cost to you if you contact us and we choose to post your book. We accept all genres except erotica."

5. Books on the Knob (blog.booksontheknob.org):

   "Bargain reads, free ebooks and book reviews for the Amazon Kindle, NOOK, Kobo, Sony and other e-readers, Kindle Fire, NOOKColor, Kobo Vox, and other tablets, along with some games, music, technology and computers tossed in now and then."

6. The Cheap (www.the-cheap.net/about):

   "This website was created in an attempt to let other Barnes and Noble NOOK users know that there really are plenty of deal priced books for NOOK readers. Here at The Cheap we, a group of deal-scouting women, inform you of free and low-cost books."

7. eBooks Habit (www.ebookshabit.com/about-us):

   "Each day we will bring you 20–30 great ebooks that are free at the time of posting, as well as some bargain ebooks with reduced prices!"

8. eReader News Today (www.ereadernewstoday.com):

   On this site, you'll find "Tips, tricks and bargain books for your Kindle."

9. eReader Perks (www.ereaderperks.com):

   "We bring you the latest free Kindle books, free NOOK books and free Kobo books and update throughout the day with the newest (and best!) free offers. Find a great new-to-you author for free!"

10. Flurries of Words (http://flurriesofwords.blogspot.co.uk):

    "All listings will be in the form of a blog post which will be shared on Facebook, Twitter and Google+ … The blogs are archived so you will be able to reference it."

11. FreeBooksy (www.freebooksy.com/about):

    "If you find an ebook you think FreeBooksy readers should know about let us know. And if you are an author and you want to tell the world about your free ebook, we'll take a look at your book."

12. Frugal Reader (www.thefrugalereader.wufoo.com/forms/frugal-freebie-submissions):

    "Submit your free books to be considered for a featured freebie post." Features most genres, aside from erotica.

13. Free Kindle Books & Tips (www.fkbooksandtips.com/for-authors):

    "If you are an author and would like to have your book promoted (for free) on our site, your book **must** be free in the Amazon Kindle store and must have an average user rating of 4+ out of 5 stars for consideration."

14. Free eBooks Daily (www.freeebooksdaily.com/p/contact.html):

    Useful website "if you have a comment, suggestion, or free ebook you would like listed."

15. Goodkindles (www.goodkindles.net/p/why-should-i-submit-my-book-here.html):

    "We are a place where you post your own article about your title and can reach the readers. We do not review your book – we give you a platform to tell everyone what you think is most interesting about your book and what you think will interest readers so much that they will go and buy your book."

16. Pixel of Ink (www.pixelofink.com/sfkb):

    "If your book will be listed as Free on Amazon in the next thirty days, let us know. Pixel of Ink may attempt to feature your book on the day it is free."

17. Writing.com (http://www.writing.com):

    "The *premier* online community for writers of all interests and skill levels, has been going strong since 2000. We provide an extremely creative environment for authors, offering hundreds of unique writing tools and opportunities for creation and inspiration.

    "Whether you are a writer looking for the perfect place to store and display your masterpieces or a reader willing to offer feedback for our writers and their work, this is the website for you. No other website services the writing world better than we do!"

And this is to name just a few free ebook promotion websites.

Here are links to even more book-related discussion forums where you can promote your book for free:

http://www.bookandreader.com/forums/

http://www.bookgrouponline.com/forum

http://digitalbooktoday.com/join-our-team/

http://www.forum.info

http://forums.onlinebookclub.org

http://www.kindlemojo.com (for Indie authors)

http://www.online-literature.com/forums

http://www.reading-forum.co.uk/forum

http://thebookmarketingnetwork.com/forum

Exercise 8. Take an hour to look over these various discussion boards to see how you can upload your book to them for free advertising and promotion.

Build an Author "Brand"

Once you have your book profile listed on various sites, it is time to raise your literary profile and start building up a recognisable brand around it.

For your book to reach as many readers as possible and for you to be a commercially successful author, you need to market yourself as well as your book, which means communicating the message that you want others to hear about you and your books to a range of audiences over a sustained period of time. You have dedicated considerable time and effort to putting your thoughts down in words for others to read, enjoy and learn from, now you need to spread the word, grow your brand and convert readers into fans who will hopefully tell their friends and fellow avid readers about you and buy your next book.

Building yourself up as a brand name

Branding is something people hear a lot about but don't fully understand how complex it can be. Examples of good branding are BMW, Microsoft and Virgin. If you buy a product with their brand name on it, you are expecting it to be reliable and great quality. Similarly, if you shop for beans at Aldi or Lidl, you know the products will be good but perhaps not the same quality as beans from Sainsbury's.

A well-documented example of poor branding is when Gerald Ratner, Chief Executive of the once-profitable Ratners Group of jewellers, made a memorable speech at the Institute of Directors in London in April 1991, and commented:

> "We do cut-glass sherry decanters complete with six glasses on a silver-plated tray that your butler can serve you drinks on, all for £4.95. People say, 'How can you sell this for such a low price?' I say, 'Because it's total crap.'"

He compounded this gaffe by going on to remark that some of their earrings were "Cheaper than an M&S prawn sandwich but probably wouldn't last as long."

He was joking at the time, but Ratners' shareholders were not laughing for long. Consumers exacted their revenge by staying away from Ratners shops. The value of Ratners Group plummeted by £500 million, which nearly led to the company's collapse. Ratner's comments are textbook examples of how you can alienate your target market with poor quality and off-the-cuff remarks. Ratner resigned the following year and the group changed its name to Signet Group in 1993 because the "Ratner" brand had suffered immeasurably from this marketing faux pas.

It takes a lot of time and promotional work to establish yourself as an author and a brand name, but only a few minutes to lose that hard-won credibility and fan base by publishing books that have not been professionally proofread or making caustic remarks on discussion boards or on Amazon. One well-known crime writer did just this, criticising reviewers of his book, which led Amazon to throw his books off the site, costing him both readers and revenue.

As an author, you cannot separate yourself from your books completely even if you use a pen name, because you still have to work with people who will be aware of your real name. In fact, writing under a pen name can hinder your marketing activities in various ways. Likewise, uploading positive reviews of your own book disguised as "anonymous" postings on discussion boards or adding five-star reviews of your book on Amazon can inhibit rather than expand your book's marketing reach because it is obvious which glowing, detailed reviews are written by authors for their own books, especially those that say "a must-read" or "I cannot wait for the author's next book."

Having said that, it still seems as if the majority of first reviews for books on Amazon are five-star and written by the author, or a close relative or friend per the author's request. In some respects, it is better for the first review to be four-star as it lends more credibility to the review.

An author acquainted with Piers Morgan once asked Piers to write an endorsement for the back cover of his book, to which Piers replied, "I'd be glad to provide a positive review, just don't expect me to read it!" Orchestrating positive reviews is of little use to you or your book as honest, genuine feedback, whether it is good, bad or just average, will give you a much better understanding of the strengths and shortcomings of your book. By all means encourage reviews from readers as part of your book promotion to build up a brand name and fan base, but do not fabricate them.

Similarly, the aforementioned crime writer who was thrown off Amazon for a spell for criticising and to some extent threatening and bullying negative reviewers, admitted that he has been posting adverse reviews of other crime writers' books on Amazon and the like, thereby causing their books to move down the "recommended reading" lists on Amazon, a baneful practice known as "sockpuppeting." Once exposed in a national newspaper for doing this, surprisingly along with a number of other well-known authors in various genres, he decided to "go to ground" and lost some of his readers as well as his credibility. Not only was he undermining other authors in this self-aggrandising way, but he shot himself squarely in the foot in doing so, damaging his author reputation and brand.

If you disrespect your readers or other writers, criticise your publisher for not doing more, upload raving reviews of your own book or harass retailers for not stocking your book, then no one will want to work with you and your books will not have a chance. Conversely, if your readers take time to review your book, even negatively, you should consider carefully what they say and respond positively to them. Do not take your readers for granted, or you will lose them quicker than you gained them. Listen closely to your readers, and give them what they're asking for – that is the key to brand building.

Having warned of the potential pitfalls that you should avoid, let's turn to what you *should be doing* to build an author brand. You and your books make up your brand. Your books are your logo and will be your readers' first impression of you; hence, it is essential that you get the title and the cover right. Along with the storylines that you skilfully and painstakingly weave together, your author brand is how you pitch your work and how you conduct yourself.

A good example of branding in the literary world is Mills and Boon. Everyone knows they publish romance novels. Stephen King is a horror writer that most people know which is why his name is larger than the title on the cover of his last five books. The publishers are trading on his brand name as an internationally recognised author. Julia Donaldson has published over 120 children's books and the covers of many of them state in bold letters "by the Children's Laureate and author of *The Gruffalo*." I took my children to see Julia Donaldson speak at the Wonderlands Festival of Writing at the British Library and expected a question-and-answer session with the author talking about herself, her inspiration behind writing best-loved children's stories, and what she is working on next. Instead, she skilfully engaged and involved almost all of the hundred-plus children in the audience over the course of an hour and invited them to act out her stories while she sang songs from her books, accompanied by her multi-talented guitar-playing husband, Malcolm.

J.K. Rowling has set a great example to writers by playing down her success and being pragmatic during interviews. Many readers will know that she wrote her first few novels in cafés in Edinburgh because she was a single mother at the time and the walk there helped get her young daughter to sleep. Her brand is her Harry Potter novels first, and her personal "rags to riches" life story adds to her overall brand because she came from humble beginnings and downplays her success. You are your brand. Get people to like you and they will want to read your books.

Forget about your book as the focus for a moment and concentrate on building up yourself as a brand. You have probably heard of the term "personal branding." It is a popular phrase with personal development types, which basically means "how you present yourself to the world."

This applies to the literary and business world and also to your extended circle of contacts. The main idea is that, whether you like it or not, the world is going to have an opinion about you which will be manufactured from how you conduct yourself in the public arena. Most people do not think too much about how they are seen by others but if you put yourself out there, you will be judged. That is just human nature. If you're an author, you can no longer just live and let the world think of you however they'd like. You have to be mindful of your actions if you are going to put your work in the public domain.

"Personal branding" is about intentionally influencing how the world sees you by behaving in a certain manner. It's about purposefully packaging "that brand called you," making sure it is a likable package, so much so that your readers want to "buy into it." The benefits are obvious. The better prepared you are to show the world who you are, the more likely the world will see you the way you want them to. Being respectful and positive adds value to your book and expands your fan base, thereby adding value to your author brand.

That means your readers and reviewers.

That means interviewers from the media.

That means people searching for you and your books online.

That means your social circle, family, friends and other professionals from the literary world.

When you have a solid personal brand, you will be more memorable, you will be more impressive and people will end up having a more favourable opinion about you. They will be much more likely to go away and look at your book and upload a favourable review if they like you – that's the same thing that good branding does for a product.

Exercise 9. What is your individual author brand? How do you project this brand in an effective way (by effective, we mean in a way which will raise your literary profile and sell copies of your book)?

How to actually do it in practice

Like most things in the world of personal development, "personal branding" is a pretty vague concept. It is a great idea in theory, but how do you sit down and plan how to do it? Discussions about it tend to be impractical or not actionable enough to be useful. If an idea is not practical, is it worth much? Here are some fundamental tips to help you develop a brand name. Follow these six easy steps and adapt them to suit your own situation and you will have worked out a personal brand strategy that you can start building on straight away:

Step 1: Choose the core focus for your personal brand

Every brand is based on a few memorable qualities that marketing people tend to focus on. For instance, BMW do not market their vehicles on their green credentials or their safety record. They market them on their quality and contemporary styling and up-to-the-minute technology. Focusing on a few key qualities or USPs (unique selling points) makes it easier to connect with the message and remember the product.

Another great example of branding is Apple. Apple sells computers, phones and software. You could say a lot about them, but their brand is focused. Apple's brand is fun, slick, stylish, cutting edge, reliable and virus free. Their brand is focused and it is positive. You need to do the same. Choose a handful of qualities about yourself that you want to be known for. Maybe you are a children's book author and when you write blogs or interact with people you come over as someone who genuinely cares about children, or maybe you are an excellent reviewer of other children's books. Or maybe you are a confident speaker, detail-oriented, serious about important issues and a crazy J.K. Rowling fan.

What core attributes as a writer do you want to be known for by the world? Obviously you want to be known for your storytelling. Make sure you do not try to focus on too many things – it'll be harder for someone to remember any of it. Concentrate on two key aspects and maybe three or four minor ones. Make sure you are honest with yourself– pretending to be something you're not never works and there are many trolls out there who will see through your description of yourself and take great pleasure in dissecting your mistakes in the public eye.

Exercise 9. Write down four or five things you want others to know about you as an author. This is your starting point for author branding.

Step 2: Prioritise your core brand focus

It is easier for people to remember one thing than several things. Equally, it is easier for people to focus on doing one thing than doing a lot of things. For example, most websites want their visitors to do a variety of things – get on an email list, bookmark the site, click on an advert, buy a product, comment, share on social media, etc. The more of those things a website "focuses" on, the less likely visitors are to do anything but go to a different website. Too many options lead to inaction. The same is true for your personal branding. The more you throw at someone, the less likely they are to remember any of it. So what you have to do is look at your list of four or five qualities about yourself and decide which is the most important. If someone could define you by one quality, which would it be? The other aspects of your character, though important, can be secondary elements in your personal brand.

Exercise 10. Rank your four or five characteristic by importance to you.

Step 3: Make your core values into priority list

As a general rule, people talk up the importance of things like personal goals and objectives, and personal mission statements too much. Even so, the process of developing a key list helps take something general (like a list of five qualities about you) and makes it easier to talk about convincingly. This is important because it can be hard to talk about something you have not already thought through. When some asks you what you do, you need to be able to sum up your core values in a few interesting sentences.

Have you ever talked about something in public without first having time to think about what you had to say? For example, has someone ever asked you to tell a story about something funny that happened to you?

You remembered exactly what happened, but it comes out in a jumble. So you then try to explain why it was funny, but your friends' eyes glaze over because you are not telling it well, and you eventually end awkwardly with "Oh well, I guess you had to be there."

It is a similar situation with your personal brand. You need to think through how to communicate it or it will not be conveyed.

Here is the best way to work through that quickly:

1. Pull up something that can record audio on your computer or phone.
2. Record yourself speaking about each of your four to five qualities, why they are important, why other people should think they are important and examples that would show the world you have them.
3. Ramble on and on until your ideas start to come together. Talk until it starts feeling more comfortable and natural to talk about them.
4. Once you start feeling comfortable with what you are saying, stop recording and listen to it.
5. Write down the most compelling things you said – the things you think are the smartest, most eloquent things you said about yourself.
6. Condense the best stuff into three sentences that emphasise your primary quality while including the others. This is your personal "elevator pitch" for the purpose of this exercise.
7. Work through your words, making mental notes and distilling it into your core values. Do not stress about getting it perfect. This is an exercise in shaving off the excess so you have a convincing paragraph of information that will be your core focus. If you practice it, it will become more convincing.

Step 4: Focus your online identity with your new core statement

Like it or not, what you do online influences how others perceive you and affects your product. If you want your personal brand to be effective, your online accounts at Facebook, Twitter, LinkedIn and your other online profiles need to reflect the ideas in your core statement. If you were a stranger looking at your online accounts, would your main message reflect your personal brand? If you look at Conrad Jones's Facebook account or fan page, you know straight away that he is a thriller writer. He does not post what he is having for breakfast or what new trick his dog learned today, but he does post every review that he carries out or receives. If you visit it, then you would be under no illusions that he is an author, or about the genre in which he writes.

If your Facebook account or blog does not do this, then you need to think about adjusting things that you have online. Take your time to get it right and stick to those key focal points. Do not cut and paste your core statement into your Facebook profile, as that will look unprofessional and somewhat retentive. Instead, emphasise the things that make your personal author brand stronger online and de-emphasise the things that conflict with it. For example, if you say you are a published author and reviewer, delete any quotes you might have on the site about disliking someone's book or criticising traditional publishers and agents for not having the courtesy to reply to your book submissions or for sending boilerplate rejection letters rather than providing constructive feedback.

> *Exercise 11. Take a quick audit of your online profiles and adjust them so they reflect the elements of your personal brand and concentrate on the core ideals.*

Step 5: Take control of your online brand identity

Most companies have a presence on social media nowadays that reflect their brand. But their online platform is a website they own. The reason for that is simple. Online profiles can be managed according to the rules of the social media platform, but they have complete control over a website they own. The same is true for you. You can clean up your Facebook account all you want, but if you really want to solidify your brand online, creating a personal website is the best way to make that happen as it provides a professional platform to showcase for your writing, sort of like a shop window for your online bookshop.

This step might take you off-guard a little. Many people think creating their own website is difficult, or that they might need to learn complex computer programming, or pay thousands of pounds to get someone to design a website for them. The truth is that it is never been easier or less expensive to create your own website these days. If you are knowledgeable enough to have bought this book online, then you are already computer literate enough to create your own website. If you do not know and want more details about how to easily create your own author website, go to www.websitefromnothing.com which has a quick, useful series of tutorials that show you how to do it.

We recommend that you build your website on a domain based on your name (rather than your book title) for the most effective personal branding. If your name is John Crowther, buy www.johncrowther.com, .net, or .org. The .com suffix is generally the most important one to have, as it gives your writing more international kudos. Often, authors' names with a .com suffix have already been taken by someone else, so you may need to be slightly more creative by adding in your middle initial, which changes the domain name to www.johnecrowther.com, or if you would prefer, add –author to your website domain name, so that it might be www.johncrowther-author.com. This tells people right away that you are an author.

Make sure your website is simple to navigate and clearly highlights your personal brand. It should show your core focus. It should communicate, "This is who I am, this is what I write, and this is why you should read it." Be creative and take your time to update and improve your pages. It is your unique online real e-state. Create your own personal website to establish your personal branding and showcase your work.

Step 6: Live your personal core brand

The last and most important step is to actually *live* your personal brand. An effective personal brand is more than how you present yourself to the world. It is also a real-life description of who you are and what you and your writing is all about. Spend your time emphasising the core elements of your personal brand in your life. Sometimes we do not act like the person we want the world to see. We think we are motivated, but we spend too much time watching television and surfing the Internet. If you post yourself as an author and reviewer, then write every day and post interesting reviews and people will see that you are an active writer and reviewer, rather than passively waiting for people to find you.

A well-thought-out personal brand will help you present yourself to the world. It can also be a clear-cut description of who you should aspire to be in your day-to-day life. No matter who you are or what your goals may be, it is helpful to go through these simple steps and develop your personal identity and author brand and concentrate on the core ideals on a daily basis. Decide that brand building in this way is going to be an integral part of your marketing strategy. If you get it right, then you can use it to your advantage in raising your literary profile and building up a readership for your writing. Are you going to sit and hope that your book will find its intended market or are you are going to go out and grab their interest?

Summary

To recap the Dos and Don'ts in successfully building an author brand:

Dos:

a. Have your book professionally proofread prior to publication.

b. Seek reviews from your readers, and especially your fan base.

c. Thank them for taking the time to review your book, whether the review is positive or otherwise.

Don'ts:

a. Resist uploading or orchestrating five-star reviews of your own book to Amazon.

b. Avoid uploading negative reviews of other authors' books or engaging in sockpuppeting.

c. Never make caustic remarks on discussion boards or Amazon.

Exercise 12. Make sure that all your profile pages reflect what you want to say about yourself. Check and update your pages to minimise the clutter and focus on your core values.

Remember to stay focused and professional at all times even when dealing with scathing remarks or poor reviews. What you write may not be liked by everyone, but focus on the positives and take any criticism as an opportunity to improve. If you take it personally, it will wear you down. Keep positive, interact daily and keep writing. Brand building does not happen overnight. It takes a lot of time, effort and commitment, just like your writing.

4

MARKET YOUR BOOK ON TWITTER, PINTEREST AND GOODREADS

Set yourself up on social bookmarking and social cataloguing sites.

When you understand that almost every author spends some of their time networking and marketing their books online, it makes sense to link with as many other authors as you can. Using other authors and their fans to generate interest in your own books is an essential tool to build up a readership. To communicate with other authors and avid readers, try social cataloguing sites like Shelfari or weRead where you can rate, review and discuss your book, as well as books by other authors. Use Meetup to find and join groups united by a common interest such as books. Sites like Digg, Pinterest, Delicious, StumbleUpon, BuzzFeed, Slashdot and Reddit are social bookmarking services that are useful for storing, sharing and discovering popular content.

Affiliate programmes offered by sites like ClickBank and Tradebit can help you to market your ebook as they provide online marketplaces for digital information products. These sites aim to serve as a connection between digital content creators (known as "vendors") and affiliate marketers, who then promote the relevant content to consumers.

We would not recommend spending much money on Google adwords and other "pay-per-click" traffic generators. There are campaigns run by authors who have a lot more marketing money than most that fall flat on their face by throwing money at their books and thus throw away their money rather than adopting a better informed, more effective DIY social media approach. Remember that free global advertising is available to you directly via the Internet. The best way to raise your literary profile, build up a readership for your ebook and engage with your readers on a regular basis so you can successfully establish a loyal fan base is through social networking, social bookmarking and social cataloguing. The most used sites are ranked below, but remember that just because they have the most users does not necessarily make them the most effective. Each author has different advice and different results. Interaction on the Internet is much the same as interaction socially. Some people are more successful than others and thus gain more interest from the communities they mingle in.

A social bookmarking site is a centralised online service that enables users to add, annotate, edit, and share bookmarks of web documents. Many online bookmark management services have launched since 1996. Delicious.com, founded in 2003, popularised the terms "social bookmarking" and "tagging." Tagging is a significant feature of social bookmarking systems, enabling users to organise their bookmarks in flexible ways and to develop shared vocabularies known as folksonomies.

Best Social Media Websites for Books

According to *eBizMBA Rank*, in January 2013 the most popular social bookmarking sites were as follows:

1.	Twitter	250,000,000 – estimated unique monthly visitors
2.	Pinterest	85,500,000 – estimated unique monthly visitors
3.	Reddit	16,000,000 – estimated unique monthly visitors
4.	StumbleUpon	15,000,000 – estimated unique monthly visitors
5.	BuzzFeed	14,500,000 – estimated unique monthly visitors

6.	Delicious	5,500,000 – estimated unique monthly visitors
7.	Tweetmeme	5,450,000 – estimated unique monthly visitors
8.	digg	4,100,000 – estimated unique monthly visitors
9.	FARK	1,850,000 – estimated unique monthly visitors
10.	Slashdot	1,700,000 – estimated unique monthly visitors
11.	Friendfeed	1,500,000 – estimated unique monthly visitors
12.	Clipmarks	1,400,000 – estimated unique monthly visitors
13.	Newsvine	1,390,000 – estimated unique monthly visitors
14.	Diigo	1,200,000 – estimated unique monthly visitors
15.	DZone	325,000 – estimated unique monthly visitors
16.	Chime.in	250,000 – estimated unique monthly visitors

If you are getting ready to publish a book then you have to "get up to speed" with social bookmarking. A lot of authors we talk to want to learn about social media and how it is going to help them sell thousands of books but they hesitate, because they are not confident with it. They know they need to be building their author platform and brand, but do not know how Twitter fits in. It is a simple communication platform to send regular updates and build an audience for your writing. There are only a few things you can actually do on Twitter but simple is good. Everything else that flows from your involvement with it comes from the network of people you connect with.

Exercise 1. Take a look at each of these bookmarking websites, read their "About us" descriptions of what they do and how they work, and think about how they might help you to sell and market your book.

It takes time and effort to build a following. If you have no followers, then you will be wasting your time trying to sell and market your book. You have to grow a community around the value of the content and ideas you share on the site. Also, you have to listen and interact with your fan base, taking on board their comments and giving them what they would like. Also, mentioning, and thus including, "superfans" in your book in a subtle fashion, perhaps by using their surnames (if they allow it) or fan page/profile names, is generally a good "hook" to keep them interested and retain them as fans, thereby helping to build brand loyalty as an author.

Twitter has more active users than any other social bookmarking site by far, with over 340 million short, 140-character messages sent across its network each and every day. It is essential for any author to be knowledgeable about how it works and how it can benefit them as an author in terms of promoting their book.

Set up a Twitter Account

Most everyone has heard of Twitter, but most authors do not know how to use it to their best advantage. Twitter is a real-time information network that connects you to the latest stories, ideas, opinions and news about what you find interesting. You can simply find the Twitter accounts that you find most compelling and follow and participate in the conversations.

At the heart of Twitter are small snippets of information called tweets. Each tweet is a maximum of 140 characters long, but do not let the small size fool you – interesting things often come in small packages. You can see photos, videos and conversations directly in tweets to get the whole story at a glance, and all in one place.

Summary of Twitter "speak"

We know that Twitter can confuse people when they first start using it. It is like learning a new language – if you know a few commonly used terms, then you can make sense of most of the rest.

Let us start by explaining what Twitter symbols and acronyms mean.

@ – The @ symbol is used to communicate with other Twitter users. For example, if you wanted to contact someone on Twitter you would have to include @someone in your message. It is like a phone number. You cannot call someone without knowing their phone number. Similarly, you cannot tweet someone without adding an @ followed by their Twitter name.

– This is a hashtag, which plays an important role on Twitter. It helps put tweets into a specific category. For example, we might use the hashtag #publishedinaday. If you search #publishedinaday in the Twitter search bar, any tweets containing #publishedinaday will appear. Notice there are no spaces between words when using a hashtag.

Hashtags are used to help people find things easier. If enough people use the same hashtag it will become a "trending topic" and will be shown on users' dashboards.

RT or Retweet – This is the equivalent of forwarding an email or a text. If you like it, you might decide to share it with your followers. Sometimes people add "Please RT" to their tweets. By sharing your tweet with more people, it is more likely to be viewed or answered if you have a question.

Tweet – A tweet is a message you can send on Twitter, comprised of up to 140 characters.

Followers – These are the people who are following you. They can see tweets you send. However, you cannot see their tweets unless you are following them.

Following – These are the people you are following.

Twitter handle – This is Twitter speak for your username.

Trending topic – If a hashtag is popular enough it will become a trending topic. You can see these on the lower left hand side of your dashboard and you can choose whether you want to see worldwide trending topics, countrywide or trending topics in specific parts of your country. If you click on a trending topic you will be shown all the tweets using that hashtag.

Tailored topic – Twitter has recently launched tailored topics. These are trending topics tailored to you based on the things you talk about. Tailored topics are really useful for promoting your book. If you see a tailored topic in your genre or area of expertise, you can tweet about it or post some relevant content to increase your marketing reach.

How to use Twitter to promote your book

Whether you tweet 100 times a day or once in a blue moon, you still have access to the voices and information surrounding all that interests you. You can either contribute, or just listen in and retrieve up-to-the-second information.

Exercise 2. Go to www.fly.twitter.com for information about what is available on Twitter for you to discover. Then go to www.twitter.com to sign up.

When setting up a Twitter account, make sure your username is not random or too long, ten or twelve characters should suffice. Remember that your username on Twitter needs to include "author" or "writer" in it if you are going to use it effectively for promoting your book. It is part of your branding strategy.

Spend time building up followers and friends. Increase your friends and contact list and then set up an event, which will be the launch of your ebook. Make sure you also set up a Twitter (www.twitter.com) account and a LinkedIn (www.linkedin.com) site *before* you set up your event as they all link through the same page on Facebook. That is one of the best things about social networking. It is all integrated for you at the click of a button. Once again, if you are not familiar with these sites, then take ten minutes to take a look at them and familiarise yourself with how they work. It will probably take you fifteen minutes to half an hour to set yourself up with a profile when you are ready to.

Set up your author page on Amazon by going to the Author Central page, and link it to your Twitter and Facebook pages. All you do is click on the icons and the software does the rest for you. Along with your blog, these three sites are crucial to any Internet campaign. Build your profiles with pictures, book covers and positive reviews. Keep it fun and interesting and people will be regular visitors to your site.

There is free software that makes Twitter a lot easier to use. Twitterific on the iPad and the iPhone are good, though there are many others so it is worth looking around to see what works best for you. The software allows you to automate your Twitter profile, which saves time.

Being able to schedule tweets in advance is a big advantage and you can auto-tweet and re-tweet which gives you the ability to plan your marketing campaign.

Here are some general pointers for using Twitter[1]:

- Do not read EVERY tweet
- Follow anyone who follows you (and unfollow spammers)
- Promote other people twelve times to every one self-promotional tweet
- Build lists to follow people who matter to you more closely
- Re-tweet good stuff from others. Sharing is caring, as they say
- A lot of @someone replies shows a lot of humanity and engagement
- Robot tweets are less effective than human tweets

1 http://www.chrisbrogan.com/50-power-twitter-tips/

- Promote the new/less followed authors much more than well-established "names"
- Set an egg timer; Twitter can be addictive!
- Everyone tweets their own way; you are doing it wrong, too – to someone

The same basic principles that apply to social bookmarking apply to social networking in general, especially in terms of building up a group of readers who are keen to hear about your publishing plans.

Exercise 3. Search out people in the book world on Twitter.com as you did online. Target your searches to find the people with the biggest followings in your genre. Once you find them, start looking through the list of who they're following to find more people to follow.

Building up your followers takes time, hence the importance of planning your book launch well in advance. Even if you have already launched your book, set up your profile and spend time regularly building followers.

Search the list pages, too. There are many ebook review groups and ebook re-tweeting groups. Some will have over 100,000 followers, so if they pick up one of your promotional tweets and pass it on the results can be incredible. There are many writers and publishers who you can follow for great information and tips. Try to find lists created by experts in your field and re-tweet any useful links to your followers.

If we assume that you are now following important people in your genre, you should check them out on a daily basis. Remember to keep adding followers, too. Keep your focus tight at first so you do not overwhelm yourself with input. Read the tweets from these industry leaders and add people with lots of followers. Click through anything that looks interesting to see what they are linking to. Watch especially for links that get re-tweeted or passed along.

There is no rush. Read tweets for two or three months before sending out any tweets of your own. Be patient and keep watching and soon you will see why some people are popular and lots of people want to follow them. It is usually because they consistently provide links and ideas that are valuable or because they make an effort to connect and re-connect with people individually.

Once you have worked out what is considered valuable in the Twitter communities that you are following, it is time to become a participant. Do a little searching and see if you can find resources that have not been mentioned recently and pass it on. If you use your Facebook account to post links then it'll automatically send it to Twitter and LinkedIn. Create a short tweet alerting people to this resource, put in a shortened link and tweet it. You will pick up followers if your content is useful.

Re-tweeting other authors like this builds brand loyalty. It is about sharing discoveries, sharing content and not direct selling. You are building trust and a trusted community of followers. At the same time, you are receiving valuable tips from the people you are following.

Be polite to all even when abuse is tweeted in your direction. There are thousands of Internet trolls out there with nothing better to do than annoy people on the Internet. If you encounter them, be professional. You will gain the respect of the rest of the literary community if you handle yourself with dignity. Remember that others can see your conversations unless they are private messages and abusive arguments in clear view of the community will alienate your readers.

In essence, you are asking people that you never met to trust you and read your ebook. This is done most effectively by adding value to others and not by tweeting anything you have not personally verified yourself. Trust is the most important element in the community you are building and it takes time to build but seconds to lose with the click of a button, so be careful what you say whenever you tweet.

Twitter is truly an amazing phenomenon. Become familiar with posting links and photographs. They will help create interest in you and your book. The creativity, energy and vitality on Twitter are astonishing. It can be a great place to connect to people who are interested in your work, and who in turn will hopefully send your message out into their own networks of followers.

Tweeters can restrict messages to those in their circle of friends or allow open access. So, if you are on Twitter, you can send your followers a tweet telling them that your new book is published and see what they tweet back. You do not want to send too many tweets to friends about how wonderful your book is, as they may begin to think that you are more of a twit than a tweeter.

You can tweet others about blog entries, your book launch and upcoming speaking engagements. When promoting your book via a short 140-character pitch, include a catchy headline and a link to every blog post or review article. But do not overdo it. Take time to forge relationships on Twitter and familiarise yourself with how Twitter works before using it to promote your book.

If you are looking to promote your book by writing articles, fortunately many magazine and newspaper reporters are on Twitter. Read up on their articles and reference them when you tweet about your book. When you tweet an editor, you can draw attention to a query or just make small talk so they will be aware of your name when they see your query. Get access to the reporter's personal website and hopefully their email address for future queries.

One of the most valuable tools that Twitter offers to authors is the ability to promote their book directly to book reviewers and bloggers. Here is a list of some of the most interesting and communicative book bloggers on Twitter. You should "follow" them:

http://twitter.com/#!/BiblioBrat

http://twitter.com/#!/Book_Faery

http://twitter.com/#!/bookaliciouspam

http://twitter.com/#!/amusedbybooks

http://twitter.com/#!/YABookShelf

http://twitter.com/#!/thebookmaven

http://twitter.com/#!/brokeandbookish

http://twitter.com/#!/NovelNovice

Exercise 4. "Follow" each of these book bloggers on your Twitter account. Hopefully, they will "follow" you in turn.

By participating in the book community on Twitter and forming and nurturing friendships and connections there, you can achieve long-lasting publicity for your book without ever having to "sell" at all.

It is about building up a community of the *right followers* on Twitter – readers, reviewers, reporters, book bloggers, other authors and publishing industry specialists. While it is easy to find authors on Twitter, how do you find *readers* and get them to follow you?

How to find readers on Twitter

The challenge authors face when trying to promote their book on Twitter is readers do not identify themselves in their Twitter profiles. An author's profile might state: "Crime thriller author." But the vast majority of their readers will not identify themselves as: "Crime thriller reader." The result is despite endless tweeting, interactions and building "follower" numbers, most authors still struggle to find avid readers for their work.

The truth is that finding readers on Twitter is actually easy, if you know where to look for them. Irrespective of which genre you write in, Twitter is truly an Aladdin's cave of information about the readers that you are looking to attract. Here are four easy ways to locate readers on Twitter.

First, readers can be found by using the Twitter search facility. Type into Twitter's search engine the words and phrases that readers of your genre might be using in their tweets. A few of these searches will start to reveal readers of your genre in significant numbers. Then just go through the search results and "follow" those readers that you feel belong to your book genre, based on what they say in their tweets. Many of them will "follow" you back!

Second, you can search using the names of successful authors of books similar to yours. For example, if you are a children's book author writing about horses, you might search for author "Michael Morpugo." This search will reveal readers in the genre in which you are writing because many of the tweets will be from people tweeting about how much they loved his book *War Horse*.

When searching, remember to click the "All" link at the top so you can see all the tweets that include a particular phrase, not just the most popular.

> *Exercise 5. Go through the search results and pick out the users who are obviously readers in your genre. Click on the names you like, and their profiles will pop up – then click each one to "follow" them, in the hope that they will "follow" you back.*

Third, you can search using titles of bestselling books in your genre. For example, if you wanted to find readers of British action thrillers, you could search for titles by author Lee Child, and his "Jack Reacher" titles. This will generate a useful list of twitter users, many of whom will be reading these books and tweeting about them. Perusing the content of their tweets, you can choose to "follow" users who are dedicated readers of action thrillers.

Fourth, you can search for readers using places and concepts that commonly arise in other books in your genre. This requires searching for locations or other unique things mentioned in bestseller books that are similar in style or content. For example, if you are writing a book about the infamous Jack the Ripper, you might search for names of people or places that commonly appear in related books like "Mary Jane Kelly" or "Whitechapel" or "From Hell letter" or "Leather Apron," which was one of the Ripper's nicknames at the time, and you will find avid Ripperologists and crime readers sharing thoughts about these subjects on Twitter.

Cherry-pick and "follow" those Twitter users who are obviously readers of books in your genre and style of writing. Well-thought-out searches will produce a treasure trove of potential readers for your books.

How to turn your Twitter followers into book buyers

Finding your readers is the first step of the process. You then need to put your book in front of them in a subtle way and persuade them to buy your book. As mentioned previously, the worst way to do this (which many authors still do unfortunately) is by proclaiming, "Here is my book, it's great, you should buy it!" People find this really off-putting, and will often "unfollow" you if you do that.

Rather, converting your Twitter followers into buyers will only happen if you interact with them *in the right way*. Twitter is all about relationship building and engagement. You need to get to know them and they need to learn more about you, so they feel connected with you and your work because you share common interests, and *then* they will buy your books.

The way to build support for your books is through *reciprocity*. You store up goodwill by going out of your way to tweet about your key followers, leaving supportive comments on their book blogs, and generally helping and encouraging them. When the time comes to launch your book, they will generally respond in kind by recommending your work and sending tweets about your book to their followers. It is the communal aspect to Twitter that makes it so effective as a marketing channel for your book.

50 Ways to Build Your Author Profile Using Pinterest

In case you have never heard of Pinterest (www.pinterest.com), it is a relatively new social networking site that allows users to create online image collages, then quickly and easily share those collages – called "pinboards" – with other Pinterest users. It is fun, easy, and catching on like wildfire. Part of Pinterest's appeal is that it is simple and beautiful.

When you enter the colourful world of Pinterest, all the troubles of your day-to-day life just seem to slip away in a stream of perfect little black dresses, baby otters, and cherubic children who never seem to get dirty or mouth off to their parents.

Because it is image-based, the core of Pinterest is overwhelmingly positive. Think of Pinterest as Facebook without words, where pictures do actually speak a thousand words. Yes, Pinterest is beautiful. And yes, its users *love* it. But do not let the cuddly hearts and flowers fool you. Behind those lovely images, Pinterest is fast becoming a heavy-hitting marketing tool for brands and businesses … like yours.

Let us take a closer look at *why* this is, and then we will get to specific Pinterest tactics you can use to your marketing advantage.

What is Pinterest and why should I care?

Once you have registered for a free Pinterest account, you can create online collages ("boards") for different topics that you are interested in, and then add images and videos to your boards by "pinning" them (the equivalent of using glue sticks on old-school vision boards, but faster, slicker and considerably cooler). Much like a television commercial or subtle product placement within movies, those inspiring vision boards result in referral traffic to websites and blogs.

In 2012, Pinterest drove more traffic to websites than LinkedIn, Google Plus, Reddit and Youtube *combined*! This is because there are multiple ways of using it to build your author brand and connect with your readers, and to translate this medium into effective means for you to promote your book in a creative way.

Here are various ways to incorporate Pinterest into your marketing campaign[2]:

Pinterest marketing for beginner pinners

1. Make sure you feature your author name or book title on your profile for maximum exposure. Use your author name as your username, or change your profile name to your author name after your profile is set up.
2. Add a paragraph about who you are and what you are interested in to the "About" section on your Pinterest profile. It will show up right under your photo, and will be one way that users can find out more about you and your book.
3. Connect your account with your Facebook and Twitter accounts. Not only will it help you gain followers, but making this connection adds social media icons under your profile picture that link to your Facebook and Twitter profiles.
4. Do not forget to add your website URL to your profile, too.
5. Pin lots of stuff. Pin content steadily, instead of in huge bursts, to maximise your exposure and engagement.
6. Come up with creative and interesting board names. They will get shared whenever you pin something, so make them enticing. But be creative – you need to keep your board names short. There is not a lot of room for long descriptive titles.
7. Tag other Pinterest users in your pins by using "@username" in your descriptions.

   Exercise 6. Network with other literary professionals by using this "tag" feature. Not many people are doing this yet, so it is a great way to build your following and stand out.

2 http://www.copyblogger.com/pinterest-marketing/

8. Comment positively on other people's pins. Just like with tagging, this feature has not really caught on yet, so use it regularly to really engage with other users. Obviously, use the same good manners and common sense you would when commenting on a blog or other social media site.
9. "Like" other people's pins to give a thumbs up when you want to recognise great content.
10. Pin from lots of different sources, instead of just from one or two sites. Variety is important on Pinterest.
11. Mix pinning your own unique finds with doing lots of "repinning," which is repeating someone else's pin to your followers (much like retweeting on Twitter). The person whose image you repin gets notified by email and they get a credit on your pin, which increases their following.
12. Pin your own book blog posts, but do not over-promote. Follow the usual etiquette rules of any other social media site, and do not be the boring one at the party who only talks about himself.
13. When you pin an image, add a description under it. Be smart about these descriptions – a good description will stay with an image as it gets repinned all over the Pinterest world. If the image is something from your own site, definitely use your author name or book title in the description.
14. After you have pinned a new image using the Pinterest browser bookmarklet, you can use its built-in social media prompts to re-share your pin on Twitter and Facebook. Again, one of the main benefits of online marketing is that it allows for viral marketing at the click of a single button.
15. Use Pinterest's embed option to publish pins as content in your blog posts and website pages. As Pinterest is catching on, you may need to tell your users that they need to click on a Pinterest image to get to the original source.

16. Optimise your website content for Pinterest sharing. Use images in every single post you write, so your post can be shared on Pinterest. When you find yourself getting lackadaisical about this, remember – not using an image in your post means no one will pin it. And the better the picture is, the more it will get pinned. The images that primarily appeal to Pinterest members are powerful and emotive, so keep that in mind when choosing your pictures.

17. Consider watermarking your images or adding text to them. If you are using your own image or cover design on Pinterest, one of the best ways to ensure that your image stands out is by adding a clear description to the image itself or adding a watermark with your author name or your book's title. It is all part of building brand awareness. Make sure it is clear and that it does not block the main image.

18. Create storyboards that relate to the storyline of your book. For example, you can have rushes or a series of images that help readers to follow your story and see the actual locations or memorable scenes that you describe in your book. Users love imaginative pins of this kind.

    Exercise 7. Use Pinterest to tell your story in pictures. A picture says a thousand words, and a good storyboard can tell an amazing story.

19. Add a prominent "Follow Me on Pinterest" button to your website to advertise that you are a pinner.

20. If you have a book signing, include pictures from the actual event. This is a good chance to upload picture of your readers and fans as well.

Pinterest marketing for intermediate pinners

1. Search for new images to pin (or for trends) by using Pinterest's search function. The search bar is in the top left of every Pinterest page.

2. Use keywords in descriptions of pins so pinners can find your images and boards when they do their own searches.

3. Make sure you have a "Pin it!" button added to the footer of each of your blog posts so your readers can quickly and easily share your content on Pinterest.

4. Your Pinterest page has its own RSS feed. Find your Pinterest feed by clicking on the RSS symbol under your profile photo, then use it anywhere you can use a feed (on Facebook, LinkedIn, for syndication on other sites, etc.). Advertise your Pinterest feed to your readers and ask them to add you to their RSS feedreaders.

5. If you have a Wordpress site, feature your recent pins in a widget in your Wordpress sidebar by using a Pinterest widget.

6. Pin your YouTube videos as trailers for your book. Pinterest has a special section for pinned videos, and there are far fewer videos than images on Pinterest at this point, so use them to distinguish yourself. Any YouTube video is easy to pin.

7. If you are up on the latest technology, get the Pinterest iPhone application so you can repin on the go, pin from your camera and add a location to your pins so others can find your images.

8. You can add contributors to any of your boards. Use this feature to further engage readers and let them contribute to your Pinterest presence. Your readers will love this, and your boards will be richer for it.

9. If you would like to find out who has been pinning your stuff, go to: http://pinterest.com/source/yoursitehere. View your page frequently to discover which posts and images are resonating with Pinterest users and use that valuable marketing information to shape your content strategy.

10. Add prices to your pins to create your own Pinterest shop. To add a price to a pin, type the $ or £ symbol followed by the item's price in the pin's description. When you add prices to your pins, they may be featured in Pinterest's "Gifts" section.

11. Create a picture board that tells the story of your literary inspirations and aspirations and communicates your core values. Make this board available to your fan base so they can identify more with you and your writing.

12. Consider creating "thank you" boards for your fans and reviewers to send special appreciative messages.

13. Watch for trends. You can click on the "Popular" link on your Pinterest home page to discover what is catching on with pinners, and then integrate those trends into your content strategy.

14. Be yourself. Pinterest is all about personal expression, so do not be afraid to pin stuff that represents who you really are, but avoid pinning photos of a personal nature.

15. Become an information curator for your genre. Gather the latest and best resources on your boards. Become a trusted source of information on Pinterest, and your following will grow considerably.

16. Integrate your Pinterest account with Facebook's timeline feature, so you post content in both places at once.

17. Highlight old content on your blog so that people can repin your archived posts. The "LinkWithin" tool will add a footer to your blog posts that features images and links pulled from old content, giving people the opportunity to pin any previous articles and books.

18. Think about freshening up old photos, or going back through your blog archives and adding photos to those text-only posts. Remember – the nicer the picture the more pins you will get.

19. Set up a literary competition with a series of images of the main character, asking readers which they would prefer with the offer to mention the winner in the acknowledgements of your book.

20. Upload a wide range of book covers, and ask readers to help you select the best cover design.

Pinterest marketing for advanced pinners

1. Find out when you are getting the most repins, likes, comments and referral traffic by regularly analysing both your Pinterest profile and your site traffic stats. Experiment by pinning on different days of the week and times of day to maximise traffic and audience engagement.

2. Connect your readers who use Pinterest by introducing them to each other. Recognise your best pinners by sending out a weekly "Best of Pinterest" email that includes spotlighted boards and pins from your readers' profiles.

3. Create moderated boards for your fans to express their support for you. They can add reviews, blog posts and photos of them with a copy of your book prominently displayed in their hand.

4. If you have a number of different author personas (say you write under one pen name as a horror writer and another pen name as a children's book writer), you can create a separate board to represent each persona, then use those boards during your sales cycle and embed them into your website pages so people are clear about the different kinds of books you write.

5. Create boards for the book-related or marketing articles that you write.

6. Create picture boards for referral sources, affiliates and strategic partners, and let them add to the boards. Engage with the partners so they know they are included and appreciated.

7. Allow your favourite readers and fans to join in on certain boards and pin hints about your next book, or themes that go along with your narrative.

8. Upload a new board with images of your book photographed in famous or exotic locations.

9. Think about creating an endorsement board with favourable quotes from positive reviews of your book on Amazon. This needs to be done in a tactful manner, not in a self-aggrandising way.

10. Use Pinterest boards to tell short stories, thereby serialising your book in pictures. This will give a real-life feel to your story.

Pinterest.com is not only picking up steam in social media circles, it has become a proven source of traffic for blogs and websites, quickly surpassing current favourites like LinkedIn and YouTube.

While lots of people are talking about the impressive statistics of Pinterest, some authors are quietly using this new site to pin their way to better reader engagement and a visually striking, enhanced author brand. Our advice is to start making your social media strategy more beautiful, one little pin at a time.

Building Your Author Profile on Reddit

Reddit (www.en.reddit.com) is a social news and entertainment website where users can post links to content on the Internet. Other users may then vote the posted links up or down, causing them to appear more or less prominently on the Reddit home page. The site has discussion areas where users can discuss the posted links, and vote for or against others' comments. When there are enough votes against a given comment, it will not be displayed by default, although a reader can display it through a link or preference. Users who submit articles which other users like and subsequently "vote up" receive "karma," which are points that a user receives for submitting interesting articles. Reddit also includes several topical sections called subreddits that focus on specific topics including writing, literature, poetry, fiction and short stories.

Here are some tips for building a good author reputation as you market your book on Reddit[3]:

1. **Name yourself smartly.** Your Reddit account will have a name attached to it that every reader will see. Make sure you pick a name that reveals that you are a published author.

3 http://businessmentor-ray.com/1050/what-is-reddit-com-how-to-market-successfully-on-reddit/

2. **Make friends.** Reddit is a communal website, and your marketing efforts will go much further the more thoroughly you involve yourself within that community. Pay attention to users who comment on your posts and check out their own posts. Cultivate relationships with other Reddit members who share your professional interests.

3. **Comment wisely.** Besides posting and ranking content, Reddit users are free to comment on others' posts. You should do so to raise your literary profile. Make sure you focus on items that are relevant to your writing, and make sure that your comments are positive and demonstrate your expertise in your field.

4. **Cross-promote.** Make your presence felt on Reddit without generating any new content. If you run a blog or post articles on your website, submit the content to Reddit. One way to improve click-through is to post part of a story, encouraging Reddit users to visit your site to get the full story.

5. **AMA.** "AMA" stands for "ask me anything." This is a post that invites other Reddit users to submit their queries to you. Doing an AMA can be a great way to market your book and expand your visibility on the site. If you have already built up a reputation as a good writer or authority in your genre, your AMA will get plenty of responses.

6. **Seek feedback.** One way to get your book mentioned on Reddit is to ask for advice. You can seek reviews of your book, or post newsworthy excerpts on the site to generate interest, combining community participation with marketing.

7. **Secure affiliate links.** Reddit is a good place to link to your publishing affiliates, but you should only submit links in places where your links will be welcomed. Always pick an appropriate category or "subreddit" for your affiliate links, and never submit links in ways that could be seen as spamming.

8. **Participate often.** Reddit does not like self-promotion more than any other online community. Even if your Reddit account is dedicated to your literary pursuits, use it for more than just marketing

your book. Make sure your posts and comments reflect your personal interests, not your marketing plan.

Becoming an integral part of the Reddit community takes time and effort. If you can gradually build up your presence, you can do some effective marketing through Reddit. Because the site relies on a democratic voting system to decide what content becomes most visible, overt marketing is counterproductive and you need to be creative in your book's placement within your submissions.

In order to understand how to effectively market your book on Reddit, to gain votes for your posts, you must first understand the community and its idiosyncrasies.

Understanding Reddit

On Reddit, any user is capable of submitting any type of content to the site. Registered users then vote this content up or down. An algorithm based on the ratio between time and votes is used to determine how visible the submitted content becomes. Content that is "voted up" by large numbers of Reddit users can see massive amounts of engagement. Content submitted to Reddit that reaches the front page of the site – the most popular content of the day – tends to receive traffic in the range of 50,000 to 200,000 referral visitors and hundreds of subsequent links to that content from outside sites.

Subreddit demographics

Over the last few years as Reddit has grown, there has been an increase in the number of categories or "subreddits" on the site. These subreddits are sections of the site dedicated to specific topics or niches, and span a wide variety of subjects. The most popular subreddits have more than a million subscribers, with over 100,000 unique subreddits. They cover nearly any topic you can imagine. Even more obscure niches like "Fahrenheit 451" have subscriber numbers in the tens of thousands.

When promoting your author brand or book, you should understand what resonates with redditors in your subreddit. For instance, the subreddit community at r/thechildtaker is primarily made up of women, whereas the community at r/criminalrevenge is overwhelmingly made up of men.

Benefits of Reddit marketing

With Reddit being a dynamic, marketing-averse, democratic community, it can be unwieldy and difficult to predict. Still, it can be a tremendous marketing channel for your writing if you can harness it because of its viral potential, the targeted nature of its users, and its syndication potential.

Because of Reddit's voting system, the visibility of content is dependent on how the content resonates with Redditors. The source of the content plays only a small role in how many people eventually see the content. This system allows innovative and creative individuals to enjoy viral success in a way that has rarely been possible previously.

With segmentation of communities provided by the subreddit format, very specific demographic information can be gleaned from the site. In many cases, the subreddit communities are among the largest dedicated to a specific subject across the whole of the Internet.

Because Reddit is a news/information hub for thousands of tastemakers online, the content that appears on Reddit enjoys wide syndication across blogs and other online and offline publications. For those whose primary goal is link building, this is a notable and important advantage.

Understanding Reddit's content-rich approach

To see a return from marketing on Reddit, you need to approach it with the intention of providing value for Redditors from the start. This is not to say that you cannot accomplish your goals at the same time. However, if you do not keep at the forefront of your mind the notion that your first priority is benefitting others in some way, your online marketing campaign will fall short of achieving its desired end of raising your literary profile, building up a readership and selling more copies of your book.

Adding value on Reddit is simply a matter of providing content that is interesting, useful, or otherwise shareable. This content can be in any form, but visual content typically performs best. It is important to keep the content you create as impartial and non-sales oriented as possible. For this reason, Reddit is a great way to launch content with the intention of gaining links (and subsequent improvements in ranking).

The secret ingredient

There is one sure-fire way to engage in marketing with Reddit that will prove effective. The approach starts with the community in mind, and expands from there. Here is the approach in six easy steps:

1. Understand that your goal is to create engagement through content creation. The indirect benefit will be increased traffic to your site, link building, author brand awareness and perhaps an increase in readers and book sales.
2. Understand that you must provide something of obvious and proven value to the community you are marketing to on Reddit.
3. Your content must be explicitly tailored to a particular subreddit.
4. Your content should be visually impressive.
5. Your content should serve as an evergreen resource for the subreddit you are targeting.
6. The only marketing the content should do is give credit to the creator of the content. Putting your author name on your content can be beneficial, or saying the content was "taken from [your book title]" is fine as well.

The keys to unlocking the potential of Reddit is to first understand its communities, and then work closely with those communities and the moderators of subreddits to provide them practical content based on topics you are certain that *they* will find interesting. When you can achieve these two things, you will set yourself up to harness the viral potential of one of the most dynamic and wide-reaching marketing channels on the Internet today.

Exercise 8. Join Reddit and create posts that are rich with content and useful to the Reddit community. Focus on your particular subreddit when doing so.

Set Up a Goodreads Account and Join Their Author Program

Goodreads (www.goodreads.com) is a book cataloguing website which allows individuals to freely search their extensive database of books, annotations and reviews. You are able to sign up and register books to generate library catalogues and reading lists. You can also create your own tailored groups of book suggestions and discussions on the site.

The Goodreads Author Program was specially designed to help authors reach their target audience; that is, avid readers. This is the perfect place for new and established authors to promote their books.

These are the steps you need to take to join the Author Program:

1. Registering is simple. Go to www.goodreads.com and type in your name, email and password. Then click "Sign up."
2. If your book is not already in the Goodreads database (most are), then add your book.
3. Search for yourself and click on your published author name. The author name is listed below the title of your book in the search results.
4. Clicking on your name takes you to your basic author profile page. This page has your name at the top and "author profile" to the right of your name. This page is part of your database of books and authors and is separate from your member profile page (which lists your bookshelves and friends).

5. Scroll down to the bottom of the page. Click "Is this you?" to send a request to join the Author Program. It may take a few days for the site to process your request. You will receive email confirmation when we successfully upgrade your user account to an author account. Joining the programme merges your author page with your member page. The email will also contain further instructions for managing your author profile.

Exercise 9. Sign up to the Goodreads website and join Goodreads' Author Program and manage your author profile, as outlined below.

Once you have set up your author profile, you can take control of your profile and make your profile a dynamic destination for curious readers. Here are some of the features you can use on your profile:

- Add a picture and a bio
- Share your list of favourite books and recent reads with your fans
- Write a blog and generate a band of followers
- Publicise upcoming events, including book signings and speaking engagements
- Share book excerpts and your other work
- Write a quiz about your book or a related topic
- Post videos and trailers about your book
- Add the Goodreads Author widget to your personal website or blog to showcase reviews of your books

Promote your book on Goodreads

Here are some of the promotional tools available on Goodreads:

- Sign up to advertise your book to the Goodreads Community with its 12,000,000+ readers

- List a book giveaway to generate a pre-launch buzz
- Lead a Q & A discussion group for readers
- Participate in literary discussions individually on your profile, in groups and in the discussion forums for your book

To start using Goodreads to its full advantage, you should select books that you have read, that you are reading or that you want to read, and add them to "your books." You can do this by searching for books on the site, by looking at your friends' lists or by entering a new book that they may not have listed yet. Rating a book automatically adds it to your books and to your "read" shelf.

You will start with three shelves (read, currently reading and to read), but you can also create your own bookshelves. Shelf categories range from classics and coffee-table books to children's lit and sci-fi – you can create categories that suit your personal taste, such as "want to reread," "guilty-pleasures," "bestsellers" and "overrated drivel."

To add books to your shelves, search by author name or book title. If the book is on Amazon, you will find it (and they carry almost everything). If not, you have the option to add it manually as a new title. When you find the book you want, you can either click one–five stars to rate the book immediately, or click on "add to my books" to choose a shelf, write a review, record the date you read the book, and even note whether you own a copy.

To sort out your books on your virtual bookshelves, click on "my books" to see all the different "views" available on Goodreads. You can sort by author, title, rating, date read, and more. One view shows you all your book covers, another shows your reviews, still another helps you collate and catalogue groups of books at once. You can change the look, feel and content of your shelves, reviews and ratings at any time.

Books are listed on Goodreads in several editions, such as hardback and paperback. Add the one you have to your books. The site has a built-in feature where their librarians combine similar editions of each book, so reviews and ratings are aggregated across all editions when you view a book.

You can personalise your bookshelf, as your bookshelf will say a lot about you. After you upload your photo and post your basic info, start adding more books to your virtual shelves. Some Goodreaders list their top 10 favourites; others catalogue everything they've ever read. You can post any quotes that you like, share your own writing for others to review and publicise your upcoming events.

The site aims to help you find new and interesting books by letting you view what your friends are reading. When you view a book, the site is set up to show you your friends' reviews firstly. When you log in, the homepage will show the latest reviews from your friends. You can also compare your book list to that of another Goodreads member to see if you share the same taste.

> *Exercise 10. Click the "Explore" tab to browse the top shelves and find popular books among your friends or all of Goodreads.*

Joining discussion groups is the perfect way to bring a group of people together to discuss literature. Some groups are for close friends or local book clubs; others are for organisations such as literary magazines, university alumni or just about any literary group conceivable. Groups can either be public, moderated, restricted by domain or kept secret.

You can click on any book title to find a lot of information about a book. Beyond the basic details such as the author's name, the book's ISBN and any literary awards the book may have won, you can also find the book's average rating, the number of people who have reviewed and rated the book, and even how those people decided to shelve it.

You can see which Goodreads groups are discussing the book, reviews from your friends, and other reviews from possibly thousands of readers. If you would like to purchase a copy of a book, you can check out the links that help you find it at an online bookseller; they will also help you discover whether it can be found at your local library. Goodreads catalogues various editions of a book, so you can find the edition that you are looking for with the cover art to make your virtual shelves look just like your real ones. Information is kept accurate and current by the site's Librarian Group.

> *Exercise 11. Showcase your book and list reviews by adding a Goodreads "widget" (in the form of a small icon) to your site or blog.*

If you know your way around Goodreads, you can also export and download your books as a spreadsheet. Or if you are using another book database, you can import it as well.

Other Useful Book Cataloguing Websites

There are other good online reading communities worth joining, including aNobii, BookJetty, weRead, LibraryThing and Shelfari, as they can also provide you with further channels to talk about and market your book, in much the same way as you have done on Goodreads:

aNobii: Where books and people meet

aNobii (www.anobii.com) is an online reading community "built by readers for readers." The site allows you to catalogue your books and rate, review and discuss them with other readers. The service is available via the aNobii website and iPhone and Android apps. The applications allow you to scan the barcodes for books and read both community and expert reviews.

aNobii gives you options to help you to shelve, find and share books:

Shelve

- Categorise what you have read, track what you are reading and log what you would like to read in your online library

Find

- Find books you might like and books you did not know existed with the help of your friends and the aNobii community
- Find readers with similar tastes and browse their shelves
- Browse popular, recently added and reviewed books

Share

- Share your favourite reads by creating your own reading groups, book clubs and discussion forums through aNobii
- Share your library and wish list with friends through Facebook and Twitter
- Use the aNobii badge and link to your library from your blog or website

BookJetty: Catalogue your books and share with your friends

Another noteworthy social book cataloguing site is called BookJetty (www.bookjetty.com). The best feature of this site is its great library integration, especially considering that most library systems still run antiquated web 0.1 systems, which are not very compatible with today's technology. The site currently links with more than 300 libraries worldwide from 11 different countries, and more are being added each week.

The site is also linked to Pinterest, which showcases some of the books on the site (see http://pinterest.com/source/bookjetty.com/).

weRead: Books, authors and more!

weRead (www.weread.com), formerly iRead, is basically an online community of book enthusiasts. The site's "Chuck a book" feature allows users to recommend books to their friends. Its "Author's corner" is billed as "a place to connect authors and their fans," and is your own little soapbox to sing the praises of your book.

weRead's "Read inside" feature allows members to browse sections of many new titles and read entire books in an electronic format.

There is a useful Q&A section on the site, which explains just about everything you might want to know about the site, how it works and how it can benefit you as an author.

LibraryThing: A home for your books

LibraryThing (www.librarything.com) is a massive online resource for all things book related. It is used by just about everyone across the literary spectrum, including authors, agents, editors, reviewers, book marketing specialists, librarians and publishers. There is "more information than you will ever require" here about books, ranging from top-rated authors to the most prolific reviewers on the site. It boasts the "world's largest book club" and as of July 2012, the site had over 1.55 million users and more than 74 million books catalogued.

The primary feature of LibraryThing is the extensive cataloguing of books on the site by importing data from six Amazon.com stores and 690 libraries (and counting), including the United States Library of Congress, the National Library of Australia, the Canadian National Catalogue, the British Library and Yale University. Should a record not be available from any of these sources, it is also possible to add the book information yourself.

The most popular tags for groups on LibraryThing (and there are currently over 9,000 of them on the site) include: challenges, group read, librarything, literature, religion, science-fiction, authors, books, history, fantasy. The most active groups include Pro and Con (progressives and conservatives), a Harry Potter discussion group, Let's Talk Religion, a few book challenge groups and something called Literary Snobs.

There is certainly a lot of text, lists and numbers on the site (some would say clutter), and it could use a tidy up. Browsing LibraryThing is like walking into the home of a compulsive hoarder. No literary facts are left unlisted. Still, if you know what you are looking for and you can figure out where to find it, much like shopping in your local supermarket, you can get most everything you might want from the site in terms of facts and figures about literati.

Shelfari: A community-powered encyclopaedia for book lovers

The last social cataloguing website for books that we will mention is Shelfari (www.shelfari.com). This site enables users to build virtual bookshelves of the titles they currently own or have read, and rate, review, tag and discuss their books (much like Goodreads, but more storage than review oriented). Users can create groups that other members may join, initiate discussion topics, talk about books and share information about developments in the publishing world. Recommendations can be sent to friends on the site about what books to read, which is useful for marketing your book.

Shelfari is owned by Amazon, so it is safe to say that it is not going anywhere and is likely to expand its reach in the coming years.

Shelfari promotes its "virtual bookshelf" as one of its main features. The virtual bookshelf displays covers of books, which the user has entered, with pop-ups to show the user's book information (review, rating and tags). Sorting by author, title, date, rating or review is available to the viewer of the shelf. Shelfarians can organise their books on different shelves, organising books according to what they have already read, are currently reading and planning to read, their wish list and the books they currently own and their favourites.

The Shelfari catalogue can be edited by users, although some changes must be approved by Shelfari site administrators or online "librarians." Users can edit each book's author, title, publication date, table of contents, first sentence and series. Users can also combine redundant books into a single entry or add new titles not found in the catalogue. Similar to books, author pages can be edited or created. In addition to general catalogue maintenance, users are encouraged to contribute reviews, descriptions, lists of characters and settings, author biographies, categories and descriptive tags.

Most books in the Shelfari catalogue come from the large Amazon catalogue with Amazon Marketplace listings added by independent resellers. These books link to Amazon and display current pricing with additional links to Abebooks (also owned by Amazon!) for used book sales. While there is some astroturfing on Shelfari by Amazon (as pointed out by Tim Spalding, creator of LibraryThing), Shelfari is a well-designed, user-friendly website for avid readers with a simple layout (unlike LibraryThing) with a strong sense of serving the book community, and we would certainly recommend it to authors as yet another useful channel to market their own book.

> *Exercise 12. Join Shelfari and create groups that other members will want to join, initiate discussion topics, talk about interesting books, and share information about recent developments in the publishing world.*

The more you can participate in literary communities of this kind, the greater the following and readership you'll develop over time for your writing.

5

SECURE REVIEWS AND SET YOURSELF UP AS A REVIEWER

There are many ways to raise your profile away from the online retailers but remember that the online stores and review sites, namely Amazon, Kobo, Tesco, Waterstones, Goodreads and Kindle Boards, are where your customers are looking for good books. Facebook and Twitter are key to your promotional platform, but your readers are in the retailers and online bookshops (or e-tailers) and therefore raising your profile in those stores is vital to your book's commercial success.

The key question is how can you do it without spamming the forums with posts and links that scream "buy my book" and turn readers off? The answer is placing strategic positive, intelligent reviews on books in your genre. You also need to encourage your readers *in the right way* to leave reviews on your book. Positive five-star reviews move your books up the search engines, but one-star reviews will knock your book down the rankings equally fast.

Where to Start

Firstly, you need to have your book or ebook reviewed by as many friends and family members as you can and ask them to post an honest review. Books with published reviews and genuine testimonials from various ebook stores or your readers tend to get more attention and interest and thus sell more. It's self-perpetuating. The more positive reviews you can secure for your book the higher up the ranking it goes; the higher up the ranking it goes the more your book will sell.

Try and reply to every review, good or bad. If it is good then you can build a rapport with the reviewer, which tends to generate more positive reviews from them in the future. If they are scathing, either ignore it or be polite and thank them for the time they spent reading and reviewing your book. We have all seen discussion threads between wounded authors and reviewers. Some of these exchanges are very heated and almost abusive, but at the end of the day a reader's opinion is just that, their opinion. You cannot change that and arguing or criticising them is only likely to make things worse.

The Nature of Book Reviews

Some publishers will work with authors to help them get book reviews, depending on the publisher's staff and promotional budget. Some will have a ready list of useful contacts that have previously reviewed their other books in the same genre. Find out how many complimentary review copies your publisher is willing to provide, and whether they will do the mailing for you. With some larger publications, your publisher will have to request a pre-publication review.

You should target magazines, journals and websites that review books in your genre. Sending books for review without adequate research is likely to result in your book being donated to the local library (at best), or tossed in the bin (at worst), without being read.

Exercise 1. Put together a list of suitable companies and individuals to approach, with the aim to send a letter or email and compliment them on their reviews, asking if they would be willing to review your book.

It might be a good idea to check with other authors to find out how they got reviews for their books, and if they have written books in the same genre, they may well have a ready-made list of relevant contacts that they can share with you for you to write to in this regard.

Even if your publisher provides review copies and a full list of contacts, you need to build up your own list as well. You should do your own research and make further enquiries. You should carefully research the reviewer's style and submission requirements. The more you can tailor your correspondence to them the more likely they'll be to positively review your book. Some publications prefer requests by email rather than post. Others only accept requests from publishers. Often, authors aim too high and send their book for review by publications such as the *Times Literary Review* or the broadsheets, whereas it might be better to seek reviews from local and regional newspapers, at least to start.

It is not just about getting reviews, it is about getting *positive* reviews, and the more thorough your research and the more professional your approach the more likely you are to secure the sorts of reviews which will help to promote your book. There are some reviewers and websites that tend to be overly critical, especially if they're sponsored by one publisher and your book submission is from another publisher, and you want to make sure you avoid sending your book to them. For example, if you published your book with Authorhouse and you send it for review by *Self-Publishing Magazine*, which is linked to the self-publishing company Troubadour Publishing, it *might* not be such a good idea.

Whom and How to Ask for Reviews

Once your book is published, you should send a tailored press release to everyone on your contact list, offering or enclosing free review copies. It is important to remember to thank anyone who does positively review your book, as they are much more likely to do the same for your next book and recommend your recently published book in their literature or on their website. It is also a good idea to focus on specific writers (both reviewers and feature writers) and send them a short informative letter or email with a line or two about the book, mentioning that you have already read a review that they wrote ("I read with interest your write-up of *Criminally Insane* and thought you might be interested in reading and kindly reviewing my new crime novel entitled *Frozen Betrayal*") and providing relevant details about your book, including the name of the publisher, ISBN, page count, retail price and publication date. Most importantly, make sure that you include your updated contact details and make it easy for them to contact you. Do not send a mobile telephone number or postal address only. Rather, include an email address and landline telephone number for them to contact you on.

It is important to tailor your letter or email to the individual who will be undertaking the review. If the reviewer thinks that you are asking them personally to review your book, they will be much more likely to take the time to review it and more disposed to write a positive review. Often, the press release that you wrote for your ebook can readily be tailored for review requests.

Checklist of Details to Include in Your Review Request

In your review letter, make sure that you clearly state the:

- Title of book
- Approximate length of book
- Genre of book
- Name of publisher
- ISBN
- Date of publication
- A brief about the book (one–two paragraphs)
- A brief about the author (one paragraph will suffice)
- Your contact details (with landline telephone and email address)

Sample Review Request Letter

Dear Editor [or preferably the editor's name, if known],

I read with interest the review that you wrote for [book title].
I am the author of a new crime novel, [insert your book description].
Would you be interested in reviewing [book title] for [name of publication or website]?
I have enclosed a review copy [or I would be happy to send you a review copy upon request].

Kind regards,

[Your name]
http://www. [Your website address]
Book Title
Author
Publisher
ISBN
Brief synopsis – about 25–50 words.

10 Best Practices for Seeking Book Reviews

There are some basic principles to follow when seeking reviews for your book. In sum, they are:

1. Do your research. Know what your potential reviewer likes and does not like.

2. Follow their submission guidelines to the letter, if they have them.

3. Do not ask for or expect glowing reviews. Otherwise, they will look artificial. Ask for an honest one, and if the person does not like your book, thank them anyway. Never respond in kind or take it personally.

4. Accept "no" as an answer. The person might be too busy, have a lot of other books in queue to be read first, have their own books to

write, and so on. Imagine if you were flooded with book review requests, and had to prioritise your day job, etc. Be very grateful for reviews, but do not expect them.

5. Endorsements are similar to reviews, only they are much shorter. So, the same practices tend to produce the same positive response. There is a famous story that when one author asked Piers Morgan to review a book for him, Piers replied, "I would be glad to endorse your book, but just don't expect me to read it." Although you would hope that your review/endorsement is based on the person actually having read your book, sometimes it is best to enclose a synopsis of your book to facilitate their review/endorsement. The point is you need to make it as easy as you can for a reviewer to say "yes."

6. Ask an author friend/acquaintance who is a respected journalist or writer, preferably one who writes in a similar genre, to review your book. This will give the review or back cover quote more credibility with readers. A children's book author or celebrity chef who endorses a crime novel will not have the same impact with potential readers as a thriller author who endorses your crime novel.

7. The best reviews of your book will often come from new readers, as they tend to sound the most sincere and authentic.

8. Sometimes it is better to have, say, three five-star reviews and two four-star reviews than five five-star reviews.

9. Do not ask someone who has left a negative review to remove it.

10. It takes time to get reviews, but the best people to review your book are readers who have nothing to gain or lose by reviewing it.

Exercise 2. Draft, tailor and send a letter or email to the companies and individuals listed in Exercise 1 and compliment them on their reviews, asking if they would be willing to review your book. For postal requests, enclose a complimentary copy of your book.

Getting the Most from Your Book Reviews

There are numerous ways that you can maximise the publicity from reviewers. First and foremost, encourage those on your mailing list to post customer reviews on Amazon.com and Barnesandnoble.com, if they liked your book. Keep an eye out for websites and publications that will agree for you to reprint their reviews on your website, although you should seek their consent before doing so as a professional courtesy. Many reviewers especially like to see their reviews and their names quoted elsewhere, so it is useful to extend this courtesy to them too.

Join online groups where reviewers will kindly review your book and encourage you as a writer. There are plenty of review websites for every genre. Many magazines and newspapers are looking for good books to review. You will be surprised how many will take you up on the offer to review your book, if you approach them in the right way.

Keep a close record of everyone who responds positively and contact them again when your next book comes out. If you treat reviewers and fans with respect and correspond with them often, they will repay you in spades when it comes to reading, reviewing and recommending your book/s to others.

Have Your Book Reviewed on Goodreads

Goodreads (www.goodreads.com) is a free website for book lovers. Imagine it as a large library that you can wander through and see everyone's bookshelves, their reviews and their ratings. You can post your own reviews and catalogue what you have read, what you are currently reading and what you plan to read in future. You can join a discussion group, start a book club, contact an author directly and even post your own writing in a positive and encouraging online literary environment.

Signing up is really simple — you just enter your name, email and a password. If you are a published author, take a look at the "Goodreads Author Program."

To start using Goodreads, you should select books that you have read, that you are reading or that you want to read and add them to "Your books." You can do this by searching for books (their catalogue already has most books), by looking at your fellow Goodreads author lists, or by entering a new book. "Rating a book" automatically adds it to your books and to your "Read" shelf.

You start with three default shelves – "Read," "Currently reading," and "To-read," but you can also create your own virtual bookshelves. Shelf names range from classics and coffee-table books to children's lit and sci-fi. You can create any category that suits your own personal taste. Some of the most popular shelves on the Goodreads website include "To reread," "Guilty pleasures," "Chick lit" and, a favourite, "Overrated drivel."

Adding your books to Goodreads

To add books to your online shelves, search by author name or book title. If the book is on Amazon, you will find it, as the sites carries almost every book with an ISBN – if not, you can add it manually if you would like as a new title. When you find the book you want, you can click on one of the five stars to rate the book, or click on "Add to my books" to choose a shelf, write a review, record the date you read the book and mention whether you own a copy. Anyone can review on Goodreads. There are no requirements. Goodreads does not moderate and police the reviews the way Amazon does. Some people complain about books being rated before they are even published, but Goodreads does allow this to happen as part of its unrestrictive approach. Many readers on Goodreads also have access to ARCs (advance reader copies).

Most people prefer not to rate a book without reading it in full, but they can add their comments based on what they have read thus far. Some people even go to great lengths on the site to explain why they decided *not* to read a book or not to finish reading it. Any text in the review box is seen as a "review" on Goodreads, but some people do use the review facility to make passing notes and on-going commentaries while reading a book.

Many people are of the opinion that the author should be able to rate their own books, but shelving their books is helpful to others because they can use genre shelves to categorise the books correctly and use shelves to share other relevant book information. Authors can also use the review box to say anything they would like about the book without actually rating it. Ratings without reviews do affect the average rating, but they do not help other readers much, which is one of the main aims of the reviews.

In sum, there are a lot of options for authors when rating and reviewing their book on Goodreads, and every published author should aim to secure positive, informative reviews for their book on this all-important social-cataloguing website.

Sorting your books

Click on the "My books" tab to see all the different views available on Goodreads. One view shows you your entire book covers, another shows your reviews, still another helps you shelve groups of books at once, and there is even one that is printer-friendly; you can sort by author, title, rating, date read and more. You can change your shelves, reviews and ratings at any time.

Reviews across all editions

Many books are listed on Goodreads.com in several editions, such as hardback and paperback. Add the one you have to your books. The site has a built-in feature where e-librarians combine editions of each book, so that all reviews and ratings are aggregated across all editions when you view a book. This is especially useful, in contrast with reviews on other websites where they are not necessarily carried across.

Personalise your profile

After you upload your photo and post your basic details, start adding books to your virtual shelves. Your bookshelves say a lot about you. Some people will simply list their top 10 favourite books of all time; others catalogue everything they have ever read. You can post quotes you like, the best opening or closing lines to books you've ever read, share your own writing for others to review or publicise your upcoming book launch or book signing events. This is a great way to build up a following for your writing.

Finding book recommendations

The central aims of Goodreads are to enable you to share the books that you love with others and discover new, exciting books for yourself. When you view a book, the site will show you all your friends' reviews first. You can compare your booklist to that of other Goodreads members to see if you share literary interests. Click the "Explore" tab to browse the "Top shelves" and find the most popular books among your friends or among all Goodreaders.

Join or start your own discussion group

Discussion groups are a great way to bring people together to discuss their shared literary interests. Some groups are for close friends or local book clubs; others are for organisations, such as literary magazines or exclusive literati; still others are for university alumni, college courses, genre reviewers, and on. Groups can be public, moderated, restricted limited by domain/address, or kept under password/secret.

Exercise 3. Start up a discussion group on Goodreads about your latest book and encourage others to participate.

Everything you need to know about a book

Click on any book title to find its relevant information. Beyond the basics, such as the name of the author, the ISBN and literary merits/awards, you can also find the book's average rating, the number of people who have reviewed it and even how those people decided to shelve it (which can be quite telling in terms of how to position your book within the market to your potential readers). You can find out if any Goodreads groups are discussing your book on the site, read reviews from your friends and read other reviews from dozens (or if your writing is popular, hundreds or even thousands) of readers. If you would like to order a copy, there are links to help you locate it at an online bookseller or even your local library. Goodreads uniquely catalogues all editions of a book (hardcover, paperback, etc.), so you can find the precise edition that you would like with the cover art to make your virtual shelves look just like real ones! And the information is kept accurate and current by the site's Librarian Group.

Book widgets

What is a "widget"? It is a device placed in cans and bottles of beer to aid in the generation of froth. It is also a rather diminutive character in Marvel Comics. In the sober yet equally imaginary world of the Internet, a widget is something entirely different. It is a software application that allows you to manage information across different publishing platforms.

On Goodreads, a widget is a personalised placeholder in the form of a dynamic image, which you can use to denote one of your chosen titles. Thus, you can show off your books and reviews by adding one of their creative widgets to your website and/or weblog.

Import and export your books

Another virtue of Goodreads is you can export your books and reviews to a spread sheet if you want to track them offline or discuss them with others. Or if you are using another book database, you can import it into the site. If you are going to set yourself up as a reviewer and secure reviews for your own book, Goodreads is a great place to start to tone your literary skills in this regard.

Exercise 4. Take 30 minutes to make sure that all of your books are listed on Goodreads.com and that they have some reviews on them.

Have Your Book Reviewed on Shelfari

Shelfari is another great social-networking site for avid book readers and reviewers. On this site you can make friends, share book recommendations, create virtual bookshelves to show off what you are currently reading, the books you have read in the past and titles that you intend to read in the future.

Shelfari is a lot like Goodreads. It offers a range of related services and has a similar aim – to appeal to book lovers. While Shelfari's interface is modern and looks professional, however, it does not connect readers nearly as well. Still, there are plenty of ways to market your book and room for securing reviews for your book on the site.

Shelfari bookshelves

The bookshelf is the mainstay you are looking for, you can add it to one of three shelves, namely "To-read," "Currently reading," or "Read." Shelfari's electronic bookshelf will display the cover image. The site will also keep track of how many books you have read in previous years or the current year. You can "favourite" books to show friends and visitors what your favourite titles are, and a small balloon will appear over the cover if you have written a review.

Every book listed on the site has a rating system of one to five stars so you can keep track of your literary preferences. The site also enables you to showcase your favourite books, as well as what you are currently reading. Since you should never join a reviews website with the sole intention of promoting yourself, be sure to add some books to your shelves and join a few groups. Other Shelfari members will be much more receptive to your messages and book recommendations if they can see your bookshelf and find areas of mutual interest in the authors and books you both enjoy.

Author page

After adding books to your virtual shelf, the first thing you should do after signing up for an account is run a search for your own book (provided it has been released and the ISBN is recognised in the database). Once you locate it, you can link your personal profile to the book and an "Unbound" author page will be created for you ("Unbound" is what Shelfari calls their author pages). Setting up just takes a quick email to the Shelfari team, and within a few days your page will be up and running.

What you can enter on your author page is minimal, but enough to tell readers a little bit about yourself. You will be able to upload a photo, as well as your date and place of birth, gender, nationality, official website and writing genres. In addition, you should include a brief bio about yourself and Shelfari will automatically display your book cover(s) and set up a discussion forum in the event that anyone wishes to discuss you or your books.

Book page

One thing that Shelfari does better than Goodreads is enable you to edit a lot of information on your book's page, and to do it quickly. Not only can you edit the details but any readers can contribute as well. This gives the website a wiki-like, interactive feel and allows people who enjoy your books to contribute helpful information for other potential readers.

While there are a number of sections to edit on your book page, here is a list of the sections that you should definitely provide information on:

- **Book description.** Drop in a short brief here to capture the attention of potential readers.
- **Ridiculously simplified synopsis.** This is a one-line description of the book, so make it good and pithy.
- **Plot summary.** This is a good place to copy/paste the text from your back cover.
- **Important people.** You can list the characters in your novel and provide some background on them.

- **Memorable quotes.** Add some great quotes from your book that will engage people and incentivise them to read it.
- **First edition.** Include edition type (hardback, paperback or ebook) name of the publisher, date of publication, ISBN, page count, and so on.
- **Awards.** Mention literary awards, prizes or special acclaim that the book or the author has won.
- **Tags.** Add a few words or key phrases that people might use to find your book when searching the website.
- **More books like this.** Here you can add in similar books from your genre or favourite authors and the covers for those titles will display on your book's page. This is a great way to link up with other books and help potential readers decide whether your book might be the sort of book they like to read.
- **Books that influenced this book.** This is the last section and serves the same purpose as above. Limit to three or four covers of the titles at most that really influenced your writing.

Exercise 5. Take the time to check that you have filled out all of these Shelfari sections on your book page appropriately.

Linking your book to other books

Since every book page is its own information link, and that info can be edited by anyone, you can go onto pages for books similar to your own, or those that helped inspire your writing, and add your book to the "More books like this" section and another section called "Books influenced by this one." Whenever people search for that classic title, they will see your book cover as they scroll about the page. This is a great way to subtly target readers who may already have a high level of interest in your genre or in similar authors, making it easy for them to find your book.

Shelfari do monitor the website closely, so only list your book on the relevant pages of similar books. Do not go crazy and link it to books in other genres, etc. or you may find yourself removed from the website completely.

Exercise 6. Make sure that your book is linked to other relevant books listed on the Shelfari website, as explained above.

Discussion groups

Shelfari encourages users to join their online groups where you can discuss different authors, genres, or specific titles. Do not try to promote your book in these groups, as this practice of overt self-promotion is strongly frowned upon both by the site's administrators and by other Shelfari users.

Writing reviews

The core of any book-based website is the writing and reading of reviews, and Shelfari is no different. After all, user reviews are what encourage us to pick up a specific title, or to avoid it like the plague. Whenever you leave a review for a book, it will show up in your profile, but also in the "Reviews" section of the book's page. If you write good reviews that contain useful information, people are likely to click to your profile to read your other reviews, and they will quickly discover that you are an author. Use your book description and biography to "sell them" on your title and hopefully you have earned both a new reader and a new fan.

Reviews for and by fellow Shelfari users

Like other social-networking sites, Shelfari gives you the opportunity to make "friends" with other writers and readers. Jot down a list of books and authors that you consider to be similar to your own literary writing and interest. Once you complete the list, search out those books and authors on Shelfari. On each book page you will see a tab called "Readers and reviews." Clicking that link, you will be taken to a page that shows any reviews that other users have left. It will also show you the profile picture of anyone who has that book on their shelf.

Exercise 7. Take a few minutes to skim through the reviews. Whenever you notice a positive review, go to that user's profile and click the link that says "Add as a friend."

You will be provided with a small, blank text box in which you can write a message to the user before they accept or deny your friend request. Use this text box to make a good first impression, as this is someone whom you know, based on your research on their profile and books, might enjoy your book and tell their friends about it.

The key is to send a short, personalised message to them that will pique their interest and have them searching to find out more about you and your book before they accept your request. Be sure to call them by name and mention that you enjoyed their review (and remember to specifically indicate which review you read).

Let them know that if they enjoyed that book then they might enjoy yours as well. Drop in a few lines summarising the book, but do not spam them with your website or Amazon.com links. Simply provide them with the title and a quick teaser and then encourage them to search for it on Shelfari if it sounds interesting.

People seem to be more accepting of self-promotion when you do not beat them over the head with it. Keep it friendly, simple and short. Often, you will receive a response to thank you for the suggestion, at which point, you can open and keep a dialogue alive with them, but only do so if they have contacted you back, following on from your initial message to them. Ask for book recommendations, read more of their reviews and offer feedback on a book that you may have both read. If they like you as a person, they are even more likely to read your book; and reciprocal relationships of this kind are the key to securing positive book reviews.

Repeat this process for many books and many users. It might sound daunting to read dozens of reviews and write dozens of personalised messages, but as an author, you need to put the time to social network in this way, building up your author brand and a loyal fan base. You are looking for those readers who will appreciate your work, recommend it to others, and look out for more books that you publish in the future. If you are not willing to take the time to cultivate those relationships, then why should anyone be willing to take the time to read and review your book? For every review that you receive, as a general rule of thumb, you need to write three times as many reviews of other authors' books.

Other Book Review Sites

There are too many review websites to mention in full, but some of the leading book review websites are:

http://www.authonomy.com

http://reviewthebook.com

http://www.oncewritten.com/About/GettingYourBookReviewed.php

http://www.selfpublishingreview.com

You can also try Yahoo groups. There are several where you can list your books and request reviews, such as The Reviewers' Choice, the Writelist and My Book Is Out.

Set Yourself Up as a Reviewer

How to write a good review

Bibliophiles the world over share the same lament: too many books, not enough time to read them all. Not only that, books can be expensive. It would be nice, book lovers will say, if we could get books for free and have all day to read them. However, in the real world, setting yourself up as a reputable reviewer is a time-consuming exercise. Still, there are ways in which you can properly and professionally review books without going broke and while having a life outside of the written page. It is not as difficult as it might seem.

Read fast and review well

A professional book reviewer's role (by "professional" we mean "paid") is to read books for a publishing house, magazine or reviewing publication, literary agency or literary consultancy and express an opinion on them. Like most jobs, becoming a *good* book reviewer requires a certain set of skills and some experience. The primary skill required is to be a fast and thorough reader. You only get paid based on how well you've reviewed the book and how many books you can review, so it pays to read quickly and comprehensively. You do not want to read too quickly and miss out on key plotlines and nuances to the detriment of your review, but you do need to find a balance between speed-reading and speed-reviewing.

In this regard, it is useful to request a synopsis of the book from the author to facilitate your review. This will give you a general steer from the outset as to what to expect when reading the book, in other words what the writer had in mind and wants to convey in the book and, for comparison sake, to make sure that you properly understood the main plotlines of the book when writing up your review. Reading the author's summary at the beginning and again after reading the book will help you to assess whether the book achieves the aims and excitement as set out in the synopsis.

Critical assessment and brevity

Another skill you need to have or develop as a reviewer is some sort of critical thinking and writing ability. Merely summarising the narrative is not enough to be a good book reviewer – that's a book report, not a book review. You need to be able to form an objective opinion of what worked and what did not work (in general, not just for you), and why. If you can do this, and articulate your views in a succinct way (reviewers should not be long winded!), you are well on your way to becoming a book reviewer.

Provide constructive criticism

Longer reviews or critiques should demonstrate the reader's own ability to write! If you are writing a full critique of a book, this should include:

a. What is particularly good about the book, citing examples

b. What is less good, with examples and suggestions for amendments

It is helpful if the main body of the review is organised so each theme is dealt with as follows:

- Structure, plot, themes, voice or voices (point of view), tense(es), pace, climax, denouement
- Characterisation: description, inner thoughts, contradictions, voice; whether characters are believable, or two-dimensional, or mere caricatures; relationships
- Descriptions of the environment: places, weather etc.; use of the senses in describing these; sight, hearing, touch, smell
- Style: use of narrative, dialogue (including use of language), imagery and the use of metaphors, similes, analogies
- Readership appeal: genre

Examples of faulty grammar, syntax (sentence construction, repetition, tautology), punctuation, spelling, inappropriate words etc. should follow, but should not be included in the main body of the review.

Watch the tone of your reviews

It is also important to express your ideas and convey your suggested changes in the right way. You should "objectify" and "depersonalise" your reviews, not so they sound dry and shallow, but so the author does not take umbrage to your review. Write every review as if you are a teacher working closely with the student-author to improve their writing.

Try not to be pedantic. The review is about the author, not about you, and if the author reads your review and thinks, *He sounds like a real literary Rottweiler and was never going to like my book in the first place because of his personal interest*, or *She sounds retentive*, then you have not removed your voice from the review, which you should do. Otherwise, authors and readers will often dismiss your review as a personal attack on the author or think that the review says more about you than it does about the book.

Here are some tips in this regard:

1. Avoid making pejorative remarks like "The plot would work better if..." or "I didn't want to read past the opening chapter;" replace them with phrasing like "The author might want to consider..." and "The pace was slow at the start but picked up later."
2. Avoid personalised remarks like "The author should take a course in English Lit" or "The author has obviously never been to the location mentioned in the book." Rather, you might want to say, "The book would benefit from a professional edit" or "In the locale mentioned, this is the case..." so your comments will be taken in a more positive light.
3. Do not tell authors how to write or what to say. Rather, provide examples and say, "The author may/might want to consider..." It is much more subtle and effective.
4. Avoid sweeping generalisations, such as "The characters just don't appeal" or "This book would not stand out on the bookshelves." Again, provide specific examples and couch your feedback in more positive terms.
5. Try to mix up your review with both good remarks and constructive feedback for improvement. You can always find something good to say about a manuscript – sometimes you just need to look a bit harder – but it's always worthwhile being genuinely positive while subtly critical.

Exercise 8. Once you have written a review, read it aloud to yourself as if you were the author and reading it for the first time. Can you guess the gender or age of the reviewer? Is there anything in the review that you might object to if you wrote the book?

Ideally, the author should read your review and should not be able to tell anything about you (age, gender, reading preferences, etc.) except the fact that you read their book carefully and you are good at providing constructive feedback, which will likely improve their manuscript.

Moving Up the Review Ladder

As a new writer will know all too well, it seems that to get your own book traditionally published you need to have an existing readership or audience and respectable sales figures in support of your proposal, which creates a vicious circle as you need to be traditionally published in the first place to achieve this! Similarly, it seems difficult to break into the world of book reviewing without some measure of previous review experience. However, this is not the case. Just as you can raise your own literary profile and build up a readership for your writing through self-publishing and self-promotion to build up a fan base and healthy book sales, there are many professional review sites and online groups that you can participate in straight away to gain useful experience – and possibly more so in book reviewing than in other fields.

If you have no experience book reviewing but are interested in getting involved in doing so to raise your literary profile and build up a following, then you can begin by voluntarily reviewing books for websites. Many booksellers offer "reader review" sections for any book they sell. If you have read a book and want to practice writing reviews, these are a great sounding board. Many of these same sites offer links to professional reviews. Study these professional reviews for an idea of how different publications handle them, and then follow their example. Once you have written a few reviews, print off copies and keep them as writing samples. Often professional review publications are more interested in how you review rather than what you have reviewed, and having a sample review to send to them will improve your chances for doing reviews.

Stepping up to larger publications

Once you have honed your skills by writing a few early online reviews and reading any feedback you can get on them, the next step is to write reviews for local and professional publications that accept freelance work. Simply contact the editor and ask how to go about reviewing books for them, and offer to email them several sample reviews that you have done for their perusal. There are many opportunities in this regard when it comes to local and regional publication – there are local newspapers, church and school newsletters and neighbourhood reports.

Exercise 9. Once your reviews are published, print them off and keep a professional portfolio of them for when you approach larger publications.

After you have run the review circuit and established a few reviewing credits, you are ready to approach the larger print publications and set yourself up as a professional reviewer online. In terms of the former, you may want to consider one of the big reviewing houses – *Kirkus Reviews* and *Publishers Weekly* are two of the biggest, although there are others. These companies publish huge volumes of book reviews every week, and they depend on freelancers to get the job done. The pay is not great, but the books are free. And having one of these larger, well-respected publications on your literary CV will help convince other print publications – the city or national newspaper, for example – that you have experience working in an intensive, professional book review situation. Now, you are ready to apply for any reviewing jobs that might interest you.

Here are a few pointers about sending in your application and CV for a professional reviewing job. First, only send in your best reviews and be selective in this regard. Even better, tailor your application by sending in sample reviews that clearly fit the same style of writing and reviews that the publication currently publishes. This requires a bit of research, so read their reviews, find out who does their reviews for them and profile and position yourself alongside those reviews and reviewers.

Do not send reviews of inappropriate books to publications. For example, do not send a thoughtful review you wrote of crime novel to a Catholic magazine as a sample of your writing. Tailor your cover letter to include all apposite writing and reviewing credits, as well as relevant experience for the types of reviewing you are doing. As a rule of thumb, the more you can talk about the organisation you are applying to and explain why you think they would benefit from your reviews (rather than talking about yourself and how it would benefit you to work with them) the more likely they will be to engage you to write reviews for them.

Book Endorsements

There are long reviews/critiques as found in magazines and periodicals and shorter, pithy reviews as found on sites like Amazon, Goodreads and Shelfari. Even more succinct, there are short, one-line snippets or quotes that you commonly find on the back cover of book or in press releases, which can be equally influential, and seek to praise or endorse a book in much the same way that a quote from a theatre critic on the side of a double-decker bus for a West End show saying, "Best musical in town…" might grab your attention.

Testimonials and endorsements of this kind are an important part of your sales and marketing strategy. Whether you need an endorsement to highlight a particular section or aspect of your book, or you would like a testimonial to lend credibility and excitement about your book, they can affirm your expertise in writing about the subject matter for non-fiction books, and affirm you prowess for fiction writing. The main purpose of endorsements is to impress your readers, and impress upon them the message that you are intending to convey.

Anytime is a good time to seek endorsements

You can request endorsements before your book is published, so you can add a short quote on the back cover of your book. For non-fiction books, especially trade books, you should seek endorsements from professionals or well-respected individuals in your field that indicate that your book provides important information and value to potential readers. For example, if you are a life coach and you are writing a new self-help guide, you might ask the head of your organisation to write a short quote for you to add to the back cover of your book.

If you have written a novel, you might ask a well-known author in your genre to promote your book. Let us say that your book is a crime novel. You might attend a crime festival, introduce yourself to an established author in this genre and ask him or her if they would mind being sent a complimentary copy of your book and possibly providing a short quote for the back cover. Alternatively, you can look up established authors in your genre on the Internet and send them a copy of your manuscript, asking if they would kindly endorse it.

Aim for the stars when requesting endorsements: ask people who are recognisable in your field and who are as well-known and widely known as possible. Keep in mind that granting endorsements is also of great benefit to the persons providing them, as it helps to build their authors brand as well, so do not be afraid to ask. Free publicity is always a bonus for both author and endorser. When your book is published, providing endorsements establishes authors as publicly recognised experts or authorities within the field or genre in which you write. So, endorsements are mutually beneficial.

Most authors will not have time to read your book from cover to cover, so send them a synopsis of the book, along with a few versions of the sort of endorsements that you would like, allowing them to choose one or two and tailor one of them. You will be surprised at how many people are happy for you to write a draft endorsement for them, for them simply to put their name to. Drafting sample endorsements will increase your chances of others agreeing to them and it allows you to emphasise the points you want to make to impress and impress upon your readers.

Write endorsements that are relevant to the expertise of the endorser. Writing "The best book I have read in some time" will not do. Similarly, being too detailed, like "This book is about John as he grows up during the war," sounds boring. The endorsement should convey the fact that the reader will find the book interesting, informative, inspirational, etc. Your endorsements must make buyers feel good or solve a problem for them. If you are selling a health-related lifestyle book, do not write, "I really liked this book." Instead, you could say, "It made me feel young again..." or if your novel is about the tribulations of growing up in the war years, the endorsement might read "Charming, moving, uplifting... it took me back to the halcyon days of my youth."

Keep endorsements relevant and terse, with one to two lines at most being sufficient. Casual browsers in a bookshop do not want to read an essay about your book on the back cover – you have only a few seconds to grab their attention and make a lasting impression. Say you were returning a book to the library, there is queue of people behind you and the librarian asks you what you thought about the book. What would you say, summing up the book you just read in a few words?

Even if your book is in print, it can be worthwhile seeking celebrity or author-related endorsements to be added to your on-going marketing. If the publisher does a further print run or revised edition of your book, you can add a strap line to the front cover or quote to the back cover of your book, which will help sell the book. It is never too early or too late to seek testimonials and endorsements for your book.

Book club endorsements

Book clubs and genre-specific organisations are also a good source of endorsements for your book. Ask one of the national book-reading groups to recommend your novel such as Lovereading.com or perhaps the National Literary Trust. These organisational endorsements will be read by thousands of book lovers nationwide. There are literary and trade organisations for virtually every genre of book (except, perhaps, erotic literature), and you might want to contact them (book clubs and literary trusts, that is) for advice and contacts in this regard.

Exercise 10. Secure high-profile endorsements/quotes for your book straight away either from individuals or book clubs. A few lines will do.

Blog Reviews

BlogTalkRadio.com is a website that allows anyone with an Internet connection to host their own Internet radio show. In fact, BTR is the world's largest social radio network where you can create your own book-related broadcast, and listen to thousands of other live Internet radio shows and podcasts. Through this site, you can reach listeners from anywhere in the world simply through your phone or computer.

The main source of information about BlogTalkRadio is from the excellent http://musingsonminutiae.com/articles/promoting-marketing-blogtalkradio/

As of January 2013, BlogTalkRadio had

- 2 million+ shows aired
- 16,000+ active hosts
- 35,000 new shows/month
- 25 million visitors/month
- 196 million page views/month

BTR Hosts schedule the air times for their shows in advance. Listeners can go onto their show's personalised pages and click a reminder button that will automatically email them when the show is going to air. If the listener is on that show's BTR when the broadcast is scheduled to begin, it will simply start playing and they can enjoy it from the comfort of their computer chair.

Internet radio allows armchair and amateur authors to claim a small part of the blogosphere and talk about their writing interests all they want. There are BTR shows about politics, finances, sports, culture, family and books!

The best part about all of these people broadcasting their shows simultaneously is they not only need interesting things (like your book!) to talk about but people to talk to. That's where you, the author, can come in to talk about your literary inspirations and aspirations.

BlogTalkRadio provides promotional badges and flash player code for placement on blogs, MySpace, Facebook and other social-networking sites. Live Internet radio shows have soared in popularity over the last few years as authors search for global channels to market and review their books.

BlogTalkRadio is doubly useful because several hours after each show has aired, the taped broadcast is available from the show's page as an mp3 download so you can store the show on your computer's hard drive and add it to your iPod. Presto – you now have an instant, readymade podcast.

Podcasting

With the invention of the portable digital audio player (such as the iPod, and other brands), podcasts are growing exponentially in popularity and are currently a large source of entertainment during many people's daily commute. Next time you are in a train, plane, underground or bus, look around at how many of your fellow passengers have a cord running from their ears to their pockets. Chances are that a good half of them are listening to podcasts specifically, and more importantly, they could be listening to you talking about your love for literature and your genre of writing, or about the future of the e-publishing industry.

Searching for your TalkRadio niche

There's a useful search facility in the upper right of the BlogTalkRadio website that allows you to type in some keywords related to what you would like to listen to or talk about. A quick search of the word "books" currently brings up over 600 archived episodes and over 300 live and upcoming episodes. Let us assume for the moment that your book is a steampunk, dystopian science-fiction novel. Believe it or not, typing "steampunk and dystopian" into the search facility on the site brings up over one hundred relevant podcasts. People are talking about every genre of writing on the site, providing an ideal channel for you to talk about your own work.

Exercise 11. Go to BlogTalkRadio.com and put the genre of your book into the search facility at the top right of the home page and make note of any upcoming broadcasts potentially relevant to your writing.

Keep in mind that as an author, you are not restricted to appearing on book and author-related podcasts. There are also plenty of BTR news stations seeking book-related content available to you as well. If the subject of your book matches up with a forthcoming event, it is more than likely that you could appear on their show as an expert on the subject. Keep an open mind and do not miss an opportunity to find additional niches. If your book is non-fiction, run a quick search for whatever your book is about. You will be surprised at the amount of people who are talking about that subject. If you can get onto one of those shows, you will be speaking directly to your target audience.

Radio show format

Each show has its own format, and we would suggest signing up for an account with the TalkRadio website and listening to a dozen episodes first to get a feel for which style would work best for you and a better idea of what you are likely to say and accomplish by participating in the discussions.

The two main formats in the world of book-related podcasts are book reviews and author interviews.

Book review shows. These shows generally involve hosts talking to a co-host or whoever happens to be listening about what books they read over the last month or so, and giving oral reviews of them. Sometimes the host will only discuss certain book genres, or they might open it up to anything. With review shows of this kind you need to realise upfront that not everyone is going to love your book, so you have to be prepared for criticism. If the host sounds like someone who might enjoy your book, you might consider sending him/her a copy.

Author Interviews. Another popular type of TalkRadio book show is the author interview where the host will hold a conversation with the writer to discuss the book, what it is about, where people can buy it, what inspired them in writing the book, future planned writings, and so on. These tend to be very informative and allow the author to connect with anyone listening. These types of shows usually get you more sales since readers will feel they know you as a person from hearing you talk and you can play a larger part in deciding what points you will cover and the topics that will be discussed.

Participate in a TalkRadio broadcast

Once you have decided what type of show you would like to participate in, make a list of the shows on BTR that you feel that you would be a good fit for. Jot down the names of the shows, or bookmark the show's page in your browser for quick reference. Get in the habit of actually listening to some episodes so you do not look foolish by offering to talk about your futuristic crime thriller on a show about fantasy novels.

Once you have narrowed down your choices, look on the show's BTR page, as hosts will typically provide details or links to sites where they tell you how to be a guest on the show. Each show has its own set of guidelines or criteria that authors and books must meet in order to be considered. You will also be provided with a contact email address or (better yet) a form to submit. The letter will help you to script the show, so that you will be talking about issues that you want to talk about.

Booking a review

If you are enquiring about being a guest on a book review-type show, offer to send a copy of your book to the host in advance (if they are not mandatory). Then be sure to actually send it. In fact, send a whole press kit if you have one with your book and a one-page fact sheet that has all pertinent info (ISBN, page count, date of publication, etc.). Once the host has received the book, you should get an email letting you know when the show featuring your book will air.

Booking an interview

Once the host gets around to fielding your request, they will usually send you an email of acceptance or rejection to having you as a guest on the show. If you get the green light, then you will likely be provided with dates and times of upcoming scheduled shows, and you can pick one that suits your schedule.

Once you have confirmed a date, the host will send you a call-in phone number that you will dial on the day of the interview and if all goes to plan, they will be on the other end of the phone waiting to speak with you. They may also send you a script for the show (see below).

Since BlogTalkRadio broadcasts live all over the world, be sure to find out what time zone the host is in to ensure you ring in at the right time.

How to be a great guest

Not every host in Internet-radio land is a professional. There are some TalkRadio hosts who do it for a living and know how to conduct them and ask appropriate and relevant questions. There are also amateurs looking to cut their teeth in the world of broadcasting, and this is their first experience. Under no circumstances should you assume that an amateur host will not have a good show. More often than not, they run the tightest ships since they are trying to prove themselves. Be flexible and understanding if technical issues arise or something unexpected happens. As the radio broadcast is live, glitches are likely to arise and expect the discussion to get you off-script. Your role, and that of the host, is to bring it back on-script and answer questions succinctly. If you are long winded, it can put potential readers off your writing.

Scripting the interview

The more professional shows will provide you with a show script ahead of time so you can follow along and know where you are in the show.

You will also see a list of the questions they plan to ask you. A few days before the show, ensure that you give them a read and jot down any hot topics you want to discuss during your interview. Is your book on sale? Have an upcoming appearance or signing? Giving something away? You don't want to forget about these things once you are on-air and the time will fly by! If you see any questions on the script that you would prefer not be asked, definitely let the host know in advance.

They want the interview to go as well as you do. They are not aiming to catch you out. Rather, they want to have a good conversation with you that will interest others and stimulate further discussion. Likewise, if there are particular questions you would like to be asked, also let them know. They will almost always be accommodating to such requests to ensure that everyone benefits from the upcoming conversation. You should have a message that you want to deliver, and they want to have a great show.

Depending on what type of show you or your book will be appearing on, take note of any special requests the host may have. For instance, they may ask you to call in to the show a few minutes early so the two of you can talk a bit and get familiar with one another. If you are doing a reading from your book, some hosts may ask that you pre-record it in order to have a perfect reading on file. This way you do not crack under the pressure of a live audience, your phone does not drop the call mid-sentence. If you do not have the facility to pre-record your segment, let the host know well in advance so you can possibly work out an alternative method. If you have any special requests of the host, just ask! They are usually professional people who will understand and do whatever they can to make your segment as easy-going and natural as possible.

Dos and Don'ts

There is nothing worse than looking forward to listening to an author interview whose writing you really enjoy only to discover that they are boring and lack personality when speaking live. Here are a few things you may want to keep in mind during your live interview:

- Come prepared. Listen to other broadcasts by your host.
- Do not be shy on the air and expect your host to dig interesting facts and funny anecdotes out of you.
- Do not give simple "yes" or "no" answers to questions.
- Expand on your ideas, but do not over-elaborate.
- Do not talk when the host talking.
- Do talk when the host is not talking. Awkward silence is bad.
- Be funny, if you can.
- Do not try to be funny, if you are not naturally funny.
- Smile when you talk.
- Do not be inebriated. You will end up saying things you regret.
- Always have your book close by in case you need to reference or read from it.
- Use the opportunity to "sell' your book because you can do it better than anyone else.
- Do not do the interview in the same room as your children or pets.
- Turn off any background noise and put yourself in a quieter room (no TV, mobile, phone, doorbell, microwave, toilet flushing, etc.).

Since you are getting a platform to discuss your work, there are some things you should always mention, such as the title of your latest book (more than once, if possible) and your next book. If the host is good, they will bring these up during the course of the conversation, but it is easy to get side tracked once a conversation has started and next thing you know, your segment is over.

Getting the most from your interview

So you have found a TalkRadio show that feels like a good match for you and your book. You have emailed the host and they are looking forward to speaking about you or reviewing your book. Now what?

Now you go and promote it! Put it on your website. Twitter about it, create event invitations on Facebook and Goodreads and let the world know. The more people who listen to the show the more books you can sell. Even if people do not tune in to listen live because of their busy schedules, they can download it later. Forward the taped interview or a link to it to everyone on your contacts list. You might not see a spike in sales immediately following the show, yet later you might be pleasantly surprised as more and more people share the show with their friends.

Following up

It might sound like common sense, but you would be amazed how often this part is overlooked. After the show has been broadcast, it is important that you take time to email the host and thank them for having you on as a guest. Depending on how your show went, they may offer to book you again in the future or invite you to email them once you have launched your next book. You may even receive a reply from the host telling you they are passing your book details to another show where it might be a good fit. You may receive guest-blogging opportunities and requests for further interviews and reviews simply by word-of-mouth.

Exercise 12. Follow the show/host on Twitter and befriend them on Facebook. They are an integral part of your social network now.

Finally, keep in close contact with your key media sources and positive reviewers and communicate with them often. Write back to each of the fans who have written to you over the year – keep all of their messages – to let them know about the book and your plans for your next book. Listen to your avid readers, keep them happy and they will return to buy your books time and time again.

6

GUERRILLA MARKETING AND DIY DISTRIBUTION FOR YOUR BOOK

When it comes to marketing your book you have to appreciate just how many books are being published every day. There are thousands of new books released daily, which means that you have to think outside of the box sometimes to attract readers' attention. You have to make your book stand out from the crowd. In this chapter, we look at some different tactics for attracting new readers to your books. There is by no means a magic wand by which to become a bestseller, more a novel way to catch the eye of readers browsing through the plethora of good reading material available at bargain prices.

Make a Good Book Trailer Yourself

If you think it is too daunting for you to make your own book trailer, think again. Anyone can do it. Besides, it's fun and easy once you get the hang of it. First, what is a book trailer? Much like a film trailer, it is a short video advertisement of a book, also commonly referred to as a book video or a book teaser. It can be done in various formats and if you are particularly keen, you can do different ones in each format. It can be acted out by family and friends, or by professional actors if you have the budget for a full professional production trailer (although it is not really necessary). You can have flash videos, animations or simple still photos set to music with text conveying a story.

Book trailers, book videos, book teasers, you name it, are one of the fastest growing, powerful trends in promoting books by way of the internet. Of course, the cheapest and easiest way to reach your target audience and generate sales is via video-sharing sites, websites, blogs, social-networking sites and book-related sites. It can cost you nothing to do it. With the help of a few simple free software applications, all you need to do is drag and drop images related to your book into the software's story timeline. Then you add video effects and transitions, and finally music or sound effects.

Getting started

This is how you get started. First, go to YouTube (www.youtube.com), or any of the video-sharing sites listed below, type in "book trailers" and observe other trailers on these sites before creating your own. This will give you a good feel for what you may want to include in your video trailer. Here are two good examples from Williams Coles:

http://www.youtube.com/watch?v=F7oUrnWiZRk

http://www.youtube.com/watch?v=FnDq3a3OObw

Choosing your software platform and images

Next, decide on what computer software you will use. You may use the following software to create your book trailer:

- Windows Movie Maker
- PhotoStory
- Stupeflix
- PhotoShow

You might want to choose Windows Movie Maker. Go to your desktop and click on "Start" at the bottom left hand corner of your computer and click on "All Programs." Movie Maker should already be installed on your computer. If you have Windows, then click on where it says "Windows live movie maker." If you do not have Movie Maker on your computer already installed, then you may download it for free from:

http://windows.microsoft.com/en-GB/windows-live/movie-maker-get-started

You can download Photostory as well from:

http://microsoft-photo-story.en.softonic.com/

As both of these programs are Microsoft products, their logo will follow your trailer wherever it goes.

Now that you have the software downloaded and open, go ahead and familiarise yourself with it. Windows Movie Maker comes packaged with easy instructions for making your book trailer, under "Movie making tips." Read it thoroughly. Play with it, dropping in a few pictures from your computer hard drive. Once, you have done so, you need to have some idea in mind for a storyline for your book. Write it out, then find some graphics or images that fit your story. Create a storyline that will arouse your audience's interest to buy. In addition, make sure the graphics and images that you choose are not copyrighted. Below are a few places you can visit for royalty-free stock images; however, you may type "royalty-free images" into your search engine and a string of them will pop up.

- Dreamstime
- Fotolia
- Microsoft Office
- Photobucket
- Clker
- Morgue File
- Shutterstock
- iStock Photo
- Free Digital Photos

Once you have decided on which images you would like to use, save them to your hard drive in your pictures folder. Book trailers should last no longer than two and a half minutes, so pay close attention to the minutes as you create your trailer. Now, we can go into the Windows Live Movie Maker and click on "Import" to include your pictures. Once your picture is imported, then you can go to that picture and drag-and-drop it into the story timeline boxes at the bottom. From then on, you can decide on what video effects and transitions you want to use.

Adding music and sound

After you have done the above, you can now add sound or music to your trailer. The same rules that apply to graphics also apply to music – make sure the music you choose is not copyrighted, or make sure you have permission to use it. You can find free sound clips at:

- Soundsnap
- Find Sounds
- Partners in Rhyme
- Brainy Betty
- Open Music Archive
- Opsound
- ccMixter
- Neo Sounds

As you did when choosing photos and images for your video, you may find some sound clips by typing "royalty-free music," or "free audio clips," or "royalty free sound clips" into your web browser. You can save them to your "Music" folder. Royalty free is the key to keep you safe from copyright infringement.

Distribution channels for your book trailer

Now, the time has come for you to put your book trailer out there for the world to see and there are many channels available for you to promote your trailer, which is one of the benefits of producing a trailer in the first place. There are myriad places for you to distribute your book trailer. You should upload it on your own website, or blog, video sharing sites, social-networking sites, and even mention it in your email signature. Video size is limited to 100 MB on most video-sharing sites, which is plenty of space for you to produce a professional-looking book trailer. Remember, the book trailer is similar to your book cover – it is the shop window for your book. If it looks professionally done, then it will draw people in. If it looks amateurish, then readers may assume (rightly or wrongly) that your writing is similarly amateurish, without having read a word!

Below are just a few channels to market for your book trailer.

- YouTube
- Revver
- Veoh
- MySpaceTV
- Godtube
- MetaCafe
- Yahoo Video
- Google Video
- Book Trailers
- Ourmedia
- Digg
- DailyMotion
- iPikz
- AuthorsDen

Having a book trailer made for you

If you do not have the time or technical know-how to make a decent trailer yourself, then go to www.fiverr.com. There are dozens of great graphic design students on there who will make you a trailer for just $5! You may not get exactly what you want if you do not make it yourself, but you can still tailor it with your own pictures and images if you would like and you will have to upload it the distribution channels listed above yourself.

Exercise 1. Set a goal to submit your trailer to one new distribution outlet a day for a fortnight.

Kickstarter Sponsorship for Your Book

Kickstarter (www.kickstarter.com) is an innovative funding platform for creative projects. Everything from films, music, games, artwork, design and technology are listed on the website by people creatively seeking sponsorship. Kickstarter is full of ambitious, innovative and imaginative new projects that are brought to life through the direct support of others. Since the site launched in late April 2009, over $500 million has been pledged by 3 million people funding more than 35,000 creative projects and enabling many great ideas and lifelong ambitions to be realised.

How does Kickstarter work?

Thousands of novel endeavours are sponsored on Kickstarter at any one time. Each project is independently created and crafted by the person behind it. The filmmakers, musicians, artists and designers you find on Kickstarter have complete control and responsibility over their individual projects. They will build their respective project pages, shoot their videos and upload trailers, and brainstorm what rewards to offer backers on the site. When they are ready, creators launch their project and share it with their friends, family and fan base in order to secure funding.

Each creator sets his or her own funding goal and deadline for each project that they upload to the site. If people like the project, they can pledge money to support the endeavour and help make it happen, in return for which they will receive benefits as stated in each listing. For example, let's say you are seeking to raise money that will enable you to write your next book, have it professionally edited and typeset and then published in digital, paperback and limited-edition hardback formats, before being turned into a screenplay that will be pitched to UK and US-based filmmakers, and you will need £5,000 in funding to achieve this.

Breaking down your costs

You can break down the costs on your Kickstarter listing as follows (the more you can break down your costs so backers can see what they are paying for the better):

Production costs (writing the book and cover design)	= £2,500
Copyediting and professional typesetting	= £450
Film trailer and distribution	= £100
Postage for reviews	= £200
Promotional material for pledges	= £250
100 limited-edition numbered hardbacks for pledges	= £1,500
Sponsorship total required	= £5,000

Listing the benefits

On your Kickstarter book listing page, you should provide a full list of the potential benefits to your backers in detail, stating clearly the likely return that your sponsors will see on their investment in you and your book.

For example, you might say:

> Pledge £5 or more…
>
> A free copy of the book in digital and paperback.
>
> Estimated delivery: Mar 2014
>
> Pledge £20 or more…

A free copy of the digital and paperback book sent personally to you, and a signed postcard version of the book cover, personalised to you.

Pledge £50 or more…

A limited-edition hardback copy of the book, signed by the author, along with a free digital and paperback version of the book. Your name added to the roll call of friends at the back of the book and a signed postcard version of the book cover, personalised to you.

Pledge £250 or more…

Your name or the name of your company or someone you would like to be in the book, as a character or as subtle product placement within the book. Three limited-edition, numbered hardback copies of the book, all signed and dated by the author. A free digital version of the book. Your name added to the roll call of friends at the back of the book and a signed postcard version of the book cover, personalised to you.

Some friends and family will support and sponsor you and your writing out of sheer kindness, without expecting anything in return. Others will be more commercially minded and will expect to see a return on their investment. You need to cater for both types of sponsors in your "benefits" package. For example, one book on the site written about a mouse living on Bodmin Moor who went in search of the small church in which he grew up (as he was a church mouse), and found his way home by following a trail of cheese, was sponsored by Cathedral City, one of Britain's best-loved cheese brands. The sponsor received a mention in the back of the book, and suddenly it was Cathedral City cheddar that helped the mouse find his way home. It was a win-win for both sponsor and author, providing clever product placement for the sponsor and a good means to secure financial support for the author.

Funding is all-or-nothing

You will need to state the funding goal at the outset, when uploading the information about your book, as well as the funding period.

If the project succeeds in reaching its funding goal, all backers' credit cards are charged once the time expires. If the project falls short of its funding goal, no one is charged and the author does not receive any of the funds.

According to the Kickstarter website, the reasons for this "all-or-nothing" funding approach are:

> **It is less risk for everyone.** If you require £5,000 to write and publish your book, it creates problems having £1,000 pledged and people expecting you to complete a £5,000 project using this amount only. It is not fair to you and not fair to your sponsors to expect you to complete this project and fulfil your commitment to them on this basis.
>
> **It motivates and mobilises others.** If people really want to see a certain project come to life, they are going to spread the word and encourage others to support you and your book.
>
> **It works.** Of the projects that have reached 20% of their funding goal, 82% go on to receive sponsorship funding in full on the site. Of the projects that reached 60% of their funding goal, 98% were successfully funded in full. It seems that projects either tend to make their goal or they find little support. There is little in-between. More information can be found in the website's FAQs. http://www.kickstarter.com/help/faq/kickstarter%20basics.

Nearly half of the sponsorship projects listed on the Kickstarter website reach their funding goals successfully. Many book pledges come from friends and family rallying around a friend or relative's talent. Others are fans supporting authors they may have long admired or want to be associated with in some way. Others are just inspired by the author's writing and excited about the idea of a new book coming out by the same author. And still others are incentivised by the book's rewards, such as a signed copy, a limited edition or, as mentioned above, the prospect of having their name or their product in the book itself.

Viral marketing plays a key role in securing sponsorship, as it does with most online book promotion. Sponsors will often spread the word to their friends on social media websites such as Facebook and Twitter, and mention the project on Kindle Boards and Goodreads.

The author retains 100% of the ownership/rights to their book project. There is no shareholding/equity exchange on offer to sponsors. Also, when full sponsorship is secured, the money is paid to the author minus a 5% commission, which is deducted by Kickstarter on the total monies raised. For UK authors, payments are processed securely through a third-party payments provider, and these middlemen tend to charge anywhere from 3–5% as well. So, the amount that the author can expect to receive on successful receipt of the full sponsorship is 90–92% of the funds pledged.

Who takes responsibility for the funding?

Kickstarter does not take responsibility for the fulfilment of any projects nor do they monitor the author's ability to complete their book project as stated in their listing. Rather, they leave sponsors with the responsibility of validity and worthiness of a project by whether they decide to fund it. Launching a Kickstarter book project is a public act, and authors put their reputations at risk when they do. Supporters look for authors who clearly state why they are seeking funding, what it is for and what the genre and content of the book is going to be, and for some, what they can expect to get for their support. Authors are encouraged to share links and as much background information as possible so supporters can make informed decisions about the book projects they support. Also, potential backers can always reach out and ask the author questions before pledging any monies through the "Contact me" button on the project page.

Authors are expected to post a book project update (which is emailed to all backers) explaining how things are progressing, sharing the story, explaining any delays regarding production or publication, and so on. Most supporters back projects because they want to encourage new talent, see something creative and help someone achieve something important to them and they would like to be a part of it. Creators who are honest and transparent will usually find backers to be understanding if there are setbacks and occasional writing blocks along the way.

It is common for projects to take a bit longer than expected to come to fruition. Writing and publishing a book is like implementing a business plan and taking a product to market, in that they both take planning but rarely go to plan. If you are making a good faith effort to complete your book project and you are giving regular updates, supporters tend to be understanding, flexible and more encouraging than you might expect.

If you cannot complete writing and publishing your book for whatever reason, then you would be expected to offer refunds, detailing exactly how funds were used, and other actions to satisfy backers. In fact, according to the Kickstarter terms and conditions, you have a legal obligation to follow through on your book project, and to give backers a full refund if the project is not completed in a timely manner, in accordance with the "Estimated delivery date" in the project listing. Again, Kickstarter does not take responsibility for issuing refunds – it is the responsibility of the project creator.

To get started, click the "Start your project" link at the top of the home page of Kickstarter.com. This will take you through the full process of creating your book listing, and it is all fairly self-explanatory. All projects must meet Kickstarter's project guidelines and authors must meet the eligibility requirements.

Exercise 2. Before jumping in and seeking sponsorship on Kickstarter, do some research. Read through Kickstarter School for additional tips on how to structure your book pledge page.

Talk to your friends about your ideas to see what they think. Look at other projects on Kickstarter that are similar to yours. Connect your Kickstarter book project to your social media websites. Finally, once your book project is up and running, email Kickstarter to ask if they could include your project in their weekly newsletter and in their "Staff picks" section, which will increase your book's visibility and thus improve its prospects for receiving full sponsorship.

Set Up a Social Networking Competition to Raise Awareness

Running a social media contest or competition can generate some quick interest in your writing and potential readers and fans. It can also build up your email list and drive quality, qualified, interested traffic to your site. For example, the author Rick Warren penned a new book entitled *The Hope You Need*. To gain pre-release publicity for his book, he announced to his Twitter followers that they could help him design the cover for his new book. The design contest for the book cover was hosted on 99designs.com, and his publisher offered a nominal cash prize for the winning book design. Much to his surprise and that of the publisher, over 3,500 cover designs were submitted, and there are now dozens of blogs and articles devoted to his book, all of which help to sell more copies.

It not about setting up any old run-of-the-mill contest. Without a clear strategy in place, your creative hard-earned promotional effort might go to waste as explained in the link below.

> http://www.agentmedia.co.uk/social-media/how-to-run-a-successful-social-media-competition

Here are five ways to turn your contest into a valuable, long-term, marketing prospect.

1. Begin with a social media plan

Competitions should only represent one part of your full social media marketing platform. If you do not have a clear strategy in place, if you fail to plan, you plan to fail.

Your plan should include:

- A clear goal as to what you want to achieve
- A calendar for your content
- Targets for your outcomes
- A swipe file of your content ideas and mind maps.

2. Have a clear goal in mind and on paper

To make sure you are running an effective campaign, a clear goal is essential. A social media promotion will generally bring in one or more of the following:

- Sales
- Fans
- Email subscribers
- PR/brand awareness

Exercise 3. Write down a list of what you want to achieve by actively participating on social media websites – this will guide you in deciding which ones are best suited to meet your expectations and ends.

Decide what you most want to achieve before you begin to run your competition, design your competition message and follow-up campaign based around your desired outcomes. Setting a clear goal also helps you to keep track of your performance, so you can make sure your contest is performing to your expected targets.

3. Use a third-party application to run your contest

You do not need your own in-house programming team and a disposable income to develop an online contest based around your book. Rather, you can use a third-party software application to host and drive your contest. This will ensure that your contest has a tried-and-tested Internet platform from which to launch and some platforms will give you a range of tools to help you begin engaging with your fans, which is what social media and engagement marketing is all about – communal participation and reciprocity.

For example, a Japanese company launched two new snacks brands, "Tyrant Habanero Burning Hell Hot" and "Satan Jorquia Bazooka Deadly Hot" in 2007. Customers were encouraged to join nightly battles in a virtual game between Habanero and Jorquia, on behalf of either snack brand, to determine the winner of the "World's Worst War."

Another good example of social engagement or "event marketing" is the "your face here" contest run by Jones Soda. On the company website, ordinary customers are allowed to send in photos that will then be printed on bottles of the soda. These photos can be put on a small order of custom-made soda, or, if the photos are interesting enough, they might be put into production and used as labels for a whole production run. This strategy is effective at getting customers to co-create the product and engaging customers with the brand.

There are three key steps to setting up a successful event marketing (also known as "live marketing" and "participation marketing") campaign:

Step 1. You must provide a memorable experience, something that could go viral, that your customers will participate in and share with others. Most people know what to expect from larger, established authors, so this where new, creative authors can make their mark.

Step 2. Incentivise participants to stay in touch. Contests are not just about making a big splash and then quickly being forgotten. You need to provide content and offer prizes to persuade readers to join your growing fan base and stay in touch, whether through email marketing or social media sites such as Twitter, Facebook or Google+. When participants stay in touch, you are able to keep the momentum going and they may buy copies of your other books and recommend them to others.

Step 3. Engage people. Social engagement means sharing content on your blog or social media channels that inspires followers. It means holding discussions about your book to topics of shared literary interest online or hosting regular book events. It means actively seeking and offering to do book reviews – activities that will engender a communal spirit and involve reciprocity and sharing information for mutual benefit.

There are various third-party applications that are suited for different forms of event marketing. Some of the more popular contest ones are:

- Binkd Promotion – http://www.binkd.com

One of the best value and most customisable contest platforms on the market today to create sweepstakes, photo contests and challenge contests available via WordPress and Facebook.

- Bulbstorm – http://www.bulbstorm.com

Allows you to create social and mobile campaign apps for established and new brands, through Facebook sweepstakes, photo contests and vote-to-win competitions.

- Kickofflabs – http://www.kickofflabs.com/contest-landing-pages

Launch your book contest with a landing page in just 60 seconds. Choose a theme, add content and start collecting entries straight away.

- Wildfire App – http://www.wildfireapp.com

Wildfire software applications enables brands to grow, engage and monetise their social audience, through Facebook sweepstakes, photo contests and vote-to-win competitions.

Exercise 4. Launch a book contest using one of these applications with free book giveaways. Explain clearly what the contest is about and make sure the message will deliver your intended outcome, and that the prizes on offer are interesting to ensure that they will attract and engage your participants/readers.

4. Mobilise your social network

Unless you have an expansive and engaged fan base already, your contest is going to need a bit of a push to get it going. To get the most out of your event marketing campaign, you should raise awareness across a number of platforms, including:

- Your current readers and reviewers
- Your Facebook fans
- Your other social media platforms (Twitter, LinkedIn, etc.)

- Your social cataloguing sites (Goodreads, Shelfari, etc.)
- Your blog and website
- Newspaper or radio interviews

5. Have your website ready for traffic

A well-run and popular contest will send traffic to your author website. Be sure to update your website before you launch your competition. You should:

- Ensure that you have your competition clearly visible on your page
- Make sure all your links work properly
- Have your opt-in links clearly visible and accessible
- Make sure your book is easy to find and easy to buy from your site

Win over the losers

The return in any marketing campaign is in the follow-up. Your well-run contest should bring you a raft of new, qualified, engaged and loyal readers. The most valuable people in your contest are not actually the winners, they are the participants who did not win! Prepare your auto-responder campaign beforehand, encouraging your new fans to take further action in the competition.

During the social media competition, you can give participants:

- Tips on how they can increase their chances of winning
- Educate and encourage them to share your content
- Engage with them through social media and really get to know them
- Publish valuable, relevant, and shareable content

A competition with a coveted prize will encourage a lot of interaction on the social media platform you run your competition on. Make sure you get in well on the conversation, and actively chat and engage with your fan base.

Follow-up is key to long-term success

After the social media competition:

- Keep the conversation open and on going with post-competition book offers, early notification of launch events, book signing updates and valuable content for them to share.
- Ensure you give participants good reason to stay on your contacts list and ask them what they would like to see in your next book and to kindly review or provide feedback on your latest book.
- Offer follow-up extras simply for having been a part of the contest such as free digital downloads, signed copies at a discounted rate, and so on.

Go forth and build your community

Make full use of the hype and excitement surrounding your contest to build your community and expand your fan base further. A community is not a place where your readers just respond to your questions, articles and updates; rather, it is a place where they actively seek to engage with you and discuss your writing. Managing the interest in your competition will help you position your author brand as a talented writer, a useful resource of information and the main person to read in your particular genre.

Other Guerrilla Marketing Ideas for Your Book

Thus far, we have talked about three novel ways to market your novel, by doing your own book trailer (video marketing), securing sponsorship for your book on Kickstarter (pledge marketing) and running a literary competition to raise awareness of your book (event marketing). These are each different forms of "guerrilla marketing." Guerrilla marketing is an advertising strategy in which low-cost unconventional means are used, often locally or with pockets of similar, co-ordinated activities in different locations, albeit carefully chosen locales, to promote a product or idea, or in this context your book.

Guerrilla marketing techniques are intended as to be an unconventional means to creatively convey the notion that your book is worth reading, that it is interesting and worth buying, in a way that relies more on timing, energy and imagination rather than a big marketing campaign. Typically, guerrilla-marketing events are unexpected and unpredictable. The aim of this form of marketing is to create a unique, engaging and thought-provoking experience and create a buzz about your book, in the hope that it will then go viral, i.e. everyone would be talking about the event and thereby you and your book.

Guerrilla marketing involves unusual approaches, such as intercept encounters in public places, street giveaways, PR stunts or any out-of-the-ordinary sales and marketing ploy intended to generate maximum interest and follow-up from minimal resource, to engage potential readers and create a memorable author-brand experience. This is where your creative talents come into play yet again, and your personal drive to succeed as a well-known and well-read author can take you to new heights, as guerrilla marketing is ideally suited to new authors. Sometimes you need to think outside the bookstore box, especially if your book is self-published, and think up new ways to capture public attention and generate a ground swell of support for your book.

Consider how the technique was used at the Frankfurt Book Fair a few years back. To promote their exhibition stand and showcase their books, the publisher Eichborn Verlag released 200 flies with an ultra-light banner attached to their legs with their stand number on it. The banner was attached with natural wax. After a short time the banner dropped off by itself and the flies flew away unharmed. Although the company organising the book fair disapproved, claiming that the stunt "flied in the face of convention," it was effective because it got a lot of people talking and numerous videos of the flies with adverts dangling from their legs went viral.

Authors often use guerrilla-marketing techniques to break into the market and create a stir about their book. Many new authors do not have the financial resources required to sustain a lengthy marketing campaign, especially when they have spent a lot their time writing, publishing and promoting their book already. Therefore, they have to be entrepreneurial and imaginative in their approach to marketing to stand out from the madding crowd.

There are authors prepared to read their book atop Mount Everest to garner publicity, or ride through the streets of Coventry in true Lady Godiva-like style to raise awareness of their book and a few eyebrows. Former basketball star Dennis Rodman showed up in a wedding dress to promote his new book. An Indonesian businessman named Tung Desem Waringin circled a soccer field in Serang raining adverts down with his book title on them to promote his book. However, these are extreme cases, and one does not have go to such audacious heights, dress in bizarre clothing or throw confetti at people to creatively market a book in this way.

Don Miller hid copies of his book *A Million Miles in a Thousand Years* in various tour stops and cities across the country. Each day, messages were sent via Twitter and Facebook with information on the location of two "bootleg" copies of the book. Each person who found a copy of the book was given a "special" reward.

Kevin Joslin, author of *See John Run* (2009) and *Run John Run* (2011), a humorous collection of BBC Radio 2 stories as read by Terry Wogan, discussed running a national competition on Twitter in conjunction with his publisher to include the name of the selective readers in one of his naughtily hilarious Janet and John parodies.

The common link in each of these creative promotional activities is the use of social settings and social media to spread the word and hook readers into participating. YouTube offers an excellent opportunity to think of innovative ways to promote your book. The prolific writers' network that branded James Patterson produced a video for *I Alex Cross* in which Patterson says he will "kill off Alex Cross if you do not buy copies of his book." He puts the fate of the protagonist in his readers' hands. Similarly, Chris Anderson's innovative and stylish promotional video for his *Long Tail* has been nominated for numerous awards for its creativity. Common favourites are the YouTube videos for *Tales of Mere Existence* by Lev Yilmaz and *Simon's Cat* by Simon Tofield.

As part of your imaginative marketing campaign, factor in how you will tell the media about what you are doing. There is no point going to all that trouble, and simply hoping that the press will hear about your great event and pick up the story and run with it. You need to let them in on the "secret" in advance so that they come along to cover the event.

Exercise 5. Summarise in a short press release what you will be doing, where and when, and let the media know so editors and journalists can see that it will be worth covering.

You should be wary about organising a publicity campaign that may go wrong, get out of control, or get you into trouble, exposing you and your publisher to potential litigation. In order to sell your book, you need to establish a positive relationship with the reader, and your book must stimulate their interest or in the case of works of non-fiction, deliver an effective message and favourable outcome. Gimmicks do not achieve this, results do. It is not good enough just to be memorable. You need to be remembered in a good way for any marketing campaign to be successful and for you to profit from your writing.

Book Sharing

People who love books enjoy sharing their favourite book with others once they have finished with them, rather than having them taking up space and gathering dust on their bookshelves at home. One way to do this is by "book crossing," which is when you leave your book in a public place – on a park bench, a coffee shop, museum, doctor's office or in a hotel room on vacation – the idea being that it might find a new reader or new home where it will be read and enjoyed again. What happens next is up to fate. You never know where our book might travel, unless, as many avid book crossers do, you leave your first name, town and date you left the book on the inside cover which gives your book a wonderful, "I was there," well-travelled feel to it, much like a message in a bottle or a time capsule.

In fact, there are book-crossing groups and websites specifically set up to encourage book sharing in this way, and it is environmentally-friendly. Rather than cutting down millions of trees each year to print more books, why not share the ones that you have which are already in print with others? By recycling good reads in this way, bibliophiles can breathe life into their favourite books and send them on an adventure of their own, releasing (or "treeleasing") their favourite book back into the wild.

If you join BookCrossing.com, which over 1 million people have done, registering over 8.5 million books since it was launched in April 2001, you can track your book's journey around the world as it passes from one person to another. There are also interesting forums to discuss your favourite authors, characters and books in every genre throughout history right up through current releases.

> *Exercise 6. Join BookCrossing.com and add your book to the site, and leave a few copies on the train, plane or park bench. Make sure there is something in the books that state that they are for book crossing, and track the books' travels online.*

Similarly, Bookhopper.com enables people to share their passion for books by mailing them to other book hoppers who have expressed an interest in reading and receiving their book. If you received a number of complimentary copies of your book from your publisher, this may be a good opportunity for you to get your book reviewed if you send copies to book hoppers who might be linked to social media. Alternatively, ask them in your mailing if they would kindly review the book on a specific book review website for you, telling them that you are the author of the book.

Once registered on the site, users must offer three books and then can choose from any in the entire collection. The site is international but book searches only display titles offered by people in the same country, to reduce postage costs. The sender pays postage, and recipients can only receive the same number of books as they send themselves to others. No money changes hands, and you do not have to make any payments. You simply need to have the goodwill to send other people your books when they request them and in return you will be able to have others send you theirs. The Bookhopper motto is "Give books to others as you would like books given to you." The only downside is that the Bookhopper website does seem to be offline for extended periods of time before suddenly reappearing again like the proverbial phoenix.

Sharing-books.com does much the same for children's books, albeit on a somewhat smaller scale and in partnership with Room to Read (www.roomtoread.org), which is a global organisation providing books for underprivileged children and helping to build libraries throughout the world in developing countries.

The first book crossing convention (aptly named the Book Crossing UK Unconvention!) was held in Edinburgh in July 2009, sponsored by WordPress and a number of traditional publishers. If you have published your book and a dozen or more copies of your book were included in the publishing package, some of which sit in a box in the garage because you have already donated a few copies to your local libraries and to Oxfam and sent a half dozen or so copies out for review, you might consider book crossing or hopping with them. If your novel finds its way around the world to exotic places, which you can track on the Book Crossing website, this in itself could be the basis for a good news story – and the more your book has travelled the wider the appeal.

Any guerrilla marketing campaign will need to be tailored to your book, and the success of your promotional activities will depend on careful planning and the time and energy that you are prepared to devote to it. Nobody is going to be able to do everything mentioned in this book to sell and market *their* book. Rather, you should focus on those activities that you feel you can do, will do and will do well, and focus on them. In terms of creativity, you have already shown that you are creative by writing a book and if you are a good storyteller, a good raconteur so to speak, you will be able to think of even more interesting and fun ways to promote your book.

For example, you might get copies of your book cover or website/blog address printed onto t-shirts, calendars or coffee mugs and hand them out to people. You might donate copies of your book to a school raffle, or sell limited-edition signed copies of your book on eBay. You might participate in a writers' workshop or attend a book festival and leave eye-catching bookmarks with your book's cover and title on them on the seats of everyone in attendance. There's one author who sells hampers and includes a copy of his book in each hamper, while passing on the price of the book by including it in the cost of the hamper!

> *Exercise 7. List five ways in which you might "guerrilla market" your book. Then, list them in order and try the first one on the list and see how you get on. If it goes well, move on to the second one on the list, and so on.*

Always remember, whatever you do in terms of selling and marketing your book reflects on you as an author, and the more professional and respectful of others you can be, the more likely they will take an avid interest in what you have to say and write.

Be Your Own Distributor

Ask yourself an important question – do you need to pay a third-party to distribute your book for you or can you do this yourself?

Self-published authors often believe they need a major distributor to sell a lot of books for them. They want to use The Book Service, Gardners, Bookmart, Booksource, Central Books, etc., because they think they need to get their book into the "brick-and-mortar" bookstores like Waterstones and WH Smiths to achieve healthy sales figures. They jump through many hoops and snags to accomplish this – only to be told once they have been passed around the houses and eventually get in touch with the "right person" that "they do not take on self-published books" or from the retailer that "all their book ordering is done centrally" or "it has to go through Head Office."

The cost of conventional distributors

One author we know wrote and illustrated three lovely children's books. His books were well reviewed and well received by anyone who took the time to read them. Still, because they were published by Authorhouse, he found it impossible to get a large distribution company to take them on and help get his books into retailers. The more he tried more frustrated he became. A few distributors said if he was prepared to underwrite the full cost on a sale-or-return basis, they would consider taking on his book, but this would mean he might have to pay to print thousands of copies to supply them to retailers and if they did not sell, he would be stuck with buying them back as well.

You do not need to do this! The same author decided to take his books on the road to local fairs and talks where he could keep all the profits. Distributors take a generous commission from the authors' sales, and once you have paid a 40 per cent or more margin to retailers, it is difficult to see how any author can make a profit the conventional way, whereas the larger publishing houses have the promotional muscle to have their books front of shop, partake in two-for-one retail offers and pay retailers a lesser margin.

Distributors will also charge the author for storage, and when books are returned, the author loses those sales and has to pay the distributor again for the privilege of returning their books! Authors lose further from the bookstores when payment is late or unreliable, as many distributors will only pay 90 days after the book has sold. And writers are not always efficient at collecting overdue payments. These much-prized middlemen not only take most of the authors' profits, they cause a lot of stress along the way as well. Authors should avoid them like the plague, as you do not need them to distribute your book for you. You can do it yourself, and here is how.

How to distribute your own book offline

First and foremost, you have to buy an ISBN (International Standard Book Number) for your book for distribution purposes. When you do, you are listed on sites such as Books-in-Print, BookFinder and BookButler, where you can find a list of retailers currently listing and selling your book. Libraries, bookstores, Amazon and Barnes & Noble all require an ISBN to list your book for sale. You can purchase your ISBN easily from www.isbn.org.

> *Exercise 8. Buy an ISBN for your book, if one has not been assigned to it already by the publisher. This is essential for your book to be listed on Amazon, etc.*

For print books (perfect-bound, spiral-bound or stapled) or ebooks (sent through email as a Word doc or PDF), there are a number of ways that you can distribute your book to your target market.

For local distribution, with each venue, make sure to include ordering information such as your website domain name, your contact address and your local landline (rather than mobile) telephone number. Here is a range of local distribution channels for your book:

1. Disseminate information about your book through your local press.
    - Draft a press release and marketing kit.
    - Secure a local interest feature story from your local newspaper.
    - Submit a how-to article to your local newspaper.
2. Distribute flyers.
    - Carry two dozen flyers with you with your book cover on it and hand them to everyone you meet in your travels.
    - Include excerpts, endorsements and testimonials.
    - Make your book easy to buy by accepting online PayPal payments or cheques.

3. Distribute through a local talk radio show.
   - Listeners want practical information. Don't sell, inform.
   - Offer free digital (ebook) copies to capture email addresses and build a fan base.
4. Distribute at local gatherings.
   - Sell your print books at scouting events, your local gym or library, local fairs and book festivals.
   - Try to capture everyone's email addresses at any talks that you give. Word of mouth takes a while, so be patient for results.

You do not need an expensive distributor to get your books out to the public and into the hands of readers. You just need to be willing to burn the shoe leather in the early days to build up a local groundswell of support. If you track your book sales closely, you will see a spike after each talk that you participate in.

How to distribute your own book online

The Internet provides a great, economical means to distribute your own book. With online distribution, the industrious author is able to keep all the proceeds from his or her efforts. Whether you have a print-on-demand (POD) paperback book or a digital download (ebook) to sell, you can be your own e-distributor in the following ways:

First, set up your email address so people you contact know that you are an author. For example, one of the co-author of this book, Conrad Jones, has the email address:

"Conrad Jones (best-selling Kindle author)" jonesconrad5@aol.com

This email address serves a three-fold purpose. First, it has the author's actual name in it! Believe it or not, there are numerous authors who have cryptic email addresses or ones that are impossible to guess. For example, let's say your name is Mary Ellen Smith and your email address is

ME_dorman79@hotmail.com, as Mary_Smith79 was already taken and you had chosen an email address that had your maiden name in it. This is going to be difficult for you fans to find either online or in their address book, which is counterproductive in terms of social networking. As an author, make sure your first and last name is in your email address.

Conrad's display name is also enclosed in quotation marks, which means when you look up a contact in your inbox or sent email, his email will always come at or near the top. The easier your fans can find you and your book the more likely they are you corresponds with you and buy your book.

It is not an accident that it also states "best-selling Kindle author" in Conrad's display name. This uniquely sets him apart from other authors, and often leads to media requests, which in turn help to sell more copies of his books. If you state "Mary_Smith (author of psychological thrillers)" or "Mary_Smith (UK author of MIND GAMES)" in your display name, you will be advertising your book and the fact that you are a writer every time someone receives an email from you.

> *Exercise 9. Set up your email address so that it promotes you as an author and your book.*

Second, send a select group of fans a free copy of your book via email. This will often generate useful feedback and positive reviews. If you do this to new people on your email list from recent talks that you have done, this will start your relationship off on the right foot. Increased sales come from trust developed during relationship marketing more than anything else.

Finally, follow-up the free digital download with more information about your next book. Each message should include a headline that will capture the reader's attention, along with endorsements and positive quotes from the press about your book, if you have them. Make sure that you always provide a link to somewhere they can buy your book, such as Amazon.

Write articles for online magazines (e-zines)

You can also distribute your book through your own online magazine. If you want to attract more credibility, trust and sales, and build up a loyal following, write your own e-zine. Your potential readers expect a lot of free giveaways, so give it to them in terms of content-rich articles. In your e-zine include a feature article, editor's note, resources and tips. Always remember to add links to your book. Keep your e-zine monthly to start and keep it short and informative.

You can also submit how-to and content-rich free articles to other key e-zines. With some of the larger online magazines, hundreds and even thousands of potential readers will see your article with your signature file on it each time one of your e-zine articles is published. Many web publishers will take your print and ebook and offer to distribute it for you for a reasonable commission. Take full advantage of this and get your book listed for sale on as many online retail (e-tail) sites as you can.

As just mentioned, you can increase distribution and promote your book by adding your signature file to every email that you send. At the bottom of each email, make sure you include your name, your book title, a link to where your book is sold, your email and website address, and your landline phone number. This is accepted practice for author emails today. If you do not include it, you are missing out on one of the easiest ways to draw attention to your book.

Exercise 10. Make sure your book is mentioned in your email signature file, as outlined above.

Sell your book on your website

You should distribute your book through your author website. There are many ways to do this. You can focus your website on you as a writer or on your book itself. You can sell your book directly via your website, or you can provide links to relevant online retailers. You do not need bells and whistles on your site to attract attention. Rather, it is much more important to have a professional-looking site and check that all the words are spelled correct, that the site is up-to-date, and that all the links are working on your site, especially the one to purchase your book!

Distribute your book through reciprocal links

E-publishers want to list your book and receive a commission from sales – both print and ebooks. Most ask you to write a blurb of 100 words or less, which should include a short endorsement quote. They sell, distribute and keep track of your sales, sending you a cheque every few weeks or so. They take different commissions. Most give you royalties of 30–50 per cent depending on whether it is a print or ebook.

There are literally hundreds of ways to creatively sell and market your own book. You cannot possibly do them all, as then you would never have time to write. But there is a lot you can do in a relatively short amount of time – much more than you think. In fact, if you want to learn more about other novel ways to sell your novel, you might want to read our other book on this same subject, entitled: "100 Ways to Publish and Sell Your Own E-Book... and Make It a Bestseller" which is available both in digital and paperback formats on Amazon.

7

SET UP A WEBSITE AND BLOG FOR YOUR BOOK

The growth of the Internet, with its global reach and ready access to information, has dramatically changed the way books are published and will be published in future. Although some people still prefer reading printed books rather than having to read them off a screen, the fact that you can order a book online from stores such as Amazon or Barnes & Noble and (usually) have it delivered within a week or two, or publish your book for free on Amazon Createspace, or surf the Internet and easily find out more about a book and its author, or upload your book in digital format for people to download around the world in minutes, makes self-publishing a much more viable option today and selling and marketing your book much easier.

Moreover, the Internet is the fastest-growing marketplace for books, with online sales predicted to surpass bookshops and other traditional retail outlets within a decade. The fact is, if you are a published author (or plan to be one soon) you really should have a website. It is your own online real estate to do with as you would like, to promote you and your book, and designing one is much more affordable these days that you might think.

Setting Up Shop

The first step in tapping into online consumer habits and technology is to create your own "shop window" on the Internet. The design and content of your website will depend on your marketing goals. If your aim is to raise your literary profile, to build up your name as a recognisable and respected author, then the structure of your website will differ from a website that focuses on just one book, for example.

Some authors, especially IT specialists, set up multiple websites to provide various shop windows for their writing. Yet, this can be counterproductive – if you promote your site on your marketing stationery and give out multiple web addresses, it could be confusing. Still, the more you know about web design and search engine optimisation, the better positioned you will be to harness the power of the Internet to market your book.

Firstly, you can either try to build your own website, and there are plenty of free websites and low-cost tools that can provide you with a website of your own. However, nothing is ever entirely for free – there is always a trade-off, and that trade-off is often click-through promotions, banner advertisements, etc., which can make your site look amateurish. Prospective readers and fans will often judge you and your writing based on the quality of your website, and if your website has all sorts of distracting links and third-party promotions streaming across it, then it will put people off. If you are not a professional web designer, then it is probably best to engage someone who has experience in designing websites, preferably for other authors, to do it for you.

Your first port of call in this regard might be someone in the family with web design experience who will help you as a favour. Alternatively, if there are no web designers in the family, the next idea is to ask someone you know who has been published and has a professional-looking website whether they could recommend their designer. The third option would be to check your phone directory for local web designers, compare costs and check out samples of their work online, or if you know your way around it, the Internet abounds with companies.

If you can find a web designer that specialises in author websites, this generally helps as they will have templates, which they have used for other authors that will keep the cost down, and they will know what questions you are likely to ask and what issues are likely to arise.

One company you might be interested in viewing is Book Promology (www.book-promotion.com).

> *Exercise 1. Put "author website" into your search engine and peruse through various author websites to get a general sense of the differences between them, as well as the common features. Write down the website addresses of three to four websites that you like most and the reasons why.*

Many readers will know this already, but for those who are still new to the Internet, a professional web designer will generally have their own hardware called a "server," which hosts websites. "Hosting" means they are reserving space or bandwidth on their server, which will enable you to have your own website on the Internet. The cost of annually hosting your website will be included in the package they offer you. For example, let us say they quote £500 to create a website for you. This generally includes registering your chosen domain name, designing a basic website (which is all you need to start), and annual hosting of your website (there will be an ongoing annual charge for hosting, generally around £20). This might include ongoing maintenance to your site if you would like your designer to make occasional changes to the wording, for example.

Depending how well established the web designer is, they might try to sell additional services to you like adding links or keywords on your website, so that when people use various online search engines such as Google and Yahoo to look for subjects related to your book, they will be able to find and access your site (this is called "search engine optimisation"). Or they might offer you email campaigns or other forms of promotional support. If you follow the simple site design and marketing advice offered here, you will not need to pay your web design company to promote your book for you. You should be able to do it yourself and track your progress, which is important in learning more about your target readership and how to reach them. This is difficult to do when someone else promotes your website and your book for you, and they do not have a weekly interest in checking the number of visitors to your site, other sites those visitors viewed before coming to your site, and so on.

As we mentioned previously, it would be better if you know someone personally, a trusted friend or family member, who can create a website for you. They should be able to help you register your domain name (such as www.davidcarter-author.com), host your website and make any ongoing changes at a substantially reduced rate. Ideally, they can train you to make your own changes in an easy and efficient way using software such as Coffee Cup Web Design, so that you can update and maintain you own website as and when you like. The more control that you, the author, have over the content on your website, the better.

Exercise 2. Choose a web designer for your book. They will usually host your site for you as part of their design package. Ask if they can teach you how to update your own website.

Choosing your domain name

The first decision you need to make is to select a domain name for your website, which will appear as its "www" (world wide web) address, or URL, which stands for "uniform resource locator (like the quadratic formula you may have learned in maths class in secondary school, you can forget this straight away; unless you are a contestant on *Who Wants to Be a Millionaire*, it is unlikely anyone is ever going to quiz you on what URL means). Just call it your "domain name." This is central to your author brand identity online.

As a general rule of thumb, the best author domain names tend to be the author's name or pen name, along with .com as the suffix. If the .com is not available, you might want to check whether .net (or others such as .co.uk or .info) is available, but if you put "-author" after your name, you will generally find that the full web address is available. Also, the best domain names are always short, easy to spell and descriptive of the site's content.

If your name is Janis Tabitha Hick, for example, then you might select "janishick" as your domain name, so your website URL would be www.janishick.com. The problem is that the more common your name is, the more likely it is that someone will have already registered the domain name. You might add in your middle initial, so your URL would be www.janisthick.com. The problem with this domain name is it could be read as "Jan is thick."

Moreover, if you add "-author" after your name – so, for example, the address would be www.janishick-author.com – then you are telling the world straight away what your profession is and what to expect on your website. This is more a matter of personal preference, but we would recommend adding "-author" to your name when deciding on your domain name.

An easy way to check whether a domain name is available is to log on to the Internet and head to www.checkdomain.com. Type in your domain name of choice, click "enter" and see whether your domain name is available. If it says "The domain that you requested is still available," then click on the link provided to reserve that domain in your own name. Alternatively, you can tell your web designer that you would like to register that domain name for your website. If it says "The domain name that you requested has already been registered," then you will need to search for a different name. Some domain search sites also have a "Lookup" facility, which enables you to find out who actually owns the domain that you were searching for initially.

You should register your domain in your own name, because the person who registers it legally owns that domain. If you fall out with the person or company that set up your author website, and they registered the domain in *their* name, they have to agree to transfer it into you, which could create problems. So, make sure you tell whoever is registering your domain you would like it registered in your own name if possible.

Having said that, it is fairly simple to register a domain name yourself on the Internet. Major online service providers like 123-reg (www.123-reg.co.uk), or better still Cheap Domain Names (www.uk-cheapest.co.uk), enable you to register a .com or .net domain name for less than £8 per year, and a .co.uk or .me.uk domain name for less than £3. They will also host your website annually for under

£30. Thus, you can organise your own domain name and hosting for less than £40.

There are some companies that offer you "free hosting," but as it is often said: if it seems too good to be true, it probably is. There is always a downside. To receive "free hosting," the ISP (internet service provider) may require you to have banner ads or some other form of gaudy advertisement on your website that benefits the ISP but cheapens the look and feel of your literary website. Also, free website hosts will limit the amount of web space you get, usually to about 20 megabytes, and some limit the number of visitors you can receive in a month – if you exceed their "limit" your site will be "turned off" until the next month.

It might be worthwhile for you to register the .com or .net and the regional suffix for your website. If you live in the United Kingdom, then you might register the .co.uk address and ask your web designer to redirect that domain name so it points to your .com address, as that will help avoid confusion if you give out your website address to others, and it will also avoid the possibility of someone putting in your domain name with a different suffix and bringing up a website that has nothing to do with you or your book.

Exercise 3. Select a .com domain name for your author website and purchase it yourself; or if you engage a professional designer to do so, then make sure that the domain name is registered in your name.

What should you put on your website?

You should design your website in much the same way that you might organise book proposals to publishers. You want to convey information about yourself and your book that is most likely to generate interest from your visitors to your site and potential readers. This is your personal real estate, your shop window. Your website is your chance to show the world what you write about and what they are going to get from reading your book. It is your signature piece, your online brand, so it is essential to get it right.

General look and feel

Keep your website simple and straightforward. Your site should have pleasing colours and be easy to navigate. One way to decide on what you would like your website to look like is to search the Internet for other author websites, and pick out a few that you like. It is important to choose one that is suitable to your budget and one that can meet your expectations. It is no use picking a website that has a lot of bells and whistles on it, such as flash design. This makes it more difficult to be picked up by the major search engines, and the more fancy gimmicks you have on your site, the less credibility you will appear to have as a writer.

Let us say you have written a crime thriller. You might start by putting the words "author of crime thriller" into your search engine (e.g., Bing or Google) and scroll down a few pages, you will find plenty of websites to choose from and there will be a wide variety of styles and content on those sites. Choose a few that catch your eye as a starter, and jot down their domain names so you can pass them on to your web designer as samples of the sort of site that you would like to have for yourself.

For example, Michael Connelly's website (www.michaelconnelly.com) is typical of a bestselling detective book author. You might want to point your web designer to this site and begin by including *some* of the categories listed at the bottom of his header such as "Home," "About," "Events" and so on (more on this later).

Or you might prefer the general look and feel of the Devon-based author Simon Hall's website (www.thetvdetective.com). By calling himself "The TV Detective," Simon is building a brand around himself as a writer of crime novels with links to his real-life work as a crime correspondent for the BBC for the South West of England. This is another alternative to having your own name/pen name or the name of your book as your chosen domain name. Perhaps you want to build a brand name around your main protagonist instead, and serialise your characters in this way.

Have a content-rich website

The most effective author websites are those that have more than just one page with their name and literary publications on it. This will give a "shallow" feel to your website, and potential readers might assume that there does not seem to be as much depth to you and your writing as they had hoped. At the same time, you need to balance this with the fact that the more pages you have on your website, the more costly it is likely to be to design and host.

Have between five and ten pages for your website. You can always add more pages and functionality later as your book begins to sell and your marketing campaign grows. Most visitors to your site will have heard you speak, read about you in the newspaper or heard about you and your book from others through word-of-mouth. They may want to know where you come from and where you may be speaking next, or what other books you may have written or are thinking about writing and your inspiration for doing so.

In choosing the categories and links that you would like to include on your website, here is a short list of the basic essentials:

- Home Page
- About the Author
- Books Published
- Other Writings
- News and Events
- Contact the Author

The home page is the first page that your visitors will see. It should be welcoming and introductory in that you should not try to convey too much information or try to impress visitors straight away. On this page you should have detail about your writing in general. It should have current information about you. You might mention forthcoming talks or book signings that you have planned in the next few months. If you do, keep in mind that you might need to keep your site updated by making frequent changes to your home page, and depending on your web designer, there may be a small cost attached each time that you do this. Again, if you can find a professional to design your site and teach you how to update it, that would be preferable.

You should not have reviews of your books or endorsements of any kind on the home page as it will look like you are boasting or trying too hard to convince visitors to your website that you are a good writer. If they have done an online search for your site, then you have already piqued their interest in your writing, so you do not need to impress them with anything other than interesting and current content.

On your "About the author" page, you should avoid using the word "I" too often. Talk about yourself and your writing in a way that may interest potential readers, such as why you set your book in Liverpool, or what books inspired you to want to write. Talk more about your inspirations rather than your aspirations (e.g., you want to be a bestselling author). You do not want your website to sound "DRY" (Don't Repeat Yourself). You might mention where you were born and grew up, what you do for a living besides writing, what your favourite books are and why, and what your interests and hobbies are.

Your "Books published" page is where you list the works that you have written (finished and unfinished, published and unpublished), along with including the cover designs for your books and a few lines about each of them. The published books that you list should include links to your publisher's website or to the book's Amazon listing, from which readers can buy a copy. You might also provide a few book reviews and links to their respective reviews on this page, but do not overdo it. I know some authors love to splash endorsements and quotes across their website, but these are generally taken with a pinch of salt and do not add much value or authenticity, unless they are senior or celebrity endorsements.

Having a quote like:

> "A riveting read, it really took my breath away and the twist at the end is phenomenal" —Claire in the United Kingdom

sounds too manufactured to have any weight.

The main purpose of the "Other writings" pages is to showcase any more writing that you may have done, such as short stories, poetry, published articles and so on. These should be limited to half a dozen at most, like a portfolio of your work rather than a library. You want your website to highlight your best work rather than seeking to impress visitors by the fact that you're so prolific, especially if the majority of your work remains unpublished. Otherwise, the impression is one of quantity rather than quality.

The "News and events" page lists press releases, newspaper clippings or magazine articles about your writing, along with a full list of upcoming speaking engagements. If you do list upcoming talks and forthcoming book signings, it is important to keep your website content current. Again, this is why it is useful to be able to make changes to your site yourself. Be sure to change them once the event has passed. Similarly, if your contact details or publishing dates have changed, make sure that they have been updated on your website.

It is also useful to have an online diary in the form of a weblog, more commonly known as a "blog," on your author website. This enables you to keep a running commentary on your progress as a writer in publishing and promoting your book. Alternatively, some authors prefer to have a separate blog or video blog for their book, and link to it from their website, as discussed later in this chapter.

It is essential to get your "Contact the author" page right. You should not mention any personal details on your website, like your postal address or telephone number or information about your family and friends. There are free "contact us" scripts that are simple and customisable so that visitors to your site can contact you via email without revealing your email address, and "spam spiders" (which scan pages for email addresses) will not locate your address and bombard you with unsolicited emails.

Exercise 4. Map out your website. Decide how many pages you would like on your site, take the same number of A4 pieces of paper and draft out the design and text that you would like on each page.

This will be the blueprint for your designer to build your website, combined with the general look-and-feel aspects that you have given to him or her from other author websites that have captured your eye.

You need to find the right balance between promoting your work and overhyping the book or boasting about your literary or commercial success. As mentioned previously, it does not really add anything to post other authors' quotes or glowing endorsements that say "this is one of the best books I've ever read" or "I cannot wait for the sequel." Too often, author sites are full of superlatives about how talented the author is or how exceptional the book is, the "next bestseller" where "Harry Potter meets Dan Brown," from people with official-sounding names and exotic addresses, intended to give visitors the impression that your writing has global appeal and has attained a global readership. As a general rule of thumb, the less the hype, the better the read.

Whatever you say on your website, it is essential that you get the details right. Otherwise, it would be like going to a job interview and providing outdated references on your CV. Even if the employer was seriously thinking about offering you a job, they would not be able to contact your references for a recommendation, which is all-important. Similarly, if you provide an email or links on your website that are broken (not working properly) or incorrect, or perhaps the details have changed since they were initially uploaded, you may miss opportunities. Your contact details need to be checked regularly and corrected straight away.

Exercise 5. Check your website (if you have one already) for outdated information and broken links and have them corrected.

Moreover, there is nothing that will lose you credibility as an author faster than finding misspelt words on your website. After all, you are professing to be a wordsmith! Many web designers will upload the website text you give to them without proofreading it for mistakes – after all, that's not their job, it's yours. You have engaged them for their IT skills, not for editorial services. And whereas it is difficult to pick up your own grammatical or wording mistakes, it might be useful to ask someone else to carefully read through the text prior to uploading it, as well as after it has been uploaded, to correct any mistakes. It is an easy assumption for readers and potential publishers to make that if you cannot spell well, you probably cannot write well. As unfair and untrue as this assumption may sound – after all, Hans Christian Andersen, Jules Verne, Agatha Christie, W.B. Yeats, John Irving and F. Scott Fitzgerald were bad spellers with learning disabilities and dyslexia, yet they were all exceptional raconteurs – still, the more professionally presented and grammatically correct your website is, the more inviting it will be for visitors and the more likely it will give them the right impression about you and your writing.

Remember, your website is your shop window. It is your online real estate. It is no good having naked mannequins in your shop window (unless you want to draw in the wrong sort of clientele), or an unmowed lawn to put off potential buyers.

Exercise 6. Take twenty minutes to check your website for spelling mistakes, or better still, ask someone you know who has a keen eye for grammatical mistakes to do so for you.

Website Promotion and Tracking

There are a number of ways in which you can track visitors to your site, and sell your book to them. Firstly, you need to make it as easy for people to find your site. The can be done by optimising your website for the major search engines through carefully chosen content and including key words and phrases in your website listing.

Key words and phrases and search engine optimisation

Search engines such as Google, Yahoo, Bing and Ask Jeeves have "spiders" that scan the internet looking for certain words and phrases, from which they will rank or position your book when someone does a search on particular words that are found on your website. That is why it is important for your name to be prominent on your website, and preferably at the beginning of your text on the site.

In web design terms:

- Every page on your site must have a unique HTML title tag, meta keywords tag, and meta description tag.
- Begin the body of your page with your keyword phrase, and repeat it a few times throughout your site. For example, it might be "Kenneth King author" or "UK crime novelist."
- Feature your keyword phrase prominently by including it in headers and making it bold or in italics.
- Use the text navigation on your site and the keyword phrases that you have selected as links. Perhaps include a footer on every page using text links.
- If you break your site into various pages, link to the most important pages from every page of your site.
- Submit your site to The Open Directory and Yahoo! Directory and build your link popularity by submitting your site to search engines, and requesting reciprocal links from related websites.

Search engine optimisation to achieve top ranking on browser searches is a specialist job in itself, and can be costly. For example, I received an email just today from an India-based SEO company offering:

150 directory submissions

60 social bookmarking submissions

20 article submissions (1 article x 20 article websites)

10 press release submissions (1 press release x 10 press release sites)

10 blog comments

1 unique, 400 word article written

1 unique, 400 word press releases

10 search engine submissions

20+ one-way directory link

On-page work activities

Meta tags/title tag changes

Keyword research/analysis

Competitor analysis

Heading tag changes

Alt tag changes

Interlinking wherever required

Keyword density in site content

HTML site map

XML site map and submission in webmaster tool

Ror.XML file creation

Robots.Txt file creation extra work activities

Google webmaster tool

Google analytics

Sounds impressive, but you do not really need most of this stuff on your website. What you do need is largely available for free and your web designer can add it for you. If you are a major multinational brand like Virgin or Sony, it might be worthwhile to invest £3,000+ to fully optimise your site. As an aspiring author with a selective marketing budget, all you have to do is make sure that the text or "copy" on your website is content-rich (providing content that is practical, informative, educational, inspiring or simply entertaining can attract and retain readers better than anything else), that the content is kept current, and that the key words and phrases (or "metadata") associated with your site are included and uploaded by your web designer. There is plenty more that can be done, but the issue is whether it is going to bring an equal or better return on your investment (i.e., whether optimising your website will sell an extra £3,000+ worth of books for you) – the answer is almost definitely not. The simpler and less expensive alternative is the one you should pursue.

Exercise 7. Draw up a list of key words and phrases associated with your site – like your name, your book title, the genre in which you write, your publisher's name and so on – and make sure they are prominently and selectively placed at the top and within the text of your website. Make sure they are included in the metadata uploaded with your site by your web designer, making it easy for someone searching for you and your books, and for similar good reads in their chosen genre, to find you.

Reciprocal links

The more your book is mentioned on other websites, the better. If there are other authors writing about a similar subject, you can email them and ask if they would be interested in putting a link to your website address on their site, and offer to do the same for them. Or, let us say your book is a charming children's story about gnomes – a simple Google search on the word "gnome" brings up www.gnomeland.co.uk, www.gnomereserve.co.uk and www.gorrinthegnome.com, each of which might be interested if approached to provide reciprocal website links. In fact, you can link directly to the Amazon Recommends service, which will list similar gnome-related books on your site.

Reciprocal links are useful in promoting your book because most search engines give higher ranking and positioning to your book (preferably on the first search page that comes up because the average click through traffic for the first ten results is over 50 per cent on Google, which currently receives 90 per cent of all search engine traffic) if your site is mentioned on other websites. The better your site is "optimised" in this way for key word searches, the more people will find your site quickly and visit your site. The more others link to your site and book, the more likely that your book will come up in the first page of listings when someone does a general search for, say, "stories about gnomes" or in your own case, stories by you or the main subject of your book.

Exercise 8. Do a general search for books on related topics to yours and contact those authors to see if they would be interested in sharing a reciprocal link with your site for mutual benefit.

Tracking visitors to your site

There are ways in which you can add tracking software to your website that enables you to monitor visitor numbers, and perhaps more importantly, which site the person visited immediately before coming to your site. This will tell you the sort of websites that it is most useful for you to link with. More sophisticated tracking software can tell you which country visitors to your site come from, which can indicate whether or not your book has international appeal.

Some websites offer free hit counters and visitor traffic logs, but this information can be misleading as it can register "spiders" that simply trawl the internet for key words and phrases, and it can reflect visits from spamming specialists looking for email addresses to add to their spurious databases. If you know how to read the data from these tracking devices, it might be interesting to see how many visitors there are to your website and whether that number is increasing with the marketing that you are doing for your book.

Pay-per-click advertising: pros and cons (mostly cons, few pros)

It is possible for banner or link advertisements for your book or site to be added to related websites, where you pay the host a small fee each time someone clicks through to your site via the sponsored banner or link. This is called pay-per-click (PPC) advertising and the largest network providers in this regard are Google AdWords, Yahoo! Search Marketing, and Microsoft adCenter. All three operate on a bid-based model – in other words, the more in demand your key word or key phrase is (e.g., "crime thriller") the more it can cost you each time someone clicks on your banner or advert link.

If your book is a work of non-fiction about a unique person or a specific period in time, then pay-per-click advertising may be worthwhile. For example, if your book is about the Cuban revolution in December 1956, then it might be worth investing a small amount and bidding on "Fidel Castro" or "Che Guevara" with Google AdWords. If you choose to promote your book in this way, make sure that you put a monthly limit on the amount paid for click-throughs.

However, a word of caution: there are various problems with this form of advertising for author websites. Firstly, it is open to "click fraud," which occurs when a site developer, automated script or computer program repeatedly imitates a legitimate click-through visitor, costing you money every time he clicks the banner/link. Also, people are often put off by unsolicited, flashing advertisements of this kind, and this can reflect badly on your book and on your literary profile and the author brand you are trying to build. Furthermore, it can be difficult to actually measure the effectiveness of pay-per-click advertising with author sites, and you should be careful not invest time nor money in something the results of which cannot be validated or quantified.

Create Your Own Blog and Vlog

Another means of promoting yourself online is by uploading information about yourself and your book in a web journal or diary commonly referred to as a weblog or "blog" for short. You can include a blog on your website, or a blog can substitute for a website and drive traffic to your site. Blogger.com, Typepad.com, Tumblr.com and Wordpress.com each provide blogging tools that enable you to create a professional blog simply and quickly as an aspiring author. There are plenty of online video tutorials found on the web for setting up your blog – for example,

Wordpress has a guide to help authors become successful bloggers at http://codex.wordpress.org/Getting_Started_with_WordPress.

The purpose of a blog is to provide you with an ongoing format to let others, especially your growing fan base, know what you, the author, are up to at the moment and planning to do next. It also provides you with a channel to share with others the latest news about the industry, forecast further developments, like the effect of digital (ebook) marketing on traditional publishers, and so on. It is your public diary of thoughts, meanderings, insights, reflections and other information that you may find useful which you may want to share with others to bring them into your literary world.

Exercise 9. Set up a blog to subtly promote your book via Blogger.com, Typepad.com, Tumblr.com or Wordpress.com.

Once you have set up your blog, you can provide a running commentary about your book and visitors to your blog can add their own insights and comments to your posting. Be sure to update your blog regularly with fresh news, relevant information, links to any book reviews and articles, and so on.

A personal blog, which is simply a running commentary by an individual generally arranged in chronological order, is the most common. Blogs often become more than just a means to communicate; they become a way to reflect on life as an author or share other works of literature that you found moving, inspiring or useful in some way. Blogging can have a sentimental quality. Few personal blogs (and there are literally millions of them on the Internet – Wordpress alone has 42 million blogs and the number is rising rapidly) rise to fame and make the mainstream, but some blogs do garner a following, such as Dr. Brooke Magnanti's diary, published initially as the anonymous blog *Belle de Jour: Diary of a London Call Girl*. Social media sites like Twitter allow bloggers to share thoughts and feelings instantaneously with friends and family, and is much faster than emailing or writing.

A good example of well-presented personal blog is Canadian author Kate Sutherland's blog "Books that Make Me Think" (http://katesbookblog.blogspot.com), which subtly highlights her collection of short stories entitled *All in Together Girls*. She adds new, interesting articles to her blog every week, lists books that she is currently reading, includes Twitter updates, provides links to reading groups and litblogs, and has received nearly 200,000 hits to her blog in the last five years. Her blog is not overtly self-promoting, and she creatively includes audio links to her radio interviews and links to her website, publisher, MySpace blog and retailers for her book.

Another blog that we like is Jennifer Barclay's diary about living on a Greek island (http://octopus-in-my-ouzo.blogspot.co.uk), which is really interesting to follow and serves the dual purpose of keeping her friends and family updated on her adventures on the island of Tilos in Greece whilst promoting her new book, entitled *Falling in Honey*. Her blog is full of interesting information about island life, about the beauty of nature, about her search for love and happiness, and is compelling and moving. Jennifer has the distinct advantage of being the former editorial director for Summersdale, so she knows how to tell a good human-interest story and spread the word in this way. That is what it takes to be a commercially successful author – not only writing a good story, but raising your literary profile and knowing which channels are most likely to get the stories read and positively reviewed. Once people start talking about it and recommending it to others – that is how bestsellers are made.

Once you have a book blog set up and you are ready to begin posting, then follow the dos and don'ts that we have listed below.

When writing a blog, do...

1. Find a theme related to your book

You should firstly ask: Who are your main blog readers going to be? Once that is decided, you can concentrate on a subject or theme directly or indirectly related to your book and begin building a brand or become the expert on it. Let us say your book is based around the

Northern Ireland conflict – you might blog about the current political climate or the ongoing efforts to resolve the hostilities.

2. Find your voice

What sets bloggers apart from the press and general news feeds is their voice. It is the fact that it is *you* speaking that makes it worthwhile, as people will start reading your blog because they find you interesting. Hopefully, they will continue to follow your posts if they find the content interesting, but it is *you* that brings them in initially. Your personalised message and how you deliver it is what draws them in, while content, if it is interesting enough, will keep them there. Let your readers get to know the real you, not the façade or pen-name (unless, of course, you are another Belle de Jour).

3. Add links in your posts

Whether you are linking to others' blogs or websites that contain useful information or linking to your own past posts via your website, link things when you can. This will increase your click-through rate whilst improving your blog's search engine rankings.

4. Add images and videos

Whilst readers visit your blog for information and personality, they also need to be engaged visually. Not all posts lend themselves to an image, but when they do, take full advantage of it. Some writers use pictures of the locations in their books to build a following. The reason the social networking website Pinterest is increasing in popularity so quickly is because it is image-based. Similarly, complement your content-rich blog posts with images and videos.

5. Respond selectively to blog posts from others

Blogging provides yet another opportunity to connect directly with the people who will be reading your book. Not all posts require a response, but make sure you respond to the ones that do, and sometimes it is worthwhile simply acknowledging posts and posting, "Thanks for reading my blog" or "Thanks for your comments."

6. Make sure your blog is linked up with your social media sites

Post to Facebook, Twitter, Google+ and anywhere else that you can, and link those postings to your blog. Do not hesitate to use your other sites to promote your posts. Any marketing channel that makes it easier for readers to find your blog and for your social network (including your friends, family and fan base) to spread the word about the publication of your book, the better.

When writing a blog, don't...

1. Overpost

Do not post every single day or flood your readers with posts – this will lead to overkill and your readers will start to drift away. Less is more in this regard. It would be like emailing someone you are in a relationship with and expecting them to reply every day. It may be exciting at first, but once the honeymoon period wears off and you start to settle in, post weekly and post regularly so your readers know which day of the week to expect new posts from you.

2. Be mundane, rather be germane

If you have something interesting to say or convey, then post it. If not, then leave it rather than saying something trivial, dull or obvious like "The sun came up from the East today." You will lose readers that way. Rather, say nothing for now and let your fellow bloggers wonder about what you have been doing and what you are going to say next.

3. Restrict your word count

Readers (and search engines) prefer substantial blog posts (500 words or more) to make clicking through worthwhile. This does not prohibit you from uploading shorter posts, nor does it suggest that you should prattle on simply to increase your word count. Rather, the point is when you have something substantial to say, feel free to mix it up and go long.

4. Rush your posts and make spelling and grammatical mistakes

Take your time, re-read your posts for accuracy, and correct them straight away if you notice any editorial mistakes. Every word that you put into the public domain will be scrutinised by others and reflects on you as a writer. If you want readers to take you seriously, then you have to take yourself (and your blog) seriously.

5. Be negative or make disparaging remarks

It is always unwise to air your dirty laundry and any personal animosity on the Internet. You'll go a lot further by being positive, inspirational and supportive to the community that you're writing to.

6. Write long paragraphs

Long blocks of text are difficult for readers to digest, especially when reading on computers and tablets. Break up your content into shorter paragraphs, bullet points and lists whenever possible. A blog is like an online diary. You might well have longer entries some days than others, especially if you have had a particularly exciting day, and your voice needs to come through as excited rather than monotonous, as if you are speaking the words rather than writing down your thoughts.

7. Avoid trying new things

Be creative. After all, that is what you are! It is important to let your blog evolve over time, and the best way for this to happen is for you to try something new every once in a while. Whether it is introducing stats or videos, or inviting guest bloggers, never be afraid to try something new. If you feel it can add something special to your blog, you should do it.

The *Guardian* recently published an article by Katy Cowan (originally published on her own blog *Creative Boom: A Blog About All Things Creative*) in which she shares her top tips for starting and running your own successful arts, culture or creative blog. This is well worth a read as it expands on many of the points mentioned above. You can find the article at http://www.guardian.co.uk/culture-professionals-network/culture-professionals-blog/2011/nov/17/top-tips-successful-blog

In summary, and by way of summarising what we have outlined above, her twenty top tips for a successful blog are:

1. Choose the right blogging platforms on which to post.
2. Integrate your blog with your existing website.
3. Choose a creative topic to blog about and stay on that topic.
4. Write about what you love and what you are passionate about.
5. Think about your posts careful and give people what they want.
6. Draw people to your site with engaging content.
7. Get people talking on your blog and encourage interaction.
8. Make posts that get people talking and commenting positively.
9. Ignore any disparaging remarks and negativity when blogging.
10. Believe in yourself and keep writing and adding useful content.
11. People love images and videos. Upload and link to them often.
12. Keep your posts as quick reads. Provide lists wherever possible.
13. Make sure your posts have catchy headlines and pithy content.
14. Keep your blog updated and regular. Use scheduling tools.
15. Keep your blog layout clean, fresh and uncluttered.
16. Link Facebook, Twitter and other social media to your blog.
17. Track how people find your site and tailor your posts accordingly.
18. Encourage people to "follow" your blog with "follow" badges.
19. Let people get to know the "real you" on your blog.
20. Check your spelling and proofread your posts again and again.

Setting Up Your Own Book Blogging Tour

Even if you plan to make the rounds of launch parties, book signings, school and library visits, there are good reasons to set up your own blog tour as well. It is a great opportunity to social network. While there are professional online services that will set up a blog tour for you and charge you for doing so, you can do it yourself instead for much less. You would not ask someone to go to a social function and meet people for you. Similarly, you need to press the online buttons yourself by organising your own book blogging tour. Here is how you do it.

Firstly, you need to initiate contact with other bloggers. Search online and locate blogs that stand out to you with related content. There are numerous databases online that organise personal and professional blogs by subject and genre. Read the blogs and pay close attention to who they link to.

> *Exercise 10. Once you have a list of blogs you would like to follow, email each blogger to let him or her know about your upcoming blog tour.*

When you contact them, show that you are familiar with their blog by including a brief reference to their actual content and why a post about you would be of particular interest to their readers. In your email, invite the blogger to join in and indicate basic timeframes ("I will post to your site two weeks in advance of the tour date"), and suggest post ideas.

When choosing which bloggers to reach out to, you want to pay close attention to the frequency of posts, reader activity (commenting) and, most importantly, the professionalism, content and quality of your posts. For example, if you find that they tend to talk about themselves all the time or criticise others on their blog, do not engage with a blogger who may give you a bad name by association. How they set up your post reflects on you, so read their past posts carefully before blogging with them in this way.

Now that you have emailed invitations to post to a few dozen selective bloggers and you are beginning to receive responses, you need to organise them and plan your posts wisely and effectively. You need to keep track of which posts go where, of who you have emailed and of what you have already said. If you have Microsoft Word on your computer, you may want to use the Scrivener for Windows software tool to do this for you, which you may have on your computer already or else you can download it from the Mac App Store online.

Scrivener is a word-processing programme designed especially for authors. It provides a management system for documents, notes, emails and posts. Scrivener enables you to organise your documents and keep track of your posts and their content for easy reference (including text, images, PDF files, audio, video, web pages, web logs and so on). After drafting some relevant text for a blog, you can export the text into a standard word processor for formatting, and this will give you an orderly catalogue of your posts.

Scrivener is a great tool for a time-monitored project like a blog tour. It enables you to keep your posts organised and keep track of dates and details without having to open lots of different Word files looking for previous posts to find out what you said and when. See http://www.ashleyperez.com/blog/item/255-how-to-plan-a-book-blog-tour-without-going-crazy

a. Whatever blog cataloguing method you use, be sure to keep track of:
    (a) the format and subject matter of each blog and post
    (b) the email address of the blogger that you are sending posts to
    (c) the blog it will be posted on (Scrivener enables you to create links)
    (d) when the post goes live
    (e) whether you have posted yet, with helpful reminders

Exercise 11. Make sure that you keep track of all the blog postings that you make, what you said in them and how they were received.

If you shoot off in all sorts of directions and blog aimlessly, then your blogging tour will not be successful. You have to do your research and plan your blogging activities carefully. Prep your preferred posts properly (try saying that three times quickly!).

Next, you need to make sure your posts on your blog tour give readers compelling reasons to purchase your book / download your ebook. You can do this by making sure that you write quality posts. Again, planning is essential. Give yourself ample time to draft your posts in advance. Think clearly about what you might post next. Spontaneous, stream-of-consciousness, quick-fly, last-minute (or worse still, late-night) posts are generally a bad idea, especially if you have children or pets running around yelling or yelping behind you (or in my case, a hamster running on a wheel), or you have had a few drinks, or you are tired. Rather, leave it and draft your posts in the morning or afternoon, or whenever you are least distracted.

How long your tour takes will depend on how much you enjoy blogging. If it feels like a chore, then keep the tour short and focus on doing a good job on a few posts. After all the time and concentration that you put into writing your *magnum opus*, after all your *ferreus opus* (hard work), you may feel that you have written enough already, but with a little effort and planning, as a writer the ideas will start flowing soon enough for you to draft rich, interesting content for your blog tour.

Here are some common subjects for blog posts for authors that you might consider:

1. Interview with the author
2. Book extract or "look inside" sneak peak
3. Review of the book
4. Rant and rave about the book
5. Top ten list of benefits
6. Story of your cover art / design

7. Literary inspirations and influences
8. Writing insights or techniques
9. Book marketing strategies
10. Hints about the content / clues to a mystery
11. "Dear Me" style letter (for YA authors)
12. Two Truths and a Lie (good icebreaker)
13. Interesting facts about the book's setting
14. Answer readers' questions

You can also invite bloggers to suggest topics of interest for your guest posts since they know their fellow bloggers best.

For your blog host, you can send them the following (when appropriate):

a. **Author biography.** Keep it brief and make sure that it does not sound like you are boasting about your literary success. If another author takes a disliking to you, they can undermine your marketing efforts by making disparaging remarks on discussion boards or blogs, or uploading a negative review of your book to Amazon. Having a published book make people envious, and commercial success even more so. Be factual about the book you published, but you might want to hide some of your literary shine under a bushel. Let the blogger or interviewer praise you and bring out your shining light for you.

b. **Synopsis and excerpts.** Other useful details for your guest posts include a brief description of your book and a short excerpt. These are essential for fellow bloggers and potential readers to get a sense of the book itself and what it is all about, and not just your publishing or blogging persona. You may want to choose different excerpts for each post, as you might have some of the same people from your growing fan base following your interviews and posts regularly, and you want to give them something new. Also, different excerpts can often lead to new angles and topics to talk about. And as we stated previously, it is important to be germane, not mundane.

c. **Promotional material.** Include press articles about you and images such as your book cover, an author photo, illustrations from inside the book and so on. You can add additional photos, images or videos relevant to each post to personalise it and add interest. YouTube trailers for your book are often useful in this regard.

d. **Book-buying and media links.** Tell people where they can buy a copy of your book and whom to contact if they would like further information, to set up an interview, book signing, request a signed copy of your book, etc. At the end of each post, provide links to your Facebook fan page, your Twitter account, your website and your own blog. The easier you can make it for people to buy your book, the more copies you will sell.

Remember to give bloggers the option of editing the material provided to suit their format and fellow bloggers based on how much promotion they feel comfortable with you doing. Book product placement is essential, but you have to strike the right balance – you do not want to overdo it and you do want to be subtle in your marketing approach or you will push potential readers away rather than pulling them in.

Also, it is a professional courtesy to send your blogger contact your post at least a week in advance, along with any images and supporting documents that go with it. In fact, you might want to have a standard digital promotional pack ready that you can add to or take away from, depending on the specifics of the post. You can also let bloggers know that they can choose to use whichever images they like, and it always helps to ask them in advance what their fellow bloggers generally want to know and tend to blog about.

Exercise 12. Have your press/marketing kit ready and tailor it for each guest post that you do when blogging.

Get to know your blog host better, as they will in turn recommend you and your book to other bloggers. It is also useful to ask bloggers if they can kindly send you a link to the post when it goes live, just as you would do when speaking to a journalist who is interviewing you for a feature article in your local newspaper. And asking for a release date often helps to shore it up. Otherwise, it can get pushed back, and all too soon it is no longer newsworthy or worthy of blogging about; things tend to move quickly in the media. Also, you will want to upload and update the information on your website and tell your readers and fans (through your other social media channels) to look out for your upcoming blog, and highlight that particular stop on your book blog tour.

Finally, you need to follow up. Be sure to visit the blogs that have hosted you and your tour and respond to any comments or questions that readers have. This is all part of the ongoing dialogue that you are seeking to create with new readers. Send the blogger and blog host a "thank you" message. They have provided you with a platform to talk about what interests you most, and this in turn helped ensure that your book blogging tour was successful.

Video Blogging and Podcasting

Known as vlogging or vidblogging, this is a form of blogging where short videos are made regularly and often combined with supporting text, images and other promotional details about your book. Entries can be recorded in one take or cut into multiple parts. Video logs (vlogs) often take advantage of web syndication to allow for the distribution of the video over the Internet as podcasts.

With podcasting, producers record videos and make them available to anyone with a high-speed Internet connection who would like them, either for free or with a fee attached. For example, let us say your book is called *Judo for Beginners* and you are using your book as a guide in a podcast to teach students about the fundaments of the sport. Programme listeners can opt in and pay a subscription fee by which they will be able to download new audio or video files that are automatically delivered to their computers or iPods for viewing.

This is an important marketing tool for books and you can create one by recording interviews with your readers over the phone (with their consent, of course) or by developing your own "show" or serialisation, thus showcasing your book. Your podcast (your showreel or training video) will be distributed to the network's subscribers and delivered to their computer or mobile device as a digital download for them to watch and listen to whenever they would like.

The benefit of vlogging and podcasting is especially relevant to practical, self-help and how-to books (such as this one), as it provides another way to package your book and share your insights and expert knowledge all around the world with others, while retaining the full rights and taking full advantage of new technologies associated with the digital revolution in which we find ourselves, to bring your writing and message to more people.

In terms of conventional book marketing, it is always best to start local, and build to regional, then national and hopefully international. Yet, the digital age and the growth of electronic publishing, combined with free self-publishing platforms like Amazon Createspace and the emergence of social media channels, is radically shaking up the industry – for the better in our view – empowering authors and enabling them to take their work directly to market, where traditional publishers have had a monopoly on the market for far too long. The ebook revolution is changing the way we think about marketing our books and reaching out to readers around the world. Going global used to be just an idea, a dream, for most authors, but the Internet makes it all possible at the click of a button, as explained in the next chapter.

8

MULTICHANNEL MARKETING TO SELL YOUR BOOK AROUND THE WORLD

It used to be that you needed a traditional publisher for your book to reach a global readership, and preferably one with a good in-house international rights team to sell your book into foreign markets. The problem, however, was that it was a closed market, in that the many traditional publishing houses republish the same commercially successful authors time and time again, focus on celebrity names, and rely to some extent on professional literary agents to introduce new talented authors and recommend books to them for consideration.

The barrier to entry into traditional publishing is exacerbated by the fact that literary agents are expected to work on a commission-only basis, i.e. they only get paid from advances and royalties on any books that they successfully place with the publishers. Consequently, this leads to a similar bias with agents who are spoiled for choice, take on very few new authors and inevitably favour representing authors who are already commercially successful to some extent and those who already have an ongoing relationship with or offer from a traditional publisher to publish their next book. It is a vicious circle for any new authors trying to break into the industry and get their first step on the literary ladder.

We have all read "no unsolicited manuscripts" in the *Writers' Handbook* under the entry of many traditional publishers. When you try to ring up publishers directly and speak to commissioning editors, they never take your call and the PA simply tells you to send in the full manuscript. You never know how much or whether it is even read because all you get back (after a prolonged wait) is a templated rejection letter. It is a closed shop, with the emphasis not necessarily on the quality of the work, but on the author's platform, i.e., their name, brand, fan base and current channels into market.

The Digital Revolution is Changing the Publishing and Marketing Landscape

Fortunately, the ebook and social media revolution is changing the dynamic in terms of empowering authors where traditional publishers have for far too long had a monopoly over who gets published. The growth of digital downloads and sales of ebook readers make it possible for authors to bypass the traditional barriers and take their book directly to market.

Moreover, it has revolutionised the way we think about marketing our books. It used to be that we needed to start locally, then regionally, and if you are successful enough through relentless self-promotion, hopefully you could secure some national media coverage. At this point you may acquire some measure of retail shelf space with a larger retailer like Waterstones or WH Smith, who will stock your book in a limited number of their shops around the country, before finally being picked up by a traditional publisher with the resources and contacts to sell your book rights to foreign publishers at international books fairs.

However, rather than working from grass roots and gradually building up more and more of a wider following, in the new model you can upload a book to Amazon and it can be bought and downloaded by someone half way around the world within minutes. The key is finding ways of raising awareness and building your author brand through social networking, social bookmarking and social cataloguing websites, organising sponsored Kindle promotions, having a professional website and actively blogging about your book, and so on.

The point is you do not necessarily need a traditional publisher these days to be a commercially successful author. In fact, if you know what needs to be done to promote your book online, you can reach out to readers around the world with very little time or expense. You can market your book locally, regionally, nationally and internationally all at the same time by planning your marketing campaign carefully and making sure that all of your efforts, posts and the general dissemination of information about you and your book are integrated online. Going global used to be a dream for most authors, but the Internet makes it all possible at the click of a button, as explained in this chapter.

The Lightning-Fast Nature of Integrated or Multichannel Book Marketing

This is where you will bring all of your marketing channels together into one fast-flowing stream of information, which we call "Blitz Marketing." It is like "blitzing" or rushing a quarterback in American football in that the marketing campaign is proactive, focused, creative, quick and relentless to force a breakthrough; it is also purposefully and strategically planned in advance so that when the circumstances call for it, you can respond quickly and with precision for full effect, or in the case of book promotion, you can mobilise your resources in an easy and cost-effective way that will get your message out there and your book in front of as many potential readers and buyers as possible.

To reach an international readership and integrate your marketing plans, there are six steps you need to take to decide how best to focus your efforts and bring them all together as an effective campaign. This is important because often authors adopt a scattergun approach where they try everything and accomplish little – like the Alamo, where the aim was to keep attacking the fort until the last man standing was toppled, hoping that something would stick. Other authors make the mistake of adopting a domino strategy, i.e., trying one channel at a time, which is also ineffective because the campaign needs to be moving together at the same time on different fronts to break through and make a real impact.

Planning your global marketing campaign

Rather than the "Alamo" or "domino" approach, as an author wanting to market your book on an international scale, you want to adopt a dynamic, lightning-fast strategy in which you can quickly identify your target market, truly understand their interests and be able to predict their likely movements, select which marketing tools to apply and when, get your message to them and your book in front of them for consideration, stay on message and track their reaction and subsequent sales.

Blitz strategic marketing calls for a structured and sustained approach where you define what you are trying to achieve, measure and analyse the markets and media options and implement an integrated campaign based on the various online marketing channels available (e.g., social networking, Amazon reviews, Kindle Boards, sponsored posts, blogging, etc.) that will help you, the author, capture a wider audience for your time and effort.

To properly understand your reader before integrating your marketing channels and mobilising your marketing force, the first step is to be clear about the nature of the task at hand and the likely result of your efforts. It is one thing to know what genre your book falls into and what gender and age group it would appeal to most (i.e., to position and tailor your book for your primary and secondary readerships) and quite another thing to know how to bring your marketing channels together into an integrated promotional campaign aimed at a more global market. It is like the difference between running as a local constituent and running for national office. With the latter, you have to develop a message and approach that will be picked up in the main media battlegrounds, where your message will receive the widest cross appeal.

As an author hoping to "hit the big time" with an international bestseller, you have to know who, what, where, when and why you are embarking on this global endeavour, and how to achieve the end that you have in mind. If you jump into international waters without knowing who and where your global readers are likely to be, your efforts will be ineffective. Here is how you should do it:

What exactly are you aiming to do and likely to achieve?

Firstly, you need to set out your objectives clearly and manage your own expectations carefully. You need to differentiate between what you *want* to achieve and what you are *likely* to achieve. If your main aim is to be a commercially successful author and make a million pounds in the first year after your book is published, then you are aiming at failure. If you set out to sell 100 digital downloads to non-UK book buyers in the first month, with incremental growth in your fan base outside the UK and visitor numbers from non-UK countries to your website over the first three months, then you are setting reasonable, achievable targets.

Or let us say that your main objective is to get as many people reading your book in as short a period of time as possible. Your blitz strategy might involve giving away your ebook for free for a limited period of time to build up a following and a fan base, with the plan to convert those new readers into buyers for your next book. Similarly, you might want to play with the pricing of your book to accommodate demand as it grows for your book.

> *Exercise 1. Write down your primary aim in seeking a global readership. Do you want your book to be read more widely? Do you want to earn more from international Amazon purchases? Then, write down what you can reasonably expect to achieve in this regard. 100 new international readers in the first month? 200 non-UK sales in the first three months? Set reasonable and achievable targets.*

Develop a general profile of your international readers

After you have defined your business objective (the "why"), the next step is to *identify* your core international readership. Again, to employ the election strategy analogy, let us say you are a Tory candidate running for national office from a traditionally conservative stronghold. You know what you need to say to garner support from them, but what about the Liberal pockets of support and Labour-held constituencies? You cannot simply ignore them if you want to "appeal to the masses." You may need to modify your approach and broaden your platform so that your message is conveyed to and welcomed by a broader base of support, or in the case of authors, by more potential readers of your work.

In identifying your global audience and international literary market:

- If you are a new author, then form a clear picture of what type of international reader you want to attract. Are they young readers and likely to be actively involved in social media and blogging? Do they read Kindle Boards or other discussion boards, and if so, which ones in different countries?
- If you are an established author looking to introduce your work and develop more of a readership in other countries, then look at your typical readers and identify the type of readers you want more of. This is where profiling your readers based on current traffic to your site or checking out the profiles of those leaving four- and five-star reviews of your book on Amazon is useful.

Exercise 2. Do a demographic profile of your global readers. Which country do they live in? What languages do they speak? Where do they typically engage with others (on Facebook, Shelfari, through writing groups, discussion boards, blogs)? How do they engage? How can you engage with them? What are their interests and general buying habits? Which e-tail (online retail) websites do they generally buy books from? Do they have an Amazon website specifically for their country?

Market your book to every country or a select few?

Again, as part of a structured marketing campaign, you need to know where most of your international readers are likely to come from. Is your book going to appeal to a widespread Japanese market if it is only available in English and has not been translated? Might it be worthwhile having your book translated into Spanish or even Mandarin Chinese (which, by the way, is the language used by the most number of people in the world, followed by English and Spanish)? The language spoken by most countries is English, followed by French, then Spanish. In fact, in terms of international languages, these are the figures:

Native Speakers

1. Chinese (1.1 billion)
2. Hindi (360 million)
3. Spanish (340 million)
4. English (322 million)
5. Arabic (206 million)
6. Bengali (180 million)
7. Portuguese (180 million)
8. Russian (167 million)
9. Japanese (127 million)
10. German (95 million)

Total Speakers

1. Chinese (1.5 billion)
2. English (1+ billion)
3. Spanish (500 million)
4. Hindustani (460 million)
5. Arabic (452 million)
6. Russian (278 million)
7. French (265 million)
8. Portuguese (215 million)
9. Bengali (211 million)
10. German (150 million)
11. Japanese (130 million)

Languages spoken in the most countries

1. English
2. French
3. Arabic
4. Spanish
5. Russian
6. German
7. Portuguese
8. Chinese

Why are these demographics important? When you are researching various international channels to market your book to, and currently the large majority of all ebooks purchased last year were from Amazon, you probably want to target English-speaking countries that have an Amazon site selling books online in their country. Amazon is currently present in nine countries, namely:

Austria	www.amazon.at	German and US titles
Canada	www.amazon.ca	English and French titles
China	www.joyo.com	Chinese titles only
France	www.amazon.fr	French and US titles
Germany	www.amazon.de	German and US titles
Japan	www.amazon.co.jp	Japanese and US titles
Italy	www.amazon.it	Italian titles only
United Kingdom	www.amazon.co.uk	UK and US titles
United States	www.amazon.com	Spanish and US titles

Exercise 3. Consider whether it would be worthwhile to have your book translated into other international languages.

Make sure your message is clear and consistent

Next, you need to consider carefully what you are going to say to your new potential readers around the world. To achieve this, you firstly need to be clear about the content-rich messages and information that you are seeking to convey, then you need to decide which of the marketing channels available you are going to employ to spread the good word, and you need to execute your plan across those selective channels and to your target global audience in a clear, compelling and focused way.

Develop a messaging strategy to effectively communicate with your intended audience. With a clear picture of your target audience in mind, determine what message and content will most effectively encourage and inspire new international readers to browse your book and hopefully buy it. This needs some careful thought to plan your general approach and what you are going to say in your basic introduction, your all-important first impression. At the same time, your approach needs to be dynamic and your message needs to be adaptable to the individual based on their own interests and reaction to your introductory remarks.

Let us say you own a shop and you want to bring new customers in. What would you say to them? Most people want to talk about themselves and serve their own interests first and foremost, especially if they do not know who you are and have never heard of you or have not come across your writing before. So, you need to say something to them that will engage them, which they will respond to positively. If you start by saying, "Here is my book. Trust me, it really is great. Do you want to buy a copy?" then they are likely to say, "No." If, on the other hand, you provide useful information that might pique their interest, and follow this up with more content-rich conversation pieces, you have a much better chance of them listening to what you have to say and following you and, hopefully, buying your book and becoming an avid fan and advocate of your writing.

Now, what is your message going to be? Let us say that you are doing a book signing and it is a bit slow, so you want to walk around the shop and press the flesh. You have written a crime novel and you know which section of the bookstore you are likely to find interested readers because the "Crime/thriller" genre is clearly marked for you. You see someone browsing that section of books – what are you going to say to them to introduce yourself and your book to them, rather than thrusting your book in front of them straight away?

Many of us will have experienced walking down the high street and being corralled, harangued and stopped in our tracks by people saying, "Do you have a minute?" or "Can you help me with a survey I am conducting?" and making believe they care about you or want to share an important public service message, only to be seeking monetary donations, generally for an animal rights cause or children's charity. This approach puts a lot of people off and if your aim is to turn them into long-term readers and avid fans of your writing, it can be counterproductive. You need a more subtle and unselfish approach.

Looking at it from their perspective, they are not in the bookshop hoping for unsolicited approaches from aspiring authors inviting them to buy a signed copy of their book. They are there to buy a book, and possibly one in your genre – but why should they buy yours? More importantly, why should they care about you because, remember, you do not want them to just buy one book from you and then never speak to you again. You want to build a dialogue with your new readers and for them to identify with you and write positive reviews of your book and recommend it to others. That is the key to international distribution, to get people talking about it in different countries.

Let us take this book and explain the message that we will try to convey when marketing it. The core message is not "This is a great book, an essential for any new author." Rather, the core message is "The digital revolution and growth of e-publishing is radically changing the way books are published, distributed and sold around the world today." This message will be the focus of any social media and traditional media that we undertake for this book, because it does not overtly promote the book, but plants the seed in writers' and readers' minds that there are fast-moving developments with regard to something they are personally or professionally interested and involved in. Once we follow up this headline message with rich, thought-provoking information, they may want to find out more. As we have a growing reputation for informing authors and the media about the current direction and future direction of the e-publishing industry, this is what leads them to buy our book, to find out what it is all about and to stay at the forefront of the digital revolution and be forward-thinking in terms of publishing and promoting their own books.

Exercise 4. Take a few minutes to write down your core message and how you plan to deliver that message in a social context to encourage new readers to take a long-term interest in you and your book. Put yourself in the shoes of your reader and consider what they would like to hear from you.

Stay on message

Once you have set out your stall and put your general message out there for global public consumption, you need to "stay on message," which means being persistent in getting your point across and not allowing yourself to be distracted from your central purpose. Otherwise, you can give out mixed messages and find yourself "following" others rather than leading them to your book. Let us say we started out by saying, "The e-revolution is changing the way the book business works," and in response, another well-known expert comes onto your blog and says something interesting and populist, like: "In five years, the digital age will make traditional publishers redundant and book retailers and literary agents practically obsolete – more on this at www.ebookexpert.com."

It does seem that other aspiring authors can be ruthless at times about hopping on the bandwagon and trying to steal your thunder and your readership. Rather than being redirected to their website and responding to them, letting them set the agenda and moderate the discussion, you need to find more channels to share your message. Online promotion and competition for readers' attention can be a tough game to play, but if you keep to your main message and find new, interesting things to say based around this core message, you will develop a following and you will find your readers and secure a loyal following.

You will need to adapt your message to selective marketing channels and keep your message current, and that is why you need a general message that tells people that the information in your book is cutting-edge, and in the case of novels, that your main character is developing and taking on interesting new cases and adventures all the time.

Let us say your books are about a young girl who seems on the outside to be unhappy and angry all the time, but in fact on the inside, her heart is in the right place and she has a unique gift for looking after others who are less fortunate and making sure they are not bullied or harmed in any way, often without them knowing about it. That is her "special power." (Think C. S. Conwell's series of "Jessica Roberts" books, including *The Girl Who Forgot How to Smile*, *The Magic of Jessica Roberts* and *The Night Fliers*.)

The message may be about bullying at school and the different forms it can take, and the narratives that are woven around this in your series of books all relate to this same pressing problem for many young people. The message you are seeking to convey will allow you to upload interesting information to anti-bullying sites and if schools discover that your books help raise awareness of this issue and inspire young people, they will buy copies of your book in bulk.

> *Exercise 5. Make sure you lead online discussions rather than following others and be consistent and persistent in sharing your core message.*

Select the marketing channels that your readership is most engaged in

Now that you have a clear vision of what you can reasonably achieve in your international marketing campaign, you know who your new readers are likely to be and where you can reach them, and you have a popular message to convey that dovetails nicely with your writing, you then need to deploy the marketing tools and mediums from your promotional arsenal that are most likely to disseminate your core message, i.e., to get your message out to the masses.

For example, if your book is best-suited to a teenage and young adult audience, such as followers of the pop singer Katy Perry, and you want to reach the North American YA market, you might want to communicate your message to them through Facebook and various American Idol channels. If your book is a practical guide for working professionals, you may want to approach the US market through LinkedIn.com, Biznik.com, Cofoundr.com and Sunzu.com.

Exercise 6. Adapt your core message to select marketing channels and keep your message current. This does not mean changing the message; rather, it means tailoring the message to the media platform.

Online bookmarking

Let us say that you are at a book writing seminar and you want to network and talk about your book. One way to achieve this is with bookmarks, which you can hand out to people or leave on seats at the event without impeding or distracting them in any way. Similarly, there are online bookmarking sites, which will enable you to discover related book content, while organising links to your core message and conveniently sharing those all-important links with like-minded and link-minded people.

For authors wanting to share the good news about the publication of their book with the world, bookmarking sites like Delicious.com provide a great way to track content and share links, as is the visually attractive and alluring bookmarking site Pinterest.com. In fact, there is a whole host of new features online within large bookmarking sites that can help you monitor and organise relevant content, and get your messages and posts viewed by more potential readers.

Here are a few other useful bookmarking facilities:

1. YouTube "Watch Later"

This works on videos that are embedded into third-party sites using the new iFrames embed code but once you click on the button the video will be saved on your own home YouTube page to watch at a later date.

2. Twitter "Favorites"

You can open up your bookmarks and add links to be read later. And if you consider that old tweets are often hard to locate, this is a great way to keep track of relevant Twitter content and organise and share your Twitter links.

3. Reddit "karma" points

Reddit is a social news website where you can post links to content on the Web. Others can then vote the posted links up or down, causing them to appear more or less prominently on the Reddit home page. The site has discussion areas where users may discuss the posted links. Users who submit articles that other users like and subsequently "vote up" receive "karma" points for highly rated links. Reddit also includes several topical sections called "subreddits," which focus on specific topics.

4. Instapaper

This is another simple online tool that enables you to save webpages for reading later, allowing you to bookmark content easily – just one click of the button and the content is saved. Where this tool becomes really useful is when you share this contact with others in such a way that they can read it on their iPad, mobile phone or Kindle and it does this in a clever way so they only see text, without unsolicited links and adverts.

5. Google "bookmarklets"

To get started all you have to do is drag their "power surfing" bookmark into your toolbar. It lacks social functionality but is linked to your Google account and you start using it straight away.

6. LinkedIn "Today"

This news-related tool allows you to save all the best business stories that you see from your network to read and share them with others later and in the format of your choosing.

7. Diigo's "Diigolet"

This cloud-based bookmarking site is similar to Delicious and an increasing number of people are using it. Their "tools for desktop browsers" menu allows you to "research, share and collaborate" information, saving your bookmarks in a cloud and viewing them from a wide range of devices at a later date.

8. Skloog "Wampum Interactive"

Like Pinterest, this site offers a more visual, iconic approach for locating, organising and sharing interesting content with others, making it easier to pick out selective sites and remember how and why you saved that particular content. You can create visual shortcuts to all your favourite sites, arrange and readily access your bookmarks, and organise your bookmarks with instantly identifiable tags and categories.

9. LiveGAP "bookmarklets"

Search, bookmark, translate and share interesting content and links from anywhere with friends and followers by linking to social media sites like Facebook, Twitter, Google+, MySpace and LinkedIn. This site allows you to search quickly using Google, Yahoo, Bing, Ask, AOL, Wikipedia, YouTube, Facebook or Twitter, to translate content using Bing or Google, and mail content and links via Gmail, Yahoo, Live and your default mail with shortcuts to your inbox and sent folders.

10. Socialmarker.com

Provides an all-in-one bookmarking button, which enables you to spread a link to the most popular social bookmarking sites in under fifteen minutes. This one-click plug-in helps you get new links to your webpage, increases your web traffic, is indexed by Google in a matter of minutes and best of all, is free!

11. Evernote

Designed primarily for notetaking and archiving, and perhaps more of a social cataloguing site. A "note" can be added as a piece of formatted text, a full webpage or webpage excerpt, a photograph, a voice memo, or a handwritten "ink" note. Notes can also have file attachments. Notes can be sorted into folders, then tagged, annotated, edited, given comments, searched and exported or shared with others as part of a notebook.

12. Onlywire.com

This site allows you to handle all of your bookmarks in one place. Filling out one form saves you time when you want to submit your postings. Just one click will send your post everywhere you would like. Automate your website content and optimise your social bookmarking with useful backlinks.

Exercise 7. Consider bookmarking and optimising your website, web blog entries and blog posts using one of the facilities mentioned above.

Time to take your message to the masses

Now that you have identified your likely global readers, you know where to find them, you have a clear message to convey to them and you know what you expect to achieve, the next step is to blitz them with your international marketing campaign through your selective, integrated marketing channels. Let us say that you decide to pay for a sponsored advert on Kindle Boards, that you give the first 1,000 copies of your ebook away free on Amazon to all countries to build up a global following and raise your global author brand, that you widen the reach of your blogging activities, and so on. There are many different ways to promote your ebook, as explained in *100 Ways to Publish and Sell Your Own E-book… and Make It a Bestseller* (How To Books, May 2013).

The time is now to push forward and blitz the international market with the full force of your promotional plans. It is essential to keep a calendar and updated checklist of your daily, weekly and monthly activities and closely track your progress, especially if you are hoping to reach wider, global readership. To do so, you will need to trial different approaches, and you may want to change the price point of your ebook at various times (which is one of the main virtues of self-publishing an ebook) to see what is most effective in terms of traffic figures, Amazon rankings and sales figures for your book. Effectiveness can only be measured if you can closely monitor and match up your activities with increments in sales activity and make necessary adjustments along the way to put your book into the hands and onto the e-readers of more people.

Exercise 8. Trial different marketing channels and consider changing the price of your ebook to suit your intended market. You might want to start by giving your book away for free to readers abroad for a limited period of time to build up a readership and for viral marketing to kick in. Sometimes you need to throw a spat to catch a mackerel.

Launching a major integrated marketing strategy without understanding where your readers are, what they like, what they are passionate about, what they consider valuable and, in the end, what might convert them into avid fans of your writing is not going to lead to the result that you would like. You may capture some new readers' attentions for a short period of time, but the long-term success of your writing in general, and your book in particular, relies on holding their attention and keeping your readers engaged and interested in your literary career.

The key to achieve this is to listen and dialogue with your new readers and give them what they want and ask for, and in response, they will recommend you and your book to others. What matters most in today's digital publishing and marketing environment is where you are actually engaging, how you are engaging and what are the results of that engagement. This is all part and parcel of an effective, integrated blitz marketing strategy.

The ground and power is shifting quickly in publishing in our digital age.[1] Traditional publishers are no longer able to control readers' attitudes and preferences through market research, customer service, commanding retail space and conventional promotional and media channels. Today, authors are taking control of their own book sales and marketing by using social media and free or low-cost publishing

1 In terms of the changing landscape with digital publishing, see *Groundswell: Winning in a World Transformed by Social Technologies* by Charlene Li and Josh Bernoff, *The New Rules of Marketing and PR* by David Meerman Scott and *Likeable Social Media* by David Kerpen.

platforms to take their books directly to their readers. They are creating their own groundswell of support and loyal readership.

Exercise 9. Focus on generating reader loyalty rather than short-term sales. You want to generate interest in your book from new readers and, more importantly, keep them engaged so they become avid fans of your writing and recommend your book to others.

A growing "groundswell" of support is garnered by carefully planned blitz marketing techniques, with authors using social media channels and new technologies strategically and effectively. In terms of book promotion, this is characterised by listening, talking, energising, supporting and tracking your readers' interests.

Listening

Firstly, authors need to listen to their readers to understand what the market is looking for and how you can meet the demand. To achieve this, you need to find out if your readers are using social technologies, and study and understand clearly how they are using them.

Talking

Instead of promoting your book directly to readers, authors need to find creative ways to connect with readers about their reading experiences and their feelings about their author brand, typically through social media channels and content-rich blogging.

Enthusing and inspiring

Avid and enthusiastic readers are an integral part of your groundswell, and authors can recognise and appreciate these readers by creating online communities and social platforms where they can connect with the author's work and brand and provide reviews and feedback.

Supporting and tracking

Authors can harness the support of their friends and family by creating social applications for them to easily connect with your book and brand, with the creative use of enterprising, dynamic social software tools and social media analytics. Some useful websites in this regard (and there are literally hundreds of them) include:

- www.google.co.uk/analytics/features/social.html
- www.adobe.com/social
- www.simplymeasured.com
- http://hootsuite.com/features/custom-analytics
- http://analytics.topsy.com
- www.peoplebrowsr.com
- www.socialreport.com
- https://socialcrawlytics.com
- http://webtrends.com/solutions/digital-measurement/social-measurement

The social analytic tools offered on these sites can help you understand which social media channel and communities are most likely to suit your book and where your audience is most likely to be. From there you can use social media monitoring tools like Trackur, Viral Heat or Radian Six. Depending on the number of conversations you are currently engaged in with your readers and the message you want to deliver, there are different types of "listening" tools available. With the data that you can collect from these social-media monitoring tools, you can see with more specificity where the relevant conversations are going on.

Once you discern where the useful conversations are taking place, you can identify the main drivers of conversation, understand where these audiences are consuming their information (are they simply browsing the Internet, are they listening to podcasts, do they pay attention to adverts, are they watching YouTube videos, are they blogging and connecting via BlogTalkRadio, and so on). You can even see what content they are sharing the most to give you a better understanding of the type of content you need to generate to engage them and to drive the conversations yourself.

Understanding the conversations your audience is having is key to blitz marketing. Your potential readers leave a clearly visible, digital imprint each time they engage in conversation with you through social media websites and their e-fingerprints will conveniently tell you what channels they find the most valuable, and clever literary marketers will take that information and produce content especially tailored for those channels, rather than producing content for the sake of producing content. It is not a scattergun approach in which you throw every marketing tool in your arsenal at your target readership. Any fly fisherman will tell you that you need to use the right fly to catch a trout. You may need to caste your net widely and go with the flow when fishing in international waters, but it helps to know where the fish you want to catch tend to forage and school, and where readers of books in your genre tend to collect and converse online, so you can focus your global marketing campaign in productive and effective ways.

Exercise 10. Track your international readers' digital fingerprints closely to fully understand their reading preferences, habits and movements.

Book promotion can seem relentless. That being said, the rewards are great because once you have a core understanding of where, when and how your audience engages it becomes easier to interact with them in a more strategic way rather than just blindly pinning the tail on the donkey. The digital revolution – or perhaps more appropriately, the digital "e-volution" – is breaking down traditional barriers and enabling new, talented authors to take their books directly to market. It is opening up exciting new channels and digital media streams for you to wade into, rather than relying on traditional means to publish and promote your book abroad.

IPR: Virtual Rights Agency

Some will say one advantage that traditional publishers still retain over self-published / ebook authors is they often have in-house foreign rights staff who actively sell the rights to their authors' books to publishers in different countries that generate subsidiary revenue streams. Or they might work closely with an international rights agency, to whom they pay an agreed commission for selling their book rights to foreign publishers on their behalf at, for instance, the Frankfurt and London Book Fairs, Book Expo America or the Bologna Children's Book Fair.

However, this traditional model for international rights sales is also changing with the recent emergence of virtual rights agencies such as www.IPRlicense.com, which gives you the opportunity to showcase your book in the global marketplace by uploading your book and listing the countries in which the rights to your book are currently available. The site enables you to make money from licensing your work in different formats. They run useful global rights campaigns and regularly send out newsletters internationally to raise awareness of your book to publishers and agents worldwide.

In this regard, there is a wide variety of rights that publishers seek to secure, including:

- Print rights (in paperback and hardback)
- Digital rights (ebook, enhanced ebook and, sometimes, app)
- First serialisation (usually sold to newspapers/magazines)
- Second serialisation (usually sold to newspapers/magazines)
- TV, film and dramatisation
- Book digest
- Radio and TV straight reading
- Book club (when books are sold through companies like Book People or Scholastic Book Fairs)
- Audio rights
- Large print rights (e.g., to Ulverscroft and Thorpe)
- Anthology and quotation

The IPR License website also offers third-party professional advice on copyright protection and registration. This digital rights platform acts as a copyright and licensing hub, making it easy to locate copyright holders and thereby seek their permission to use or cite their work. This virtual rights agency offers authors and publishers the opportunity to license, monetise and find the best new content in a global marketplace.

The e-publishing landscape is changing quickly and if you can identify the right markers, find your way and settle in quickly into this new literary scene, you can be in full control of your literary career from writing your book the way you want to write it, choosing your own publishing platform and formats, setting the price that you want for your book, promoting it as much as you would like and reaping the financial rewards in full.

The ebook revolution is empowering authors, and now more than ever you *can* realise your lifelong dream of seeing your vision and ideas in print and sharing your storytelling, experiences and insights with the world.

APPENDIX 1

UK WRITERS' GROUPS AND LITERARY WORKSHOPS

Writers' Group	Email
Abbeydale Writers	Online Form
Aberdeen Writers' Circle	Online form
Alistair Paterson	prism.atic@virgin.net
Alston Hall College	alstonhall.general2@lancashire.gov.uk
Andover Writers' Workshop	admin@andoverwriters.co.uk
Anglia Ruskin University	answers@anglia.ac.uk
Angus Writers' Circle	nicolasjw@hotmail.co.uk
Ann Newbegin	annnewbegin@hotmail.com
Apples and Snakes	george@applesandsnakes.org irenosen@applesandsnakes.org
Apples and Snakes East Midlands	stephanie@applesandsnakes.org
Apples and Snakes West Midlands	natasha@applesandsnakes.org
Armagh Writers' Group	kevin@abcwritersnetwork.co.uk
Ashford Writers	yym@btopenworld.com
Ashton-in-Makerfield Writers' and Literary Club	woodwigan@aol.com
Ayr Writers' Club	f.mcfadzean@btinternet.com

Writers' Group	**Email**
Bangor Cellar Group	lowri_ann@hotmail.com
Bath Spa Univ. College	enquiries@bathspa.ac.uk
Bath Writers' Group	clancy.inc@blueyonder.co.uk
Battersea Writers' Group	jasonyoung72@yahoo.com
Belstead House	belstead.house@educ.suffolkcc.gov.uk
Birmingham Group	join.bwg@googlemail.com
Bournemouth University	enquiries@bournemouth.ac.uk
Bradford Writers' Circle	bradfordwriterscircle@hotmail.com
Brentwood Writers' Circle	ena.love@tiscali.co.uk
Bridgend Writers' Circle	boswell258@talktalk.net
Brighter Writers	brighter_writers@btinternet.com
BrumQueerInk	brumqueerink@aol.com
Burton Manor	george.cooke@burtonmanor.com
Cambridge Wordfest	admin@cambridgewordfest.co.uk
Cambridge Writers	cambridgewriters@hotmail.com
Cannon Poets	info@cannonpoets.co.uk
Cardiff Centre for Lifelong Learning	train@cardiff.ac.uk
Cardiff Writers' Circle	niva@nivapete.freeserve.co.uk
Cecily Bomberg	cecily@bombergwriting.co.uk
Chandlers Ford Writers	info@wyvernwriters.co.uk
Charnwood Arts	kevr@charnwoodarts.com
Chelmsford Writers	secretary@chelmsfordwriters.org.uk
Cheltenham Writers' Circle	carol.sandiford@blueyonder.co.uk
Chiltern Writers	info@chilternwriters.org
Chris Leonard	mail@chris-leonard-writing.co.uk
Chrysalis to Butterfly – The Poet in You	jay@ramsay3892.fsnet.co.uk

Writers' Group	Email
City Lit	infoline@citylit.ac.uk
City University	enquiries@city.ac.uk
Commonword	Online Form
Company of Writers	mazzy@unfurling.net
Coventry Writers' Group	krismonsen@btinternet.com
Creative Ink	creative.ink@lycos.co.uk
Creative Writers' Network	info@creativewritersnetwork.org
Creative Writes	creativewrites@hotmail.co.uk
Creative Writing Ink	enquiries@oca-uk.com
Croydon Writers' Circle	battenberg@yahoo.co.uk
Dean Writers' Circle	rachel.hayward@tesco.net
Della Galton	info@dellagalton.co.uk
Denman College	hq@nfwi.org.uk
Derwent Writers	mail@derwentwriters.co.uk
DESIblitz Writing Group	editor@desiblitz.com
Dillington House	dillington@somerset.gov.uk
Dunholme Writers	john@bloodaxe.co.uk
East Anglian Writers	chair@eastanglianwriters.org.uk
East Dulwich Group	info@edwg.co.uk
Edinburgh University	cce@ed.ac.uk
Edinburgh Writers' Club	kate.blackadder@talk21.com
Elaine Everest	elaineeverest@aol.com
Ellipsis Writing Group	feedback@ellipsiswriting.org.uk
Euphoric ink	info@euphoricink.co.uk
Euroscript	ask@euroscript.co.uk
Eve Menezes Cunningham	eve@applecoaching.com
Exiled Writers	jennifer@exiledwriters.fsnet.co.uk

Writers' Group	Email
Falmouth Poetry Group	pdshuttle@aol.com
Fareham Writers	enquiries@farehamwriters.co.uk
Farncombe Estate Centre	enquiries@farncombeestate.co.uk
Felixstowe Scribblers	scribblers@ntlworld.com
Fiction City	fictioncity@gmail.com
Fiction Writing Workshop	louise_gethin@hotmail.com
Fire in the Head Creative Writing Programme	roselle@fire-in-the-head.co.uk
Free Spirit Writers	freespiritwriters@tesco.net
Gamlingay and District Writers' Group	tracey@twotodes.seriouslyinternet.com
Gloswordshop	gloswordshop@blueyonder.co.uk
Grace Dieu Writers' Circle	tonygutteridge@live.com
Guildford Writers	margravejen@googlemail.com
Hackney and East London Creative Writing Circle	nerosiri@yahoo.co.uk
Harlow Writers Workshop	anne.neuhaus@ntlworld.com
Harrow Writers' Circle	ocmonteiro@hotmail.com
Hastings Writers' Group	hastingswritersgroup@gmail.com
Higham Hall College	admin@highamhall.com
Highgreen Arts	highgreenarts@aol.com
Hills Road Sixth Form	jaberdour@hillsroad.ac.uk
Hogs Back Writers	secretary@hbw.org.uk
Initialize Films	Online Form
Institute of Continuing Ed.	aeb53@cam.ac.uk
Interchange @ IDL (Bradford Network)	joedot@blueyonder.co.uk
Katherine Gallagher	mail@katherine-gallagher.com

Writers' Group	Email
King Alfred's College	press@winchester.ac.uk
King's Lynn Writers' Circle	enquiries@lynnwriters.org.uk
Knuston Hall College for Adult Education	enquiries@knustonhall.org.uk
Lancaster University	v.tyrrell@lancaster.ac.uk
Learn Writing	info@learnwriting.co.uk
Leeds Writers' Circle	chair@leedswriterscircle.co.uk
Leicester Poetry Society	david.bircumshaw@ntlworld.com
Leicester Writers' Club	rod@rodduncan.co.uk
Liberato Breakaway Writing Courses	Online Form
Lincoln Phoenix Circle	allens.athome@virgin.net
Linda James	writingunderwater@tiscali.co.uk
London Comedy Writers	londoncomedywriters@gmail.com
London Writers' Café	lisagoll@hotmail.com
London Writers' Workshops	londonwritersworkshop@hotmail.co.uk
London Writing Workshops	londonwritingworkshops@ googlemail.com
Magnetic North	pgfreeman@yahoo.com
Malvern Writers' Circle	malvernwriterscircle@hotmail.co.uk
Marsh Ink Writers' Group	Online Form
Marylebone Group	jkispal@hotmail.com
Maureen Osborne	maureen@nightowl.wanadoo.co.uk
Mead Kerr Limited	info@meadkerr.com
Missenden Abbey Adult Learning Centre	eva.nj@missendenabbey.ltd.uk
Mole Valley Poets	membershipsecretary@ molevalleypoets.co.uk

Writers' Group	Email
Mole Valley Scriptwriting	tim@molevalleyscripts.co.uk
Monday Night Group	info@mondaynightgroup.org.uk
N16 Writers and Readers	sue.gee@tiscali.co.uk
National TV School	info@nfts.co.uk
Neath Writers' Group	llewelyn37@talktalk.net
New Rivers Group	duffusjj@hotmail.com
Newham Workshop	nwwstjohns@googlemail.com
Norden Farm Creative Writers	matthew.biss@nordenfarm.org
North Herts Writers Circle	victoria@snelling00.vispa.com
North London Group	northlondonwriters@yahoo.co.uk
Northampton Group	piedpiperrecords@aol.com
Northampton Lit. Group	dizsampson@supanet.com
Northwest Playwrights	newplaysnw@hotmail.com
Nottingham Trent Univ.	its.servicedesk@ntu.ac.uk
Nuffield Theatre Group	info@nuffieldtheatre.co.uk
Oxford Film and Video Makers	geron@ofvm.org
Petersfield Workshop	susanneleigh@gmail.com
Petersfield Writers Circle	Online Form
Pier Playwrights	admin@newwritingsouth.com
Pitshanger Poets	nala.ques@virgin.net
Pitstop Refuelling Writers' Workshops	barbara.large@winchester.ac.uk
Plymouth Library Group	plymouthproprietarywriters@googlemail.com
PMA Training	training@pma-group.com
Poetry at The Troubadour	info@troubadour.co.uk

Writers' Group	Email
Poole Writers' Circle	enquires@writerspoole.co.uk
Queen's Park Writers	queensparkwriters@gmail.com
Queen's University	e.larrissy@qub.ac.uk
Redwell Writers	info@redwellwriters.org
Richmond Adult Community College	info@racc.ac.uk
Richmond Writers' Circle	info@richmondwriterscircle.org.uk
Ripon Writers' Group	maggie@maggiecobbett.co.uk
Rising Brook Writers	Online Form
Riverside Writers	Online Form
Roehampton University	enquiries@roehampton.ac.uk
Royal Holloway	drama@rhul.ac.uk
Ruskin College	enquiries@ruskin.ac.uk
Scarborough Society	katie@savonarola.fsnet.co.uk
ScriptTank	Online Form
Script Yorkshire	admin@scriptyorkshire.co.uk
Scriveners	scriveners@lycos.co.uk
Shaun Levin	Online Form
Sheffield Hallam University	enquiries@shu.ac.uk
Shepherds Bush Group	anjan@anjansaha.com
South Manchester Writers' Workshop	Online form
South West Writers	southwestwriters@yahoo.com
South Yardley Creative Writing Group	spcnac@yahoo.co.uk
Southend Poetry Group	dorothy@southendpoetry.co.uk
Southport Writers' Circle	southportwriterscircle@yahoo.co.uk
Southwest Scriptwriters	Online Form

Writers' Group	Email
Spread the Word	info@spreadtheword.org.uk
Spring Tides Group	listmanager@northeastwriters.co.uk
St Helens Writers' Circle	gavin@citadel.org.uk
Stanton Guildhouse	info@stantonguildhouse.org.uk
Strathkelvin Writers	enquiries@strathkelvinwriters.org
Suffolk Poetry Society	ian@poetryanglia.org
Survivors Poetry	Online Form
Sussex Playwrights Club	Online Form
Sutton Writers' Circle	teresa.tipping@hotmail.com
Swan Playwrights	webmaster@swanplaywrights.co.uk
Teifi Scribblers	simone@simonemb.com
Tenbury Writers' Group	sallytenbury@yahoo.com
Thames Valley Circle	sawdonsmith@hotmail.com
Thameside Poetry Workshop	fionamoore@aetos.freeserve.co.uk
Thatcham Writers	martha@thatchamwriters.co.uk
The Arvon Foundation	hurst@arvonfoundation.org m-mhor@arvonfoundation.org t-barton@arvonfoundation.org
The Complete Creative Writing Course	maggie@writingcourses.org.uk
The Fielding Programme	info@fieldingprogramme.com
The Goldfish Bowl	admin@writingincircles.co.uk
The Indian King Poets	indianking@btconnect.com
The Inklings	aninkling@blueyonder.co.uk
The Inn Scribers	lesleymjames@talktalk.net
The Institute	Online Form
The Medway Mermaids	rockyhorror75@hotmail.com

Writers' Group	Email
The Norwegian Writing Circle in London	brit.warren@btinternet.com
The Plough Group	sarah.lawson1@btinternet.com
The Poetry Business	poetrybusiness@gmail.com
The Poetry School	Online Form
The Poetry Society's Poetry Café	Online Form
The T Party	Online Form
The Windows Project	windowsproject@btinternet.com
The Write Coach	bekki@thewritecoach.co.uk
The Writers Summer School at Swanwick	Online Form
Training and Performance Showcase (TAPS)	Online Form
Tŷ Newydd	post@tynewydd.org
University of Newcastle upon Tyne	press.office@ncl.ac.uk
University College Chichester	website@chi.ac.uk
University College Falmouth	shortcourses@falmouth.ac.uk
University of Aberystwyth	mss@aber.ac.uk
University of Bradford	press@bradford.ac.uk
University of Bristol	tom.sperlinger@bristol.ac.uk
University of Cumbria	admissionslancaster@cumbria.ac.uk
University of Derby	askadmissions@derby.ac.uk
University of East Anglia	admissions@uea.ac.uk
University of Exeter	s.d.franklin@exeter.ac.uk
University of Glamorgan	press@glam.ac.uk
University of Glasgow	dace-query@educ.gla.ac.uk

Writers' Group	Email
University of Hull	m.p.arnold@hull.ac.uk
University of Kent at Canterbury	cfl@kent.ac.uk
University of Leeds	business@leeds.ac.uk
University of Liverpool	kate.spark@liv.ac.uk
University of Liverpool Creative Writing Society	thomas.mcbride2@sky.com
University of Oxford	john.ballam@conted.ox.ac.uk
University of Plymouth	prospectus@plymouth.ac.uk
University of Salford	u.k.hurley@salford.ac.uk
University of St Andrews	english@st-andrews.ac.uk
University of the Arts	info@arts.ac.uk
University of Warwick	engd@warwick.ac.uk
University of Westminster	course-enquiries@westminster.ac.uk
Verulam Writers' Circle	info@verulamwriterscircle.org.uk
W.E.A.	info.alingtonhouse@gmail.com
Walsall Writers' Circle	walsall.writerscircle@hotmail.co.uk
Walton Wordsmiths	words@stickler.org.uk
Ware Poets	rockpress@ntlworld.com
Watford Writers	watfordwriters@gmail.com
Ways with Words	admin@wayswithwords.co.uk
Westminster Writers	westminsterwriters@hotmail.com
Wight Fair Writers' Circle	carolbridgestock@hotmail.com
Willesden Green Group	willesdengreenlibrary@brent.gov.uk
Women's Ink Writing	womensink@hotmail.com
Woodham Scribblers	webmaster@woodhamscribblers.co.uk
Worcester Writers' Circle	secretary@worcesterwriters.org.uk

Writers' Group	Email
Word for Word	wordforword@london.com
Wordplay	tonya@wordplay.org.uk
WordWatchers	peterpheasant@aol.com
Write in Bexley	Online Form
Write Now	george@wickerswork.co.uk
Write of Eden	lynette54uk@yahoo.co.uk
Writeopia	writeopia@gmail.com
Writergrrls	londonwritergrrls-subscribe@ yahoogroups.com
Writers Holiday Caerleon	enquiries@writersholiday.net
Writers Of Our Age	pjbruce@ukonline.co.uk
Writers Together	writers.together@ntlworld.com
Writers' and Poets' Circle	veronicaspaintbox@yahoo.co.uk
Writers' Centre Norwich	info@writerscentrenorwich.org.uk
Writers' Workshops	info@crescentarts.org
Writing Events Bath	Online Form
Writing in Wales	rebeccajwoods@blueyonder.co.uk
Writtenwords.net	henrietta@writtenwords.net

APPENDIX 2

SELECTED UK LIBRARY CONTACTS

England	
Buckinghamshire	lib-ahq@buckscc.gov.uk
Cambridgeshire	your.library@cambridgeshire.gov.uk
Cheshire	libraries@cheshiresharedservices.gov.uk
Devon	phil.bater@devon.gov.uk and/or jean.hall@devon.gov.uk
East Sussex	chris.desmond@eastsussex.gov.uk
Essex	answers.direct@essex.gov.uk
Gateshead	heleneddon@gateshead.gov.uk
Hampshire	heritage@hants.gov.uk
Kingston upon Hull	jessica.heathley@hullcc.gov.uk
Hertfordshire	hertsdirect@herts.gov.uk
Leicestershire	countyhalllibrary@leics.gov.uk
Manchester	j.shadbolt@manchester.gov.uk
Newcastle	information@newcastle.gov.uk
Norfolk	info.services.dcs@norfolk.gov.uk
North Yorkshire	roland.walls@northyorks.gov.uk
Northamptonshire	centlib@northamptonshire.gov.uk
Nottinghamshire	contactlibraries@nottscc.gov.uk
Portsmouth	libraries@portsmouthcc.gov.uk
Shropshire	rob.woodward@shropshire.gov.uk

England	
South Yorkshire	centrallending.library@sheffield.gov.uk
Stockton on Tees	penny.slee@stockton.gov.uk
Suffolk	libraries.direct@suffolk.gov.uk
Surrey	libraries@surrey.gov.uk
Warwickshire	katemackie@warwickshire.gov.uk
West Sussex	libraries@westsussex.gov.uk
Wiltshire	jessica.phillips@wiltshire.gov.uk
Worcestershire	david.pearson@worcestershire.gov.uk

Wales	
Anglesey	rfrxlh@anglesey.gov.uk
Cardiff	centrallibrary@cardiff.gov.uk
Carmarthenshire	shmorgan@carmarthenshire.gov.uk
Ceredigion	gareth.griffiths@ceredigion.gov.uk
Conwy	cheryl.hesketh@conwy.gov.uk chris.jones@conwy.gov.uk
Denbighshire	jeff.harrison@denbighshire.gov.uk
Gwynedd	covered by Conwy and Anglesey
Monmouthshire	juliagreenway@monmouthshire.gov.uk
Newport	rhodri.matthews@newport.gov.uk
Pembrokeshire	gill.gilliland@pembrokeshire.gov.uk
Powys	louise.ingham@powys.gov.uk
Swansea	ulie.clement@swansea.gov.uk

Scotland	
Bute & Argyll	sue.fortune@argyll-bute.gov.uk
Clackmannanshire	libraries@clacks.gov.uk

Scotland	
Dumfries & Galloway	anne.rinaldi@dumgal.gov.uk
Dundee	janis.milne@leisureandculturedundee.com
East Ayrshire	libraries@east-ayrshire.gov.uk
East Dunbartonshire	eryl.morris@eastdunbarton.gov.uk
East Lothian	ahunter@eastlothian.gov.uk
Edinburgh	jenny.hayes@edinburgh.gov.uk
Fife	christine.cook@ffe.gov.uk
Glasgow	gerry.torley@glasgowlife.org.uk
Highlands	alison.forrest@highlifehighland.com
Inverclyde	john.rushton@inverclyde.gov.uk
Inverness	june.mcmillan@highlifehighland.com
Midlothian	library.hq@midlothian.gov.uk
North Ayrshire	amcallister@north-ayrshire.gov.uk
North Lanarkshire	walesc@northlan.gov.uk
Perth & Kinross	ammacdonald@pkc.gov.uk
Scottish Borders	knairn@scotborders.gov.uk
Shetland Isles	karen.fraser@shetland.gov.uk
South Lanarkshire	heather.maclean@library.slanark.org.uk
Stirling	mcarav@stirling.gov.uk
West Dunbartonshire	mary.maclean@west-dunbarton.gov.uk

London Boroughs	
Barking & Dagenham	zoinul.abidin@lbbd.gov.uk
Barnet	mandy.stebbings@barnet.gov.uk
Brent	emma.palmer@brent.gov.uk
Bromley	janet.pullan@bromley.gov.uk

London Boroughs	
Ealing	jwilliams@ealing.gov.uk
Greenwich	jean.wright@greenwich.gov.uk
Hackney	monica.sever@hackney.gov.uk
Harrow	simon.smith@harrow.gov.uk
Havering	matthew.wright@havering.gov.uk
Hillingdon	wrussell@hillingdon.gov.uk
Hounslow	elaine.collier@laing.com
Kingston	alison.townsend@rbk.kingston.gov.uk
Lewisham	mark.challen@lewisham.gov.uk alan.morrison@lewisham.gov.uk
Newham	richard.durack@newham.gov.uk
Redbridge	nick.dobson@visionrcl.org.uk
Richmond	rosie.piasecki@richmond.gov.uk
Southwark	soulaf.rizki@southwark.gov.uk
Sutton	karyn.isaac@sutton.gov.uk
Tower Hamlets	kate.pitman@towerhamlets.gov.uk
Wandsworth	gread@wandsworth.gov.uk

Miscellaneous	
Guernsey	sue.laker@priaulxlibrary.co.uk
Jersey	je.library@gov.je

GLOSSARY

affiliate marketing: Performance-based marketing in which other sites are rewarded for each new visitor or customer brought in by its own marketing effort.

Amazon.com: The leading online retailer of books in the world today.

Amazon profile page: Amazon link where people can learn more about you. It is where you access and manage your community and book content on Amazon. You also see how people are reviewing and voting on your reviews, along with other useful lists.

author brand: How much your books are recognised and how well you are known as a published author.

author platform: How well-positioned you are to sell and market your book, including your readership/fan base, availability/visibility and authority to help your book reach its intended target audience.

Bebo.com: An acronym for "Blog Early, Blog Often." Bebo is a social networking site with a section dedicated to writers called "Bebo authors."

Blitz marketing: Integrated, strategically planned marketing campaign that is quick, economical and effective.

blog (short for web log): Discussion or informational site published on the Internet and consisting of discrete entries ("posts") typically displayed in reverse chronological order (i.e., the most recent post appears first).

BranchOut: Facebook application designed specifically for professional networking.

Delicious.com: Popular social bookmarking site that enables you to discover, organise and share interesting and relevant web content and links.

digital download: The process of copying an ebook to a computer or e-reader (i.e., handheld devices like Nook and Kindle).

digital footprint: Personal data trail left by interactions in a digital environment (e.g., what you clicked on, searched for, "liked," where you went, your location, your favourites, your IP address, what you said, what was said about you, etc.). This data can be used in demographic profiling your target audience. In social media, a *digital footprint* can refer to the size of a person's "online presence," measured by the number of individuals with whom they interact and engage.

ebook: A book-length publication in digital format, consisting of text, images or both, and produced on, published through and readable on computers or other electronic devices.

e-reader (electronic reader): Hand-held device such as Kindle, iPad, Nook, iPhone, Sony Reader and Kobo to download and read ebooks.

e-tailer: Online retailer like Amazon or Barnes & Noble for listing and selling ebooks.

Facebook.com: Social networking website on which you can add friends to your Facebook page and send them messages, alerting them about new events in your life, such as the publication of your ebook.

fan page: A facility on Facebook that enables you to build up a following for your ebook by sending regular updates to an unlimited number of people, and keep the focus on the organisation without revealing the administrator (unless you want to).

Flickr.com: An image hosting and video hosting website, web services suite and online community.

Gather.com: A social networking site designed to encourage interaction through various social, political and cultural topics.

Goodreads.com: A social cataloguing website that permits individuals to register books and create library catalogues and reading lists. It also allows users to create their own groups of book suggestions and discussion topics.

groundswell: This is defined by what your readers are writing about your books on blogs and by recutting your book trailers on YouTube.

guerrilla marketing: An unconventional way of performing promotional activities on a low budget, relying more on time, energy and imagination than a big marketing spend.

IPRLicense.com: An international rights website that enables authors to list and sell the rights to their book to a global marketplace.

Kindle: The world's bestselling handheld e-reader (ebook reading device).

Kindle Boards: Forum and discussion group facility available on Kindle to discuss and promote ebooks.

Kobobooks.com: Major online retailer of ebooks. Kobo e-readers are handheld ebook reading devices.

LinkedIn.com: Social media site for professionals, including publishing.

Lovereading.com: UK's largest book club. Along with its partner site, Lovewriting.com, offers advice on publishing your work, making it easy for people to sample, review and purchase your book.

Mass-Ebooks.com: A popular website offering free ebook downloads.

multichannel marketing campaign: Undertaking a select number of marketing activities to raise your literary profile as a published author and promote and sell copies of your book.

Ning.com: A social networking site enabling you to create your own social networking site based on a particular subject, such as your ebook.

Nook: Hand-held electronic book reader developed by American book retailer Barnes & Noble.

offline marketing: Traditional methods of marketing such as television/newspaper/magazine adverts, billboards, posters, jingles, etc.

online marketing (webvertising or e-marketing): The promotion of products like ebooks over the Internet through search engine marketing and optimisation, social media, affiliate marketing, pay-per-click and banner ads, and email marketing.

outposts: Developing your social media postings to help attract your target audience and build brand recognition for your ebooks.

pay-per-click (PPC) advertising: A form of online marketing where you bid on specific key words and key word phrases relevant to your website or ebook so when someone puts those words into an internet search engine, banners and links are provided to your website.

Pinterest: An image-based content-sharing service that allows members to "pin" images, videos and other objects to their pinboard. The site also includes standard social networking features.

podcasting: Making audio and video recordings and making them available on the Internet to download.

publishing platform (for ebooks): An e-publishing platform that allows the management of content, the definition of digital rights, authentication scenarios, the management of customers and e-commerce transactions, and the incorporation of marketing tools and text retrieval.

reader profile: Information about where your book readers live, what language they speak, what their online presence is, which sites and blogs they visit most, and what their buying habits and preferences are.

reciprocal links: A mutually agreed link between your website and another site intended to increase the numbers of visitors to both sites, and thereby achieve higher ranking on search engines, giving your site more prominence and (hopefully) your ebook more sales.

Ryze.com: Free social networking website designed to link business professionals and entrepreneurs.

Scribd.com: A digital documents library that allows users to publish, discover, share and discuss original writings in various languages. Allows users to post documents in various formats and embed them into a webpage.

search engine optimisation: Tailoring your website so that when people search online for subjects related to your book on various search engines (such as Google and Yahoo), they might find and access your website more easily.

Shelfari.com: A social cataloguing website for books. Users build virtual bookshelves of titles they own or have read and can rate, review, tag, discuss and recommend books to others.

Smashwords.com: A DIY ebook self-publishing and distribution platform.

social bookmarking: A service on the internet for storing, sharing and discovering popular content. Instead of saving website links to your web browser, you save them to the Web. Because your bookmarks are online, you can easily share them with friends.

social cataloguing: Refers to web-based applications that help users tag and track books and other materials in their own e-inventory or filing systems. Social cataloguing sites make it possible to discuss books and review them while being *social* online.

social media: Web- and mobile-based technologies and software tools, which turn communication into interactive dialogue among organisations, communities and individuals. This includes internet discussion groups, weblogs, social blogs, micro-blogging, wikis, social networks, podcasts and social bookmarking.

social networking: Expanding your contacts by making connections through attending events and meeting individuals. Online, establishing interconnected communities (commonly known as personal networks) that help people make contacts that will benefit them in some way.

target market: A group of people identified as those most likely to buy your book.

Twitter: A free, web-based service enabling its users to send and read text-based messages of up to 140 characters, known as *tweets*.

Typepad: Online service for hosting and publishing weblogs and photo albums, and supports a LinkedIn application that pulls blog posts into LinkedIn.

URL (uniform research locator)/Domain Name: The internet address for your website, generally beginning with http://www or simply www. and ending with .com, .co.uk, .net, .org and so on.

video blogging (vlogging or vidblogging): A form of blogging where short videos are made regularly and often combines embedded video or a video link with supporting text, images and other data.

viral marketing: Increasing awareness of you as a published author and your ebook through people talking about your ebook and recommending it to others.

WeRead.com: A popular online community of book enthusiasts.

word-of-mouse marketing: Using social media sites on the Internet to create a buzz about your ebook.

word-of-mouth marketing (see viral marketing): Speaking with people and groups of people directly to create a following for your book.

Wordpress: A free and open source blogging tool.

YouTube: A video-sharing website on which users can upload, share and view videos, enabling authors to showcase their books.

Zinepal.com: Enables authors to create ebooks from online content or read ebooks created by others.

ABOUT THE AUTHORS

Darin Jewell is Director of The Inspira Group Literary Agency in London. He published *How to Sell and Market Your Book* in 2010, which tells authors how to raise their literary profile and promote their books in easy and effective ways. As the director of a professional UK literary agency, he regularly participates as a panellist in writing seminars and speaks to writing groups. Darin has placed over a hundred books with traditional publishers, and represents Michael G. R. Tolkien, Kevin Joslin, David Barry, bestselling business book author Fergus O'Connell, bestselling humour writer Mark Leigh, bestselling ebook author Conrad Jones and mind, body, spirit author Simon Brown, whose book *Practical Feng Shui* has sold over a million copies.

When **Conrad Jones** turned his novels into ebooks, his thriller series stormed the Kindle charts. Within 3 weeks of launching them he had two titles, *The Child Taker* and *Slow Burn*, in the top ten Kindle lists, and all seven of his thrillers were in the top 40 for nearly 12 months. His eighth book, *Nine Angels*, went straight to #3 in the horror charts. He garnered over 120,000 digital downloads in 2011 by building a solid market base and applying everything he has learned to the launch of his ebooks. His credentials are actual book sales, a growing fan base and over 250 five-star reviews across his *Soft Target* series.

www.ingramcontent.com/pod-product-compliance
Lightning Source LLC
Jackson TN
JSHW020016141224
75386JS00025B/542
9780857281661